DESIGNING INTERNATIONAL PARTNERSHIP PROGRAMS:

How to Structure for Sustainability, Efficiency, and Development Impact

A PRIMER FOR PARTNERS

Andrea E. Stumpf

STRUCTURED
PARTNERSHIPS

STRUCTURED
PARTNERSHIPS

Like rock, like water, all life needs balance.

To my father, Dr. Walter Stumpf, who revealed our internal balance through vitamin D, *soltriol*, in our ultimate connection to the sun.

To my brother, Martin, my best bud, who encouraged me to follow my path and—pause for balance on the stepping stones of life.

FOREWORD

We are as effective as the partnerships we keep. This has been our lesson over time: that we can do more together. We each build our own institutions to leverage experience and expertise, but that is not enough for the complexity of our world. Wherever we look, there are challenges that need collective efforts on a global scale. In partnering across the international community—from the United Nations and other multilateral and international organizations to governments, civil society, academia, nonprofits, for-profits, and more—together we can expand our resolve and our reach to make a greater difference.

Sometimes that is easier said than done. It takes more than vision to effect change on the ground in a sustainable, impactful way. Time and again, we have seen partnership programs be their most meaningful and effective when everyone knows their part and takes their place. This is the way to keep it simple. The common ground achieved in building partnership programs, and the smooth decision making and implementation needed to maintain them, come from careful attention to structure and deliberate design choices shared by partners as a whole.

International collaboration takes effort and time, but the trends are positive, and opportunities abound. We have more experience, knowledge, connectivity, and data now than ever before. Partnership programs can bridge us from data to decisions, from funds to action, and from goals to results. In promoting values like inclusion, mutual respect, and country ownership, well-structured partnership programs represent the values we seek to promote in society as a whole.

This book provides essential nuts and bolts to improve our partnering. As we address some of the most protracted issues and enter some of the most challenging environments of our time, our ability to collaborate determines our effectiveness. As individuals and institutions, we each have our unique perspectives and comparative advantages. It is with humility, hope, and purpose that we join in structured partnerships to do and become more together.

Franck Bousquet
Senior Director,
Fragility, Conflict and Violence Group,
World Bank

ACKNOWLEDGMENTS

My thanks go to many friends and supporters over the years, especially those who encouraged me to be creative and explore ideas. I thank all those who were game to engage in our iterative exchanges, as we honed our way to more solutions and better results. Every client, every colleague who brought a challenge gave me another piece of learning that is reflected in these pages. I owe great thanks to the World Bank for letting me redirect my career to international development. I am especially grateful to my very able, amiable, and unflappable Chief Counsel of many years, Tom Duvall, who believed in my abilities and gave me free rein. Under him, I had a privileged part in hundreds of international partnership initiatives, all of which made their mark and many of which continue to improve the world to this day. I cherish my continuing ability to contribute at the World Bank, including under the inspiring leadership of Franck Bousquet. In preparing this book, I received support from Daniel Balke, Colin Bruce, Ivar Cederholm, David Gray, Duncan Kiara, Nancy Marder, Kristen Milhollin, Kristina Nwazota, Atsuko Okubo, Sarah Rawz, Julie Rieger, Seema Thomas, and my awesome proofreading mother, Ursula Stumpf—my thanks to all of them. Lauri Sherer on copyedit and Joe Bernier on layout were terrific in helping me do the book my way, following my cues and queries through all the iterations. I also extend special thanks to Eija Pehu, a faithful touchstone for this project and my professional journey, and Omri Sender, a valued friend and resource on all things international. Finally, here's a grateful shout-out to my greatest supporter, my daughter and illustrator, who indulged the hours and hours I spent on "my book" with loving encouragement.

This book is my chance to give back to all who shared in my learning. To the team members who walked into my office with a wealth of sector expertise but not so much on structuring partnerships, I hope to empower you to make sound decisions based on informed choices. To the lawyers, accountants, and other professionals who live in the nitty gritty and do all the plumbing, this is for you to keep the flow, as you navigate between the shoals. To the innovators who want to do more and better, this is an invitation to be creative with ideas that build on solid ground. Hopefully my personal views and experiences can stimulate more thinking and engagement on the subject, as we collectively expand the repertoire.

———————————————•———————————————

Because there is so much to share, this Primer for Partners, geared more toward business teams, will be followed by a Book for Builders, geared more toward lawyers and other professionals.

PREFACE

This book is an outpouring of experience and lessons learned over more than a decade of working on partnership programs at the World Bank during a time of great partnership enthusiasm. As a lawyer supporting business teams and central units, and as a guardian of this international financial institution with its twin goals of ending extreme poverty and promoting shared prosperity, I played a part in helping orchestrate the World Bank's many roles, including as partner, supporting entity, fiduciary, and implementer. In all those years, I was connected to an incredible array of partnership engagements across all parts of the World Bank, on practically every conceivable development topic, using every available funding mechanism, to interact with hundreds of donors and other partners in every region of the world.

This was a creative space in which staff and partners with great ideas and ambitions were looking to make things happen. When I began, there was little to guide me other than my private sector experience—invaluable, as it turned out—and common sense. Even today, there is still little to guide those of us seeking to structure and design international partnership programs that are sustainable, effective, and impactful. There is indeed little appreciation that there is a gap. And yet, this *is* a practice area. I hope these pages show that in spades.

Deep in the trenches, always with a dozen or more partnership initiatives happening at the same time, I kept an eye on the big picture of what we were creating, as the same issues appeared over and over again in their infinite variations, and as task teams pushed the envelope in whatever directions seemed promising. Those forays did not all work, but in my own little space, from my singular, privileged vantage point across all manner of issues and initiatives, I collected experiences to bring to bear the next time. Drawing from my ever-increasing repertoire of examples, I could offer more alternatives, words to the wise, and answers before the questions arose.

Coming from the private sector and now my own business, I can see that these topics are universal, reflecting how we convene and collaborate across the world, with development as a particular gateway to our common humanity and inevitable connectedness. Partnership programs speak to our human and interpersonal dynamics, as we pursue global public goods and promote local well-being. They show that when we engage internationally and organically, two strands that are the warp and woof of this book, we can be more sustained, efficient, and impactful in our endeavors.

This book is offered to all who believe in the benefits of inclusive collaboration and synergies of international partnership. I am downloading the breadth and depth of my practice to draw attention to this wonderfully complex and refreshingly simple area. As you will see, it's not rocket science, but rocks and water. Let the organic nature of international partnership programs keep you on course and take you far.

Andrea E. Stumpf
January 2019

TABLE OF CONTENTS

TEN LISTS OF TEN

OVERVIEW

PART ONE: MAIN FOUNDATIONS

In this Part, we review basic types and core elements of international partnership programs, a particularly popular form of structured partnership for international collaborations.

Chapter 1: Ten Take-Aways
Every writer has a point of view, so this is full disclosure—here are ten one-liners that carry throughout the pages of this book.

Chapter 2: Like Rock, Like Water
It takes stability to have flexibility, and it takes both to have sustainable, effective, and impactful international partnership programs.

Chapter 3: Typology
In locating international partnership programs on the spectrum of structured partnerships, we pay special attention to one-stop-shops and international platforms.

Chapter 4: International Partnership Programs
Deconstructing international partnership programs, we identify six main "collectives": decision making, funding, support, activities, knowledge, and brand.

Chapter 5: Governing Bodies
Taking the first collective, we consider informal governing bodies—as distinguished from formal, corporate bodies—from both institutional (partner) and individual (representative) perspectives.

Chapter 6: Secretariats
Here we shine a light, with great appreciation, on the essential and wide-ranging secretariat support functions that hold international partnership programs together.

Chapter 7: Trust Funds
Not all partnership programs have them, but when they do, it helps to understand trust funds as accounts in relation to donors, recipients, roles, money flows, and the mechanics that make them so popular.

PART TWO: BUSINESS CONSIDERATIONS

In this Part, we pick up aspects to help partners—as organizations and individuals—make business decisions.

Chapter 1: Ten Tried and True Tips
Clear, clean, modular, flexible, comprehensive, balanced, contextual, ready, aware, and simple—these are watchwords for designing international partnership programs.

Chapter 2: Structure
Different ways of seeing structure make for more informed choices: upstream/downstream, bilateral/ multilateral, contractual/structural, follow the power/follow the money, and more.

Chapter 3: Trade-Offs
Trade-offs abound. Examples like the horizontal buy-in spectrum, the central harmonization spectrum, and the vertical continuity spectrum reveal how structural choices can manage and maximize trade-offs.

Chapter 4: Risk and Review
How partners see and assess partnering opportunities and risks, from start to finish, affects the stability and effectiveness of their engagement in international partnership programs.

Chapter 5: Partners and People
We come as partners—institutions structurally and people operationally—and convene and collectivize organically. Remembering this can help us manage our partnering dynamics.

PART THREE: KEY ELABORATIONS

In this Part, we take some deeper dives on select topics that can make a big difference.

Chapter 1: Partnering Internationally
Benefits of partnering in the international arena are best preserved if they are better appreciated, including in terms of what law applies and how that affects governing bodies.

Chapter 2: Decision Making
Here we explore the virtues of consensus decision making and the benefits of no objection decision making, breaking each mode down and showing exactly how it works.

Chapter 3: Supporting Entities
In full recognition of the central supporting entity role, we unpack what that means for partners, including the supporting entities themselves.

Chapter 4: Custodial Effect
In this chapter, we highlight the unacknowledged role of the partnership program "custodian," which usually attaches to the legal entity function and fills in as needed.

Chapter 5: Synergistic Conflicts
By taking a closer look at "conflicts of interest" in partnership programs, we discover inherent and intentional features that are in fact valuable partnership synergies.

Chapter 6: Trustee Types
From full trustees to limited trustees, and modular combinations and downstream variations, different options let partners position trustees to fit partnership program purposes.

Chapter 7: Use of Funds
This chapter gives us a chance to consider fund use not just as a trust fund matter but more broadly from partnership program perspectives.

Chapter 8: Fund Use Responsibility
As a corollary to fund use, here we look at different kinds of responsibility: implementation responsibility, two kinds of fiduciary responsibility, and collective oversight responsibility.

KEY TERMS

For ease of reference, here are brief descriptions of frequently used terms that are more fully described throughout this book:

CUES

>@   see "more at" a cross-referenced chapter or section

ABBREVIATIONS

AKA   also known as

COI   conflict(s) of interest

CSO   civil society organization

IFI   international financial institution

M&E   monitoring and evaluation

MDB   multilateral development bank

NGO   nongovernmental organization

ODA   official development aid

P&I   privileges and immunities

TAC   technical advisory committee

TOR   terms of reference

UN   United Nations

WBG   World Bank Group

STRUCTURES

Coordination partnerships: A type of international partnership program whose partners convene through an informal governing body for coordination and light collaboration, primarily to share knowledge and experience, without dedicated pooled funding and with separate downstream implementation outside the partnership program; AKA learning platforms.

Dedicated entity partnerships: Legal personality partnerships that consist of new entities under domestic law that are created to convene and implement the partnerships, often mobilizing major funding; with no reliance on existing legal functions, these are not partnership programs; AKA, for example, international institutions under the Swiss Host State Act.

Embedded partnerships: Partnerships with all partnering inputs provided upfront and actual implementation delegated to a supporting entity; with no shared governance, these are not partnership programs.

International partnership programs: Partnership programs with mostly international partners, like national governments and international organizations, that engage and convene in the international arena.

International platforms: A type of international partnership program with a strong informal governing body that convenes around a trust fund with a limited trustee, usually with multiple downstream fiduciaries.

One-stop-shops: A type of international partnership program for which the supporting entity plays multiple roles, including as full trustee for a dedicated trust fund.

Partnership programs: Structured partnerships that are not legally incorporated entities and instead feature shared governance through informal governing bodies, rely on existing supporting entities, and may have dedicated funding sources, like trust funds.

Structured partnerships: Partnership arrangements by which partners participate through collective terms and mechanisms that include the use of structure to define and delineate roles and responsibilities.

Trust-funded partnership programs: Partnership programs that are supported by one or more dedicated trust funds.

Umbrella arrangements: A type of international partnership program that links multiple funding vehicles and programs through a common, overarching informal governing body.

structured partnerships in the international arena

international partnership programs

one-stop-shops

international platforms

COMPONENTS AND ROLES

Contributions: Funds flowing to trust funds from donors, including paid cash contributions and to-be-paid contributions receivable.

Donors: Contributors of funds to trust funds under terms agreed with trustees; AKA development partners.

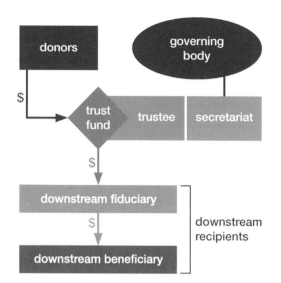

Downstream beneficiaries: Recipients that directly receive funds from either trustees or downstream fiduciaries for fund use, usually under supervision; AKA grantees, beneficiary recipients (including beneficiary countries).

Downstream fiduciaries: Downstream recipients that directly receive both funds and fiduciary responsibility from trustees; or, by continuity of function, full trustees that keep downstream responsibility; AKA fiduciary entities, fiduciary recipients, implementation support agencies.

Downstream recipients: Recipients of funds disbursed from trust funds either directly from trustees (as downstream fiduciaries or downstream beneficiaries) or subsequently from downstream fiduciaries (as downstream beneficiaries) under agreed terms,

Full trustees: Trustees that have fiduciary responsibilities (including supervision) for any use of funds from their trust funds, including by their direct downstream beneficiaries, potentially along with other roles, like secretariat-type functions.

Governing bodies: Shared governance, either decision-making or advisory, through informal bodies with agreed participants, roles, and responsibilities; AKA governing councils, steering committees, advisory committees (preferably not "boards").

Grants: Funds flowing from trustees or downstream fiduciaries to downstream beneficiaries.

Implementers: Entities with implementation responsibilities, including some trustees and downstream recipients.

Inhouse secretariats: Secretariats that are part of supporting entities; AKA embedded secretariats.

Limited trustees: Trustees that have fiduciary responsibilities for funds in their trust funds only as long as they hold the funds, up to the point of transfer to downstream fiduciaries; AKA pass-through trustees, fiscal agents.

Members: Decision-making participants in governing bodies of international partnership programs.

Multi-donor trust funds: Trust funds that receive contributions from more than one donor.

Observers: Non-decision-making participants in governing bodies of international partnership programs.

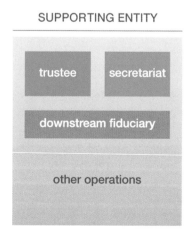

Secretariats: Administrative units, usually in supporting entities, that have agreed partnership program roles and responsibilities, particularly vis-à-vis informal governing bodies; AKA coordination units, focal points, management units, program teams, inhouse secretariats, embedded secretariats.

Supporting entities: Existing international organizations, like MDBs or in the UN, that provide support to partnership programs in addition to their regular operations, including as secretariats, trustees, and downstream fiduciaries.

Trustees: Administrators and financial managers of trust funds, including full trustees and limited trustees, that manage funds on behalf of donors and are part of supporting entities; AKA fiduciary entities.

Trust funds: Accounts managed by trustees on terms agreed with donors that support international partnership programs and are usually operated by international organizations outside of domestic laws.

DOCUMENTS

Charters: Baseline establishment documents adopted by informal governing bodies that set forth agreed terms defining roles, responsibilities, governance, and other essential partnership aspects.

Constitutive documents: Baseline establishment documents, such as charters and fund flow agreements, that set forth agreed terms for structured partnerships.

Contribution agreements: Fund flow agreements between donors and trustees for trust fund contributions.

Fund flow agreements: Agreements with trustees to accompany either the receipt of funds into, or disbursement of funds out of, trust funds, including contribution agreements, grant agreements, and transfer agreements.

Grant agreements: Fund flow agreements between downstream beneficiaries and full trustees or downstream fiduciaries for trust fund disbursements.

Transfer agreements: Fund flow agreements between downstream fiduciaries and limited trustees for trust fund disbursements.

CHARACTERISTICS

Downstream: The part of partnership programs that involves activities and results, which in the case of trust funds includes trustee disbursements and implementation, often by downstream recipients.

Formal: Governed by domestic statutory frameworks and jurisprudence, as with incorporated legal entities established under domestic law.

Informal: Not governed by domestic statutory frameworks and jurisprudence, as with international partnership programs, which are not incorporated.

Upstream: The part of partnership programs that includes donor contributions and shared governance, potentially including fund allocation decisions by governing bodies.

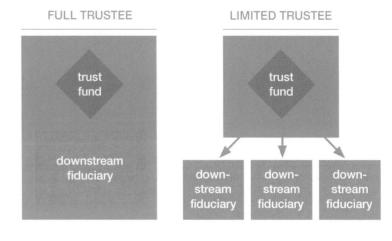

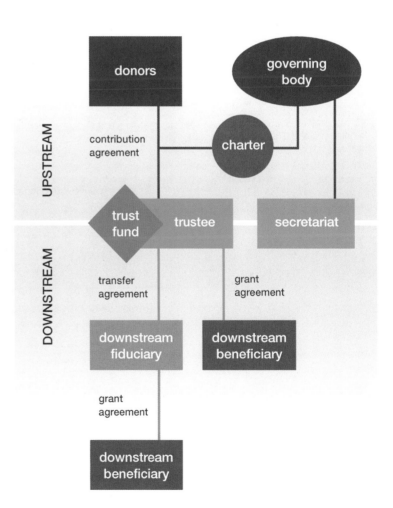

INTRODUCTION

In structuring international partnerships, it all depends.

Perhaps that is why until now, no one has put forth a book of this sort. It may also explain why attempts to sort out and standardize this area so often fall short, if they are attempted at all. And it probably explains why the subject area doesn't even have a name—so let's try "structured partnerships" in the international arena. By launching this phrase, I hope to highlight the importance of "structure" for international collaborations. When it comes to structuring, the international community can do more to cultivate expert practitioners and enrich partnership participants. In giving this topic its due, partners can design and create better international partnerships—ones that are sustainable, effective, and impactful.

It's about contextualizing.

Our focus in this book is a favorite subset of structured partnerships in the international arena: international partnership programs. These partnership programs have been proliferating in humanitarian, development, and other international settings with astounding variety. For some, this is distracting and draining; for others, including myself, it is inspiring. Some say this is too much customization, but the point is really contextualization. The variety and fluidity of these international partnership programs is a sign of healthy, fit-for-purpose arrangements that can rest on solid foundations and connect effectively to partnership ambitions.

Why International Partnership Programs?

Partnership programs are found all over the international community, particularly in international development. They are crucial to meeting development needs and targets, like the Sustainable Development Goals (SDGs) that were adopted by the international community through the UN in 2015. The SDGs even include SDG 17 for partnerships, last but not least, with an appeal to "strengthen the means of implementation and revitalize the global partnership for sustainable development." With SDG 17, the international community underscored that partnership is vital to achieving the world's targets for 2030, so much so that partnering itself would be monitored and measured. SDG 17 says out loud that the act of international partnering—done sustainably and effectively—is essential to achieving all other SDGs.

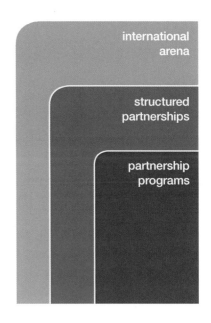

International partnership programs have become venues of choice for many international partners seeking to join forces and leverage resources to meet global and local needs. Over the past couple of decades, international partnership programs have evolved into major north-south income transfer instruments. Donor funding has become much more than just money in the kitty, as donors have increasingly stepped up to partnership program engagement. In the same way that developing country voice came to claim a space at the table through the Paris Declaration on Aid Effectiveness in 2005 and the Accra Agenda for Action in 2008, donor voice has also become a more consequential part of development in partnership.

This burgeoning and fortifying collaborative environment, where all participants engage, inform each other, and learn from each other, has reflected a genuine interest on the part of donors, recipients, supporting entities, and other partners to further development and achieve meaningful and sustainable results.

Name the development challenge, and an array of partnership programs has been established to provide support and flow funds. Many of them channel resources from donors to beneficiaries, but they also seek to amplify knowledge and innovation in search of solutions, while harnessing insights and experience for greater impact. Over the past two decades, partnership structures created by international partners have come to cover a vast landscape of causes, partners, and contexts. It is hard to imagine the international arena, particularly the aid arena, without international partnership programs.

As one of the most common forms of structured partnerships for and by international partners, international partnership programs typically feature an *informal governing body* financed by one or more international *trust funds* and supported by an international *supporting entity*. A prominent example of such a supporting entity, one I know well, is the World Bank, which has virtually all countries in the world as its shareholders. Most of these same countries either provide or receive the funds of these international partnership programs.

It takes structure for international partners to get together on a sustained basis, with allocated roles and responsibilities. When they do this in the

> What works here may not work there, but good design can get you there.

international arena, outside of domestic legal frameworks, they have a particularly wide range of design options that can respond to their interests and ambitions. As a result, how an international partnership program is structured and designed depends on many things. The who, what, how, where, and why pose innumerable variables that can be contextualized to reflect circumstances, preferences, politics, and other parameters, while maximizing trade-offs and minimizing risks.

It may be presumptuous to attempt to bring some order to this abundance of variables. However, those who work long enough on structured partnerships in the international arena may notice that themes repeat, patterns reveal, good practices emerge, and concepts solidify. These are worth cataloguing, while always remembering that everything is relative, with each case to be considered in its own specific context.

So It Begins

Say you are concerned about disparities in access to artificial intelligence that will undermine development efforts and exacerbate economic inequality. Your multilateral organization has been approached by a few of its shareholders and other like-minded partners to convene an effort to develop a code of conduct and set of standards as international baselines for national legislation and corporate behavior. Your donor partners have convinced their respective ministries to commit significant sums of development aid to this initiative. You are now tasked with making this happen.

There is no time to waste; expectations are high and so is the risk of industry capture before safeguards are in place. You need a collective forum to share views and develop agreed terms in what is still a poorly understood and widely underappreciated area. You need a way to route donor funds to any number of activities, like studies, proposals, advocacy, outreach, and meeting participation. Ideally, the global outputs will influence local activities, including through technical assistance and capacity building.

So what do you do? Who will be invited to the table? What topics will you all address? What do you all want to achieve? Who will provide the administrative support and legal entity status? Who will handle the funds? Who will implement the activities? How will everyone work together?

This is how international partnership programs start—much like any business—with vision, ambition, interest, and lots of questions. Founding partners embody the foundation and usually seek out, or get sought out by, a supporting entity as one of the partners. Once that support function is identified, things can take off, including creation of a governing body, placement of dedicated support staff, establishment of a trust fund, and identification of implementation channels. It's a process of articulation, negotiation, agreement, and implementation—and in that process, there is lots to figure out.

And so it begins, as it has for hundreds and thousands of international partnership programs. As we'll see in these pages, a good beginning includes a good foundation for good continuation.

By Way of Example

Numbers tell only part of the story, and the World Bank Group (WBG) is only one supporting entity among many for international partnership programs. However, by way of example, here are Ten Tallies for the five years ending mid-2017:

1000

The number of WBG trust fund accounts climbed steadily to about 1,000 in 2017, with over two-thirds as top-level, main trust fund accounts, and over half as multi-donor trust funds, of which a sizeable number supported partnership programs.

$30 bn

Throughout this time, about US$30 billion was held in trust by the WBG as trustee, roughly two-thirds in international platform-type arrangements, of which 80 percent belonged to the four largest.

300

In 2017, the WBG had over 300 donors, with roughly three-quarters of all donor contributions coming from sovereign governments (mostly traditional donors), about 20 percent coming from intergovernmental organizations (of which over 80 percent were from one regional union) and just under 5 percent coming from private sector entities (of which almost 50 percent were from one private foundation).

$7 bn

The top three largest cumulative donors paid in almost US$7 billion over five years, although two of the top three decreased their 2017 contributions relative to 2016: one by one-third to US$430 million, and one by almost two-thirds to US$204 million, while the third was highest for 2017, at US$443 million.

$10 bn

Total annual cash contributions fluctuated around US$10 billion and more, with roughly two-thirds paid to international platform-type arrangements (these cash contributions do not include about 50 percent more signed up as contributions to be paid later).

even

Total annual cash disbursements roughly mirrored cash contributions, somewhat under for international platform-type arrangements and somewhat over for the rest (not including amounts committed but held in balance for later disbursements).

15%

About 15 percent of all WBG funding to low-income countries came from WBG trust funds and equaled roughly two-thirds of all grant disbursements from WBG trust funds.

80%

Total grant disbursements from WBG trust funds were US$16.3 billion over five years at about 80 percent of all disbursements, with just under half of all grants going to fragile and conflict-affected states (and almost two-thirds of that to one state).

25%

Non-grant funding went directly to the WBG to administer its work program and rose by 2017 to about one-quarter (at almost US$1 billion) of all such WBG expenses, including a significant portion of staff salaries and benefits.

>50%

Of total non-grant funding, over half went to country-level support, while about one-fifth went to global-level activities that were not driven by specific country use.

Source: 2017 WBG Trust Fund Annual Report. Notably, statistics are more available for trust funds than partnership programs, consistent with the tendencies described in this book.

Who Should Care?

Hopefully this book will find its intended audience. Only then can it become a meaningful guide and empower partners to own and shape their partnership programs.

The immediate audience is anyone who engages with the World Bank Group (WBG) and other multilateral development banks (MDBs), international financial institutions (IFIs), and United Nations (UN) agencies in the context of international partnership programs for development purposes, especially those with dedicated governing bodies and trust funds. This book is meant as a resource for any partner in these contexts, including staff of international organizations that provide supporting secretariat, trustee, and other downstream fiduciary functions, as well as staff of donor and recipient countries, and staff of other participating stakeholders, like private foundations, nongovernmental organizations (NGOs), and civil society organizations (CSOs) that participate in informal governing bodies.

This book may also be useful for anyone seeking to establish other forms of collaboration in the international arena. Many of the basic concepts, business considerations, and deeper dives can be instructive for any international partners interested in structured, sustained collaboration that uses informal, unincorporated mechanisms. Even more generally, this book can shed light on any number of other contexts in which governing bodies, fund flows, activity implementation, and branded initiatives come into play. There is much in these pages that informs a general approach to partnering. Basic typologies, vocabulary, visualizations, and paradigms introduced here may be useful for any partner looking for practical perspectives and interested in new ways of thinking.

What Does This Book Cover?

1. Structured
2. Informal
3. International

"Partnership" is a broad word, and there are many ways to slice and dice the topic. This book zeroes in on the slice of partnerships that use **structure** to operate *informally* in the *international arena*, outside of domestic legal frameworks, with a particular focus on international partnership programs.

The Structured Part

The first qualifier is that this book addresses structured partnerships. The goal is to study and understand structure as a defining feature, as in architecture, infrastructure, design, and plumbing—things that hold together by connecting to each other. There are certainly partnerships that play down structure, like partnerships in principle, institutional collaborations, and partnering around high-level memoranda of understanding. There are also unstructured networks that partner, like communities of practice, newsletter lists, and other forms of "rolodex" partnering. There are even partnering engagements that explicitly state they are not partnerships (nor the whole legal litany of joint venture, agency, employment, franchise, association, or unincorporated business). Structure comes in when partners insert themselves into ongoing decision making or divvy up responsibilities in ongoing partnership business.

Before we plunge in, *nota bene* on two points:

First, this book avoids making specific references to actual international partnership programs. It draws from many of them, primarily the hundreds I have worked on, some of which are well known and others not so much. You may recognize familiar contours as you read. However, in saying that things depend on context, I want to walk the talk with ample room for business judgments, rather than second guessing. Instead of labeling cases as good or bad, or commenting judgmentally on their specifics, they may all reflect reasonable choices based on options at the time, and they may evolve from experience over time. It seems more productive to see the big picture, study trends and tenets, glean lessons learned, and formulate good practices without naming names.

Second, I acknowledge the occasional broad statement, presented more didactically than literally. Already the text is overrun with *often, typically, usually, can, may, potentially, generally,* and the like to allow for exceptions or differences that inevitably also exist. Please allow for generalizations that may overlook your specifics, as I try to frame topics and make points without choking on too many caveats and clarifications. As I am also writing from my own frame of reference, where I have more to offer, there will surely be blind spots. Hopefully these will get filled in over time as more of a community of practice around the subject of international partnership programs emerges and evolves.

As the term suggests, "structured partnerships" are when partners define their participation by creating structure. The structural design can be haphazard, like when participants are forced into prescribed templates that fit like a Procrustean bed, or when they forge ahead blindly making trade-offs like *Hans im Glück* without a plan. Or the design can be thoughtful, inclusive, engaging, and strategic. Structure can be at once solid and fluid. More than anything, it can be fit-for-purpose and designed for context. In so doing, it all depends.

The Informal, International Part

The second qualifier is that this book primarily addresses informal partnerships in the international arena. It does not directly address partnerships established under or couched in domestic law, which are considered "formal" because they are incorporated, thereby separating the legal personality of the venture from the personalities of the institutional or individual partners. International approaches based on informal, unincorporated partnership structures are fitting when the main participants are states and their multilateral, intergovernmental organizations, like UN agencies and MDBs.

Because informal, international partnerships are not governed by domestic law, much of the applicable law comes from "laws" set by the parties for themselves, first as negotiated in their agreed terms, like charters and fund flow agreements, and second, operationally through the governing environments of their supporting entities and implementing partners. For international organizations, the "rules of the organization"—usually understood to include the entity's constitutive documents, policies, decisions, and established practices—often do little to regulate international partnerships, so there is considerable room for partners to add their own creative, contextual structuring.

At the same time, despite all this latitude on the partnership plane, individual partners that come from national contexts, like country governments and incorporated entities, are still affected by the laws of their respective local jurisdictions, and locally implemented activities must still comply with relevant local laws. The informal elements that are possible in the international arena fit within the interstices of what applies elsewhere. For those who relish the complexity, we look later at what governs international partnership programs and how that affects partnering among partners. (>@ Partnering Internationally)

The Focus on International Partnership Programs

International partnership programs are easy to find in practice, but any established or coordinated practice for designing or structuring them is harder to find. And yet there is lots to unpack. The chapters that follow systematically lay out the elements, both as to their essentials and in relation to each other. The focus here is not on partnerships or partnership programs that have their own legal personalities, created as dedicated legal entities, but rather on the informal kind of international partnership that relies and builds on the resources of other, previously existing, legal entities. Much that appears in these pages applies to a wider range of partnerships, but the point of this primer is to tease out the special elements that arise from this reliance by all partners on support from one or more designated partners—more specifically, this reliance on international supporting entities that play their support roles as partners in partnership. International partnership programs are partnerships through and through to the core, with partners operating even at the very crux of their structure.

What's in the special sauce? An international supporting entity that is more than support. It is first and foremost a partner.

Conclusion

Each case offers lessons for the next case, and every case is unique. For international partnership programs in which partners orchestrate collectivized features, manage acceptable trade-offs, seek innovative approaches, and position sustainable, effective, and impactful structures, this book aims to show that the science of delivery rests on the art of design.

So here goes the first ever structuring and design guide to partnership programs for development and other endeavors in the international arena. The wide and wonderful world of these partnership programs is about to be revealed to you—in all its complexity, simplicity, efficiency, and opportunity. (>@ the rest of this book)

It's about making better partners in better partnerships.

How Best to Read This Book

For a smooth ride to a sustained, efficient, and impactful destination, please follow these guideposts:

1   *Nothing in this guide is gospel.*

Whatever your circumstances, this guide is meant to give you principles, placeholders, and pointers. Read proposed approaches, potential pitfalls, and accompanying commentary, and check them against the reality of your own circumstances.

2   *Use this guide to get the gist.*

This book goes out on a limb to take positions and suggest good practices, but only as starting points to get you going. You are your own architect and can leverage the creative space in the international arena to your advantage.

3   *Look up your specific topic.*

This book intentionally breaks material out into lots of topics and subtopics. It tries to treat each topic comprehensively—apologies in advance for any overlaps—with ample cross-referencing (look for >@). Zero in on what you need.

4   *Read for common threads.*

Many of the issues covered here are crosscutting and correlated. The themes speak to each other, and undergird, layer, complement, and circle back. Wherever you start to read, let the concepts carry you.

PART 1

MAIN FOUNDATIONS

In this Part, we review basic types and core elements of international partnership programs, a particularly popular form of structured partnership for international collaborations.

1 Ten Take-Aways
Every writer has a point of view, so this is full disclosure—here are ten themes that carry throughout the pages of this book.

2 Like Rock, Like Water
It takes stability to have flexibility, and it takes both to have sustainable, effective, and impactful international partnership programs.

3 Typology
In locating international partnership programs on the spectrum of structured partnerships, we pay special attention to one-stop-shops and international platforms.

4 International Partnership Programs
Deconstructing international partnership programs, we identify six main "collectives": decision making, funding, support, activities, knowledge, and brand.

5 Governing Bodies
Taking the first collective, we consider informal governing bodies—as distinguished from formal, corporate bodies—from both institutional (partner) and individual (representative) perspectives.

6 Secretariats
Here we shine a light, with great appreciation, on the essential and wide-ranging secretariat support functions that hold international partnership programs together.

7 Trust Funds
Not all partnership programs have them, but when they do, it helps to understand international trust funds as accounts in relation to donors, recipients, roles, money flows, and the mechanics that make them so popular.

1 TEN TAKE-AWAYS

1 International partnership program design can be contextual and fit-for-purpose.

KEEP
CALM
AND
COLLABORATE

2 International partnership programs are organic, about people more than funds.

3 Effective partnership programs need good, like-minded partners.

4 International partners have a stunning number of business choices.

5 Clarity and modularity promote stability and flexibility.

6 Informed trade-offs and leveraged synergies are reinforcing.

7 Money talks; donors drive for results with the power of the purse.

8 Supporting entities join as partners and bring their policies and risk profiles.

9 International partnership programs are in the hybrid sweet spot.

10 Best to keep it simple; it will get complex enough.

2 LIKE ROCK, LIKE WATER

G ood partnerships are organic, centered and stable, responsive and flexible. They sit on solid ground and go with the flow. They are patient and sustained, yet nimble and adaptable.

Their design is about connections and delineations, as the water flows, as the rock divides. They are structured to be secure in their settings, contextual, and modular, all the while seeking new ways and evolving over time.

In international partnership programs, where the partnership and the program are defined by their agreed terms, the establishment documents are not there to simply check the box, but to reflect reality and direct operations. Context gives terms their meaning, and agreed terms shape the context. To connect what is said with what is done, it helps to think of rocks and water.

Both structure and contracts are foundational elements of international partnership programs. Together they provide the agreed baselines and infrastructure for partnership operations. What gets interesting is the interplay between the two. (>@ Structure—Connecting Fund Flows and Decision Flows) Like rock, like water, partnerships can benefit from this two-tone setting by crafting a combination of stable and versatile elements that are matched appropriately to partnership needs.

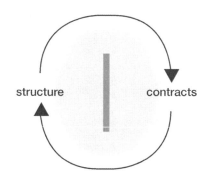

structure   contracts

- On the one hand, partners can avoid giving leeway on things that need to stay set, like upholding agreement hierarchies or having a say where needed.

- On the other hand, partners can invite leeway on aspects that need flexibility, like topics that can be put under collective purview in a charter.

All of this can be transparent and well-considered, with a discipline that ensures the clarity and integrity of the foundational documents and related procedures. What follows are Ten Tools of the Trade to start us off.

Like Rock

It all starts with a solid foundation. Here are four steps for building a rock-solid partnership program:

1 **Establish solid common ground.** Partners do well to establish specific terms of their partnership program early and clearly. For all the investments and intentions at stake, no one wants to see a partnership hit the shoals of missed expectations or failed operations somewhere down the line just because different partners assumed different things at the start. Particularly in these as-negotiated environments, where the fluidity of informal, unincorporated partnership structures can be both friend and enemy, partners should be highly motivated to create a solid foundation of clearly articulated and confirmed common ground. One of the best ways to test partner commitment and common ground is to **converge around a well-articulated charter** or similar constitutive, establishment document.

2 **Centrally position the governing body.** Establishment documents mean the most and last the longest if they belong to the partnership as a whole. In practice, this usually involves leveraging the central governing body for buy-in, especially if that body represents all partners. How? The first step to putting a foundational document like a charter in the hands of the governing body is to have the body **adopt the charter.** This way the governing body takes direct ownership, and participants view this central, definitional piece as theirs. Giving the governing body direct purview over the charter lets partners convene with consensus, transparency, inclusion, and other partnership values. (>@ International Partnership Programs—Shared Decision Making)

3 **Communicate in plain English.** Baseline documents that speak to lawyers but no one else are misplaced in partnership programs. If foundational terms are not clearly understood and knowingly confirmed, they cannot provide solid footing. They cannot orient roles and responsibilities, inform expectations and operations, or become baselines for change over time. The accessibility of establishment documents sets the tone for direct and shared engagement from start to finish. Some amount of legalese is probably unavoidable, and fund flow agreements can be dense. However, there is no excuse for charters to be anything other than direct and to the point. Circumlocution in defining partnership programs is not a virtue. Separating plain English terms into a separate document adopted by the governing body is in fact a good reason to have a charter. This is the piece that participants themselves can **create and own**—*if they make it their own.*

1. Establish solid common ground.

2. Centrally position the governing body.

3. Communicate in plain English.

4. Watch for readiness.

———————•———————

Which version would you prefer in your charter?

1) Notwithstanding any statement to the contrary, and subject to the following proviso, the parties are deemed to be in a satisfactory position to proceed on the basis of all heretofore agreed terms; provided that the foregoing is understood to be applicable as of the date hereof and for such period as the parties shall agree.

or

2) We're good to go!

———————•———————

4 *Watch for readiness.* Launching a partnership program prematurely is like pitching a roof without rafters—watch out below. And yet there is always pressure to get going, as deadlines for delivery steamroll prudent preparations. This is another one of those trade-offs that partners regularly face in establishing partnership programs: Go now with loose ends or tie them down and go later. (>@ Trade-Offs) What to watch for? Among the critical milestones for launching a partnership program is the receipt of funds, a concrete step that pins fiduciary responsibility and can be hard to unwind. A responsible trustee avoids taking funds while terms are still half-baked and big issues are unresolved. It is usually worth *taking the time to get a common foundation* and broad buy-in (points 1 to 3 above) before pressing "go."

Like Water

1. Opt for a living, breathing charter.

2. Collect essential, amendable terms.

3. Define processes for change.

4. Add the carry-over effect.

5. Take advantage of two speeds.

6. Keep current.

Flexibility is possible if you have stability; otherwise, it breeds complexity and confusion. Indeed, part of being stable is anticipating change and including change processes upfront. Anything organic needs to evolve to keep from deteriorating—for international partnership programs that means adjusting to changing contexts, shifting circumstances, and enriched understandings. Partners who let an appreciation of adaptability inform the original design can include pre-agreed change mechanisms that are easy to implement later. Here are six steps for letting the water flow:

1 *Opt for a living, breathing charter.* Since partnership programs are organic, their establishment documents need room to evolve. What is memorialized on day one may not be the whole story, nor the final tale. This is why charters and the like are best considered living, breathing documents. Charters are for adopting, not signing. Once the governing body has adopted the charter, it can later adopt amendments over time. In this way, the charter can be gently tweaked or massively overhauled—once, twice, or many times, as the partners desire—and every time, no more than one specific decision point at a time. It is infinitely easier to approve a charter amendment at a governing body meeting than to engage in arduous, legal signing exercises for individual, formal amendments across all relevant agreements (for example, all contribution agreements for a commingled, multi-donor trust fund). And with adopted charter amendments, the timing works well, too. Charter *amendments can go into effect immediately*, as opposed to waiting for every last partner's signature, which can take a remarkably long time. Imagine having gotten consensus to add a new member to the governing body, but then having to wait months or

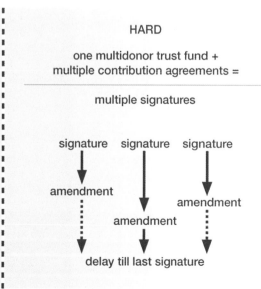

EASY

one charter +
one governing body =

one decision point

decision

↓

amendment

↓

done ☑

HARD

one multidonor trust fund +
multiple contribution agreements =

multiple signatures

signature   signature   signature

↓   ↓   ↓

amendment   amendment

            amendment

↓   ↓   ↓

delay till last signature

longer while participants muck around with their legal formalities for the amendments needed for this change to become official. Living, breathing, adopted charters can avoid this difficulty and delay.

2 *Collect essential, amendable terms.* Putting amendments in the hands of the governing body through a charter means the charter must contain relevant terms, the ones that are prone to change. What are those terms? Basically they include any *key terms that make up the contextualized, collectivized framework*, like the mission and scope of partnership activities, governing body membership, and partner roles and responsibilities—all those elements that reflect the specific partnering circumstances and define the basic partnership program contours. Fortunately, those are already charter-type terms, so this part of the exercise comes naturally. Charters by nature are foundational documents that contain these key definitional points, exactly the ones that are most likely to change over time. What is left is a systematic sorting and parsing to make amply sure the charter collects everything that should be readily amendable (and leaves for elsewhere, as in contribution agreements, what should not).

3 *Define processes for change.* In addition to the amendability of their text, partners can think about changes in terms of process. Although partners cannot foresee actual changes to be made, they can pre-plan and fill the gap with steps to be taken. Or, to put it another way, partners can have *firmly agreed content and firmly agreed procedures*. Both are rocks, but the procedures let in the water. Procedures can set up processes for change by defining *who*, *what*, and *how*. For example, the governing body (who) can expand the list of eligible countries (what) if they meet certain criteria and also have the trustee's consent (how). This triptych can be memorialized bilaterally, by including it in all signed contribution agreements, or multilaterally, by including it in charters or other governing body–approved documents, depending on who is affected. Clarifying procedural mechanisms upfront to be invoked later can enable stable flexibility.

4 *Add the carry-over effect.* That brings us to an added element for trust-funded partnership programs. Partnership programs with trust funds can usefully combine adopted documents (like charters) and signed agreements (like contribution agreements). This way, signed contribution agreements comprehensively cover trust fund operations by cross-referencing terms that are spelled out in a charter. As a result, for full effectiveness in the legal sense (full operability), it is important for charter amendments to also amend contribution agreements when the subject matter overlaps. An efficient way to do this is to *give charter amendments automatic effect* across all contribution agreements, as something to be worked into the drafting from the start. In this way, when the governing body approves a charter amendment, the set-up also reaches over and changes the signed agreements as part of the overall package. With this kind of one-stop amending, the circle is closed, everything fits together, and the governing body's view carries.

Got unknown content? Get a known process.

———————•———————

Sample Carry-Over Clause

"The Contribution may be used for the activities and in the manner set forth in the Charter, as may be amended from time to time. Any amendments to the Charter shall become applicable to this Contribution Agreement as such amendments take effect without further need to amend this Contribution Agreement."

———————•———————

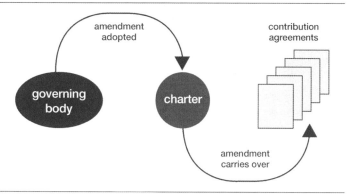

LIVING, BREATHING FRAMEWORK

ROCK & WATER STRUCTURE

5 **Take advantage of two speeds.** Careful decisions can be made regarding what stays firm vs. what can readily change. Agreements, with their binding effect and signature formalities, are usually more rigid. It takes more to get them signed, whether initially or for changes. This is particularly noteworthy for trust funds with multiple donors, where any contribution agreement change that affects the commingled funds or trustee operations requires signed amendments by each and every donor before the change can go into effect. Charters, by contrast, can be made responsive to the governing body and amendable through a single decision. This gives partners, and their lawyers, two speeds to work with. Embedding less negotiable terms in agreements keeps them in an institutional safe zone and more off-limits for change. Including more variable terms in the charter—ones that reflect a growing, maturing partnership—opens them up to adjustment through a more efficient decision process. For example, governing body membership terms are typically clear candidates for the charter, open to future adjustment as agreed by the governing body. More institutional aspects, like the trustee's standard operating terms, are typically non-negotiable and non-adjustable over time and are thereby good candidates for the contribution agreements. The process of **choosing what clauses go where** can be quite deliberate, favoring either institutional pulls or partner prerogatives by virtue of placement.

6 **Keep current.** Baseline documents of international partnership programs need to stay current. Although contribution agreements and charters may be easily forgotten the minute they go into effect, they are not mere formalities. They continue to be operative and vital to the partnership program's existence. Without them, what else is there to define the partnership program? Not all aspects of a partnership program are in these establishment documents, but those that are need updating to reflect partnership program changes as they occur. In fact, this updating through amendments should cause the change, effectively getting permission from the partners first. This is a **basic courtesy and legal necessity** for partnership programs where everyone is in it together. Everyone deserves to be on board for changes that affect everyone, and everyone should be able to rely on the continued stability and currency of foundational documents over time. The only thing worse than not having establishment documents is having inaccurate, out-of-date establishment documents, especially if they start conflicting with each other. Partners do not want to end up in the twilight zone, where establishment documents say one thing and the partnership program does something else—especially the trustee, who picks up all manner of contractual obligations, cannot afford to operate in two contradictory universes, bound by one set of terms and expected to perform on another.

If it's worth having a charter, it's worth keeping it current.

Conclusion

Like rock, like water is ancient wisdom for people as they navigate life, but it also speaks to partnerships that are navigating programs. International partnership programs are about helping people—and the planet, peace, and shared prosperity—as beneficiaries. That gets talked about a lot, with attention placed on progress, results, and impact. But the partnership itself is also about people—as in partners who are convening to make a difference. Like rock, like water includes putting people first *as partners* for the sake of collaboration. Only in this way can progress, results, and impact make the maximized, intended difference for beneficiaries. By following the principles in this chapter, embedding stability and enabling flexibility, partners, as institutions and individuals, can make sure their partnership serves them, and ultimately their beneficiaries; not the other way around.

Embed stability,
enable flexibility.

3 TYPOLOGY

With some practical philosophy behind us, where do we begin to map the landscape? This is a winding path, and we can easily go down a rabbit hole. The point is to stay above the weeds; or better yet, reach the trees, where we can see the forest. Structured partnerships in the international arena are prone to variety and variability, especially the beloved species of trust-funded partnership programs. A little categorizing and parsing can sharpen the focus.

Introducing Two Mighty Oaks

Speaking of trees, we might as well start with what pops up the most. Let me introduce two seedlings that met a need and grew into mighty oaks, facing each other across the grove: *one-stop-shops* and *international platforms*. This may not be everyone's standard terminology, but both are trust-funded partnership programs that say what they are. Once we have those firmly in view, we can put them in context and consider the broader terrain.

One-Stop-Shops

As a common form of structured partnership in the international arena, one-stop-shops are vertically integrated operations. They typically function with a supporting entity that is an international organization, like an MDB or UN agency, and also a partner. Partners fully leverage the supporting entity partner and give it multiple roles, sometimes more, sometimes fewer, including as convener, founder, donor, decision maker, chair, secretariat, trustee, implementer, and supervisor. Offered as a comprehensive package, these multiple roles are considered more synergistic than in conflict. (>@ Synergistic Conflicts) Some of the supporting entity's roles are explicit and agreed, like the secretariat or trustee role. Some are more implicit and organic, like the custodian or even rescuer role. (>@ Secretariats—Inhouse Secretariat Roles) The defining feature of one-stop-shops is the willingness of donors and other partners to rely on the supporting entity to carry the partnership program. One-stop-shops take full advantage of the supporting entity's legal status, resources, operating framework, expertise, experience, country reach, reputation, and more.

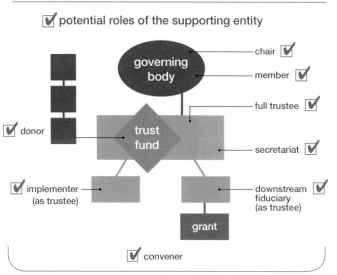

Full Trustee

One-stop-shops include trust funds because fund management is a big part of what supporting entities can offer. In fact, trust funds are usually the center of gravity for one-stop-shops, and a key characteristic is the "full" trustee. (>@ Trustee Types) Because trust-funded partnership programs often start with the trust fund—there is enough money to get something going—the focus on the trustee comes naturally. In a one-stop-shop, the trustee typically has the main role on stage, so much so that secretariat functions may be merged into the trustee role, rather than identified separately.

The full trustee connects the legal entity for the partnership program, the supporting entity, to the partners. It is the supporting entity as trustee that serves as the contractual pivot point through agreements containing or incorporating the full scope of what donors need to know to contribute. Other functions then emanate from this trustee function, like implementation and supervision under the trustee's fiduciary responsibility.

To put it chronologically, funds are handed over, the trustee deposits them in the trust fund, and then takes off from there, using those funds to follow through on the program—including, for example, putting up the brand and website, considering proposals, allocating funds, implementing activities, handing out grants, monitoring and evaluating progress, reporting back, arranging governing body meetings, and keeping records, all as agreed with the partners.

Supporting Entity

Some form of shared governance is part of the one-stop-shop structure, as with all partnership programs, although in this case, more as an offshoot from the main trunk, rather than the other way around. Shared governance gives the donors and, potentially, other partners some degree of say or engagement as the partnership program proceeds. How much and on what depends on what is negotiated, but always against the backdrop that the one-stop-shop supporting entity has the lion's share of the operating responsibility. Linking in others means extra exposure and associational risk for the supporting entity, enough to justify its large role in the decision making from start to finish.

To match accountability with authority (>@ Ten Tried and True Tips), the one-stop-shop is accordingly supporting entity–centric. It represents a specific choice by the partners to give the supporting entity soup-to-nuts responsibility and affords the supporting entity commensurate control and influence over the partnership program and its operations. Even in one-stop-shops with shared governance, partners lean on the supporting entity to carry the critical mass of responsibility, and in turn the supporting entity gets the matching reins for the ride.

It is always useful to consider who has what role in a partnership program, in addition to looking at who has multiple roles and how all roles relate to each other. Every participant has an interest in promoting, protecting, and preserving its own participation and standing. This is true with a multiplier effect for the one-stop-shop supporting entity and its multiple touch points. For everyone's sake, these entities can work with other partners to be more effective. That includes minimizing encumbrances, both substantive and procedural, that could keep supporting entities from maximum functionality for the partnership program.

Even as other partners push expectations, expect visibility, and seek to have things their way, the supporting entity has a legitimate interest in protecting its track record and reputation. Mindful of its extensive associational exposure to partners, it aims to preserve its prerogatives and privileges, including particularly any privileges and immunities (P&I). (>@ Supporting Entities—Basic Elements) Partners do well to recognize that the work program performed by the supporting entity as part of the partnership program is also the supporting entity's own work program that it needs to keep intact and on track.

How do one-stop-shops spell release and relief?

Hand it all over to the supporting entity.

One-stop-shops represent an overall trade-off: apportioning more responsibility to supporting entities in exchange for less responsibility for donors and other partners, but that also means more control for the supporting entity and less control for others. That this trade-off works well is evident in the numbers, which show that hundreds if not thousands of trustee-driven partnership programs populate the international landscape. Donors may choose this approach by default—that is, they may not have the resources or operating frameworks to carry the load themselves—but there is both release and relief in handing the whole bundle of functions over to the supporting entity.

The one-stop-shop package is in many ways plug-and-play, since it relies so heavily on existing functions. However, not everything is pre-defined, and especially contributions, objectives, activities, and governance vary case-by-case. As a result, there may be some tug-of-war between donors and the supporting entity during and after the establishment phase, as they position their respective interests. Ideally, however, the supporting entity can be clear on its offer from the start, and donors and other partners can be clear on their acceptance, as they all benefit from well-tread terms that let one-stop-shop partnership programs rest on solid foundations.

International Platforms

Whereas one-stop-shops are vertically integrated, international platforms are horizontally expanded. International platforms still showcase a trust fund and feature a main trustee, but the added components carry more weight overall. In addition, rather than one supporting entity with many roles, as in one-stop-shops, international platforms emphasize multiple supporting and fiduciary entities, each with specific, separate roles. These roles are meant to be complementary and modular, and entities can play multiple roles or just one.

In general, international platforms are big on mutual respect. Governing bodies are typically more inclusive, and each supporting or fiduciary entity is expected to operate on the basis of its own rules. With more players and more roles, international platforms tend to be more as-negotiated and less standard in their structure and design, potentially allowing for more innovation. International platforms are, as the name suggests, platforms for greater international collaboration and deeper international engagement.

Limited Trustee

Whereas one-stop-shops feature the "full" trustee, international platforms feature the "limited" trustee. While the full trustee takes on full fiduciary responsibility for the funds it receives all the way down to their end use, the limited trustee takes on only limited fiduciary responsibility. To put it simply, the limited trustee is responsible only for the funds that it holds. As soon as those funds are transferred to another entity, responsibility transfers with them. The downstream entity then becomes the fiduciary, on the basis of its own rules.

From a trust fund perspective, in its most basic form, limited trustees act on **three essential elements: (1) money in, (2) instructions in, and (3) money out**. This means the limited, pass-through trustee takes and holds the funds until it gets instructions for their use and then disburses them accordingly. Donors essentially trust the trustee to manage and disburse the funds properly, end of story. In doing its job, however, the as-negotiated narrative can get complex, with different windows and currencies, commitment letters and cash transfer requests, investment income and refunds, reports and audits, and all the various features, bells, and whistles that can constitute the trustee's operations.

The limited trustee plot twist progresses from this commingling chapter one to chapters featuring other protagonists. Downstream actors enter stage

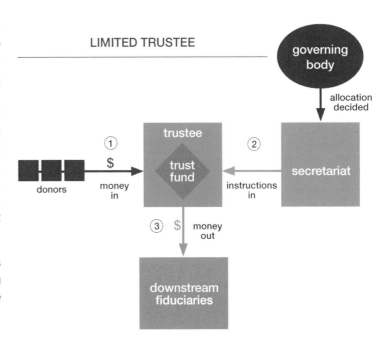

How do international platforms spell release and relief?

Crowd in multiple downstream fiduciaries.

right, having been validated by the partners and empowered (ideally) to play their part under their own respective rules. For a classic pass-through fund, this is usually an essential element: agreed eligibility of downstream fiduciary entities based on the adequacy of their own rules. In this way, international platforms crowd in multiple downstream entities.

This limited trustee approach works for donors as long as the transfer of funds and transition of responsibility is transparent, clear, and seamless, and as long as the donors' recourse travels with the funds. (>@ Fund Use Responsibility—Transferred (No) Responsibility) It also works for downstream fiduciaries as long as the trustee stays neutral and handles all downstream entities without favoritism—on a level playing field, as it were. The latter is especially important when the supporting entity that acts as trustee also acts as one of the downstream fiduciaries, a not uncommon occurrence (and a multiple role vestige of one-stop-shops).

Limited Secretariat

The limited trustee has an important legal entity function in international platforms. However, as the opening pivot for fund flows and their accompanying contractual terms, it is not the only or even primary legal entity role. The secretariat has an equally pronounced legal entity role, usually as a separate, identified function, often within the same supporting entity as the trustee. The trustee is the *financial* entry point and centerpiece, and the secretariat is the **programmatic and governance** focal point and glue. Ideally, these support functions are ringfenced on both fronts, and the division of labor is clean. For example, when it comes to "follow the money, follow the power," (>@ Structure—Whiteboarding) the trustee basically follows the money, and the secretariat basically follows the power.

In international platforms, the interplay between trustee and secretariat is paramount for the efficient functioning of upstream decision making and downstream implementation. For example, information from the trustee about funding availability flows through the secretariat to the governing body, and information about funding allocations by the governing body flows through the secretariat to the trustee. Similarly, regular financial reports from the trustee—and regular financial and progress reports from the downstream entities—also flow through the secretariat to the governing body and other partners. This positions the secretariat as essential hub and clearing house for the overall partnership program. (>@ Secretariats—Inhouse Secretariat Roles)

Despite its central position, however, the international platform secretariat is usually also expected to have a limited role, in tandem with the trustee. Just as the limited trustee is not inclined to overstep its limited fiduciary bounds, so too must the secretariat take care not to become a backdoor trustee or overstep its limited support role. For example, when receiving reports to distribute to the governing body, the secretariat's role is one of compilation, rather than review, comment, or clean up—which is to say, administrative, not substantive. (>@ Trustee Types—International Platforms—Limited Trustees)

In general, the international platform secretariat is better off guarding against overdelegation from the governing body. That includes resisting requests to check on downstream beneficiaries (not a fiduciary supervisor) or producing or applying eligibility criteria for downstream fiduciaries (not a standard setter). In international platforms, these are substantive roles that belong to the governing body, with a potentially fine line on how much support the secretariat should provide. There have certainly been zealous secretariats. However, putting it contextually, limitations on the secretariat function, as an administrative support function, are meant to carry upwards, so as not to infringe on the governing body's substantive role, and also downwards, like the trustee, so as not to favor one or the other downstream fiduciary or slip into fiduciary assignments.

Governing Body

Shared governance is usually the crux of the matter for international platforms. Here the governing body takes the front seat, directing the partnership program. The limited trustee and limited secretariat take the passenger seats, while designated downstream fiduciary entities follow in the caravan behind. Each role has its primacy for what it does, but the governing body usually has the overarching role. It is responsible for the strategy and substance of the partnership program, including who participates, on what terms, for what purposes, and to what ends. As the governing body steps up to the helm, international platforms choose to array the support functions. Individual roles are stacked and aligned to give each function clear prerogatives and responsibilities, each within its own realm.

If an international platform is well-designed, the collective whole becomes more than the sum of its parts. The governing body informs the rest of the partnership at the same time that other functions inform the governing body. This works especially well if the governing body cleanly delegates down, rather than creating a central overlay. The more that partnership-originated policies and procedures are instituted and imposed by the governing body—either augmenting or supplanting existing downstream operational frameworks—the more unwieldy the sum of the parts becomes, as partnership-specific requirements do more to detract than add.

Of all the things to be collectivized in international platforms, the one thing to be diversified is the downstream implementation. (>@ Fund Use Responsibility) Too much overlay and deviation from existing frameworks is a recipe for inefficiency and delay, not to mention human error, when processes travel outside established management systems. Even as everything flows into decision making at the top, the actual operations of an international platform are best left to the respective downstream entities that are included precisely for their implementation capacity and operating frameworks.

One-stop-shops:
Build inward with critical mass in the supporting entity.

International platforms:
Build outward with critical mass in the shared partnership.

WHERE IS THE CRITICAL MASS?

★ supporting entity	governing body

one-stop-shops

supporting entity	★ governing body

international platforms

One-Stop-Shops vs. International Platforms

One-stop-shops are the ***ultimate packaging act***. They can provide virtually turnkey support to donors and other partners as an extension of the supporting entity's own work program, making it appropriate that the supporting entity's imprimatur is on everything the partnership program does. Shared governance is usually an appendage, although to varying degrees, as partners find they cannot delegate responsibility to the supporting entity and eat their cake, too—except to the extent the supporting entity lets them. It is not always clear where the negotiating balance lies, since supporting entities have become hugely reliant on one-stop-shops to advance their own agendas, just as international partners need supporting entities to advance theirs. In a world of scarce resources, donors, in particular, seek to increase both their leverage in partnerships and their impact on the ground. In the end, though, this can still be a match made in heaven if, after a little push-me-pull-you, partners manage to maximize the supporting entity role as partner.

By contrast, international platforms are the ***ultimate balancing act***. They invite more active players to the table and thereby also invite complexity, making it all the more important to keep the division of roles and responsibilities clear and clean. The governing body is vested with primary jurisdiction on the substance at the same time that it is heavily dependent on the respective support functions, and dependent on those support functions functioning well with each other. There are many ways international platforms can go, and many have pushed the innovation envelope. Negotiations can be labyrinths, and closure takes serious time, cost, and compromise. However, international platforms are still the ultimate statement of sharing. Their greatest gift lies in their inclusiveness, synergies, and exponential potential for cooperation and collaboration.

ONE-STOP SHOP

INTERNATIONAL PLATFORM

In general, partnership programs can point either inward or outward. From a supporting entity–centric view of the world, this means that supporting entities can either pull the structure into their own operating environments, or they can support an open structure that extends beyond their own operating environments. This dynamic is a stark play in contrasts, which is why one-stop-shops and international platforms are such excellent foils for the study of International Partnership Programs 101. A whole host of elements emanates from this point of reference, not least the spirit and vibe of the initiative. Deciding whether to build inward, with critical mass in the supporting entity, or outward, with critical mass in the shared partnership, can pivot all the rest.

Which of these is more in the spirit of multilateralism? That is a valid question. One-stop-shops typically leverage multilateral supporting entities, and the more they look inward, the more they build on that multilaterally built base. International platforms typically reach out to multilaterals, and the more they reach out, the more they draw in that multilateral diversity. It is hard to say whether multilateralism is amplified or undermined by international partnership programs, especially if one recognizes that these structured partnerships and their dedicated funding vehicles are integral parts of the business of multilaterals. Suffice it to say that multilateral institutions are critical drivers and essential parts of international partnership programs, and there is no chance of either leaving the other behind.

The Broader Landscape of Partnership Programs

Judging by the popularity of one-stop-shops and international platforms, partnership programs deserve more attention when it comes to structured partnerships in the international arena. Broadly speaking, international partnership programs are hybrid arrangements that position new partnership-specific governing bodies with existing, non-partnership-specific supporting entities. Within the international partnership program subset of structured partnerships, the range of possibilities is endless. Here is just a slice of the variables at play:

- different players, different donors, different recipients, different requirements

- different supporting entities, different roles, different degrees of engagement

- different governing body compositions, different responsibilities, different standards

- different funding sources, maybe one or more trust funds, different scopes and activities

- different goals, different challenges, different politics, different personalities

The many variations on this hybrid theme add up to many business choices that go into creating these multifaceted, multidimensional structured partnerships. Designing these hybrid partnership program arrangements calls for thinking in layers, in roles and responsibilities, in modularity, clarity, and flexibility. By keeping both the forest and the trees in view, it is possible to see that the term "partnership program" is deliberate. The partnership supports the program, the program drives the partnership, and *all elements converge* to turn challenges into results. All support is geared toward amplifying the partnership and the program together.

Lawyers refer to this environment as "sui generis." That is derived from Latin for "of its kind" to recognize a unique item, apart from all the rest. For international partnership programs, this means being contextual and flexible, allowing the uniqueness of every situation to drive the structure and design of each case to maximum benefit.

Sui generis symbiosis:

The partnership supports the program,

the program drives the partnership,

together turning challenges into results.

Trust-Funded Partnership Programs

International partnership programs not only collectivize governance into a common governing body but most also collectivize funding into one or more common trust funds. (>@ International Partnership Programs—Collectivizing) For many of these initiatives, the trust fund is the impetus that creates the common venture, even more so than the shared governance. The addition of a trustee function—to administer the partnership program's dedicated funding source—is such a widespread modality that this category deserves even more attention, plus a label of its own: trust-funded partnership programs.

It is under the header of trust-funded partnership programs that we find one-stop-shops and international platforms, those two prominent, but quite different, mighty oaks.

Having simplified to this point, let me hasten to add that the mind is the limit on how international partnership programs can be stacked. For every generalization, there are exceptions; for every standard approach, there are alternatives; for every tried and true arrangement, there are innovations. The two counterpoint typologies presented here are but broad brush strokes with which to frame the discussion. They point to individual trees that give some profile to an abundant forest. We have already seen that the sub-sub-category of trust-funded partnership programs can be split into two variations as diverse as one-stop-shops and international platforms. Now add multiple governing bodies, multiple funding sources, multiple classes of participants, multiple supporting entities, multiple implementation modalities, and so much more, and these profiles are just the front end of a telescope beyond which a whole vista lies.

Among the many variations, two more plays on the international partnership program theme merit typologizing as well.

Coordination Partnerships

1. Coordination partnerships
2. Umbrella arrangements

Sometimes, all partners want to do is coordinate with some light collaboration. They each have their own decision-making structures for what to fund and how to do it. They each have separate funding sources that are individually tracked and attributed. They each have their implementation channels, either through their own means or through others. The only collective they seek is a common table—whether physical or virtual—where they can share and learn. The inputs to these kinds of partnership programs are only what it takes to meet and share, and the outputs are whatever partners can glean from those meetings and sharings.

On the theory that two minds are better than one, collective consideration of opportunities and challenges can brainstorm innovations and garner lessons learned. In the interest of avoiding gaps and overlaps, greater visibility of concurrent engagements in the same space, on the same themes, can create more seamless, harmonized, leveraged interventions. Putting it all together, coordination partnerships can even link multiple partnership programs. Even the simplest coordination partnerships can be highly appreciated by the participants and highly effective in making a sustainable difference on the ground.

This may be partnership programming on a shoestring, but it goes to the essence of partnership programs with a human face. The light touch puts the emphasis squarely on the partners, and the related low costs and simplicity reflect that. With all the emphasis on trust fund–driven endeavors, this kind of convening platform may be given short shrift, but that is not the intent. There is plenty of room for just plain coordinating. Indeed, there are more coordination partnerships than meet the eye, since they are not as visible or lauded in the "structured" pantheon. And yet, they still merit a few structural considerations.

Setting up a coordination partnership takes but a few elements:

- a group of like-minded institutions or representatives, open to sharing and able to pay for their own participation

- some leadership, like a designated, and possibly rotating, chair

- a central convening logistics function, perhaps rotated among partners or in the hands of the designated chair

- a statement confirming the group's interest and intentions, both to connect to each other and to project to others

The last point can be considered a charter-light. It does not need all the trappings of a full-fledged charter, but coordination partnerships can nonetheless benefit from a page or two saying why partners are meeting, how they expect to approach their engagements, who has what roles and responsibilities, and what they hope to achieve. As for central support, depending on how often the partners want to meet, how much they want to do together, and how broadly they want to advocate or disseminate materials, an appropriately sized function can rely on in-kind engagement from the partners. Beyond that, costs are absorbed by each partner. There is no pooled funding and no implementation infrastructure, since all of that is handled by the respective partners in their own decentralized fashion.

Lest this category fall between the cracks because it takes so little space to describe, it is worth emphasizing how incredibly beneficial coordination for the sake of coordination can be. It does not take much to convene and collect activities, experience, knowledge, concerns, and ambitions in ways that can leverage significant value, worth more than the price of admission. Where every institution has its own profile and comparative advantage, and where institutions tend to sit in their silos, just the chance to convene can be meaningful— including across the humanitarian-development-security-peace-and-every-other nexus.

Interested institutions coming together as partners can achieve much by simply creating and crowding in knowledge and amplifying their voices for advocacy. As public sources of funding get more scarce and international challenges get more complex, partners will discover more and more how much value-for-effort there is in simple coordination partnerships.

COORDINATION PARTNERSHIPS

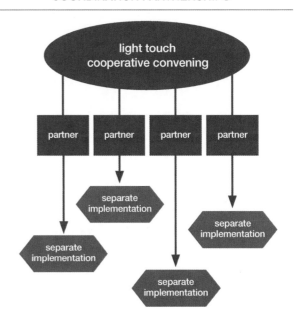

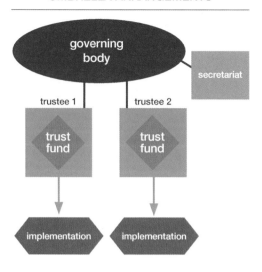

Umbrella Arrangements

In the same vein as coordination partnerships, creating a common governing body across multiple funding vehicles puts the emphasis on coordination. These umbrella arrangements can be light or heavy on structure, depending on the degree of engagement by the governing body. Umbrella arrangements share a common theme with coordination partnerships in the separate downstream implementation by different entities, whereas they differ in their shared upstream decision making about implementation. Unlike light-touch coordination partnerships, umbrella arrangements direct downstream implementation through an upstream, overarching decision-making body.

Umbrella arrangements are also one collectivizing notch shy of international platforms, which rely on a common trustee. For umbrella arrangements, funds are not commingled into one primary pool under one central trustee, but are instead separated by fiduciary institutions, like positioning a WBG trust fund alongside a (coordinated but separate) UN trust fund. While there is likely still a centralized secretariat function for the common governing body, umbrella arrangements can feature multiple trustees, each linked to the common governance framework but still doing its own thing.

Umbrella arrangements can be spanned broadly across not just multiple trust funds but also many different kinds of funding vehicles. It is all a matter of agreement among partners and definition in the documents. And best of all, once an umbrella has been spanned, the program can continue to be expanded later to include new funding vehicles or other funding sources or activities under whatever terms the partners define for themselves. It

Single Country Set-Up

A common venue for umbrella arrangements is a single country setting. If, for example, a conflict-battered country reaches a point where it can agree with the international community on a compact or other strategic framework for recovery and reconstruction, an umbrella structure can facilitate future implementation of that compact. Collaboration is set up with at least three elements—the relevant country willing to host, interested donors willing to fund, and international organizations (as fiduciaries) willing to implement—for the sake of matching country priorities with international trust funds or other funding vehicles.

just takes a platform that anticipates amendments with an agreed process for streamlined amending. (>@ Like Rock, Like Water)

The beauty of umbrella arrangements, as with so many of these variations, is that they neatly fit the context. Settings that can benefit from umbrella arrangements need a high level of collaboration among international players to stay strong and engaged. They also often highlight the beneficiary country's role in owning and driving its own future. And they give downstream entities room to coordinate without confusing responsibilities, cleanly achieved by connecting upstream decisions while separating downstream implementation.

Even among umbrella arrangements there are many variations on the theme. But in their essence, they mix and match connections and delineations in yet another way to maximally fit the setting.

What's In and What's Out

Say you want to create a platform to coordinate and stimulate country-level funding for a zero plastics, all organics campaign. Upstream the emphasis is on financial mapping by country—who has what resources available to fund the cause—and downstream the emphasis is on crowding in funding sources and projects. Some implementation from these downstream activities can be branded as part of the partnership program, while some implementation can be separate but complementary. This structure combines elements of coordination partnerships with umbrella arrangements in ways that can be organic and fluid, varying from country to country and varying over time.

You are in good company. This is a worthy model, as international partnership programs seek to do more with less. Rather than carry the whole load of implementation within the partnership program, the shared agenda trends toward catalyzing and gap-filling. Country-by-country, this kind of financial mapping can be leveraged in response to country priorities. Partners, including the countries in question, can drive their common cause based on country-centered activities, like domestic resource mobilization, policy changes, strengthened institutions, and on-the-ground projects, while also aligning bilateral donor activities, crowding in the private sector, and linking to trust-funded and other MDB operations.

Exactly what is in and what is out—what belongs to the partnership program (read what gets labeled by the brand) and what doesn't—may be less clear in this scenario, but is still worth defining. There are at least three distinct categories: (1) what is actually funded by and belongs to the partnership program; (2) what is newly catalyzed with funds outside the partnership program; and (3) what is already separately planned but complementary and actively coordinated with the partnership program. Only the first category is clearly "in," while the other two are "out" unless they are collectively designated as "in."

In other words, partners as a whole can choose to spread the tent wider if the association works for everyone, or they can keep the partnership program scope more natural and narrow. Adding the partnership program label to more activities may not be worth it if the point is simply getting the projects done—in or out, they're the same projects. And partners may prefer to keep a little distance from each other's projects, rather than crowding everything into the tent. However, sometimes partners may want to leverage a bigger portfolio for a bigger name, which in turn can turn up the volume for bigger engagement and bigger effect. That just takes more deliberate defining.

The Even Broader Landscape of Structured Partnerships

Light to Heavy

One-stop-shops, international platforms, and other international partnership programs are like mini businesses; some very mini with hundreds of thousands of dollars, and some not-so-mini, with hundreds of millions and even billions of dollars of operations. They populate a large space in the development arena that features collectivized decision making and collectivized funding, with centralized support, to run the partnership program. And yet, these partnership programs as a category are but midpoints on a larger spectrum of structured partnerships involving international partners. This spectrum runs the gamut on a range of costs, regulations, formality, and the need to create something new.

From this view of the forest, taking an infrastructure point of view, the landscape of structured partnerships for international partners can be broadly categorized into three points on the spectrum of light to heavy lift, with international partnership programs—the hybrid type—squarely in the middle:

- **_Light._** An existing supporting entity handles virtually all functions. Partners piggyback almost entirely on the existing supporting entity. Partnering decisions are made upfront—for example, in annexed common terms that attach to every contribution agreement—after which decisions and implementation are left in the hands of the supporting entity trustee/secretariat. We can call these **_embedded partnerships_**.

- **_Medium._** An existing supporting entity handles many or most functions, along with shared governance. This is where one-stop-shops and international platforms reside. These partnerships are hybrid, part in, part out of the supporting entity. Decisions can be collective affairs that take more to tee up and get done, but with lots of supporting entity support. These partnerships do not have their own legal personalities but borrow from the supporting entity's legal status as needed. They are commonly called **_partnership programs_**.

- **_Heavy._** A new, dedicated legal entity, usually with governance from a corporate board, handles all functions. The whole kit and caboodle is established specifically for the partnership. Instead of benefiting from existing entity support, these partnerships take on all that goes into setting up and running an independent legal entity. As a result, this partnership form has its own legal personality, able to contract directly with others. With significant long-term funding promised in the face of great global challenges, some sizeable cases have, for example, emerged in health and climate change. We can call these **_dedicated entity partnerships_**.

1. embedded partnerships
2. partnership programs
3. dedicated entity partnerships

| LIGHT | PARTNERSHIP INFRASTRUCTURE | HEAVY |

EMBEDDED PARTNERSHIPS **Integrated**	PARTNERSHIP PROGRAMS **Hybrid, Partially Integrated**	DEDICATED ENTITY PARTNERSHIPS **Stand-Alone**
existing supporting entity governance	new shared governance with existing supporting entity support	new dedicated entity governance
no ongoing shared governance	shared decision making or advisory inputs	dedicated corporate governance
no dedicated governing body	dedicated decision-making or advisory body	corporate board
upfront partnership agreement on key terms; supporting entity receives funds, decides funding allocations, and manages activities	combination of supporting entity trustee/secretariat with a dedicated governing body that makes decisions or provides input, depending on allocation of roles and responsibilities	separate, independent legal entity embodies the partnership, receives funds, and manages activities; partners participate in corporate board, oversee entity, and make decisions

Many partnerships in the light and medium categories operate in the international arena, where the partnership itself is not incorporated under domestic law. Embedded partnerships and partnership programs are big business for MDBs and other international organizations precisely because of the advantages of operating outside of domestic legal frameworks. (>@ Introduction—The Informal, International Part) By contrast, dedicated entity partnerships are almost always set up under the domestic laws within a specific country. Despite major structural differences, however, all of these partnership structures operate alongside each other as part of the international community, addressing many of the same challenges with many of the same participants.

A helpful way to talk about this range is in terms of fully or partially integrated partnerships vs. stand-alone partnerships. The integrated variants, embedded partnerships and partnership programs, lean on the support of existing entities to varying degrees, whereas new dedicated entities set out on their own to create unique entities specific to their particular partnerships. The decision to strike out separately is a big one and suggests a long-term mandate and funding stream. The decision to leverage existing support is usually less of a stretch.

Another way to think about these types of structured partnerships is that the first category does not create a new partnership body and instead relies entirely on existing entity decision functions. By contrast, the third category creates all new partnership elements and relies entirely on new entity functions for its governance. The middle category—some might say not too hot, not too cold, but just right—takes the best of both. Partnership programs use existing entity support functions, while creating new governing bodies to engage the partners. Creating a new body instead of a new entity is a big difference.

Circling Back

So now let us revisit our two mighty oaks. Placed on this broader structured partnership spectrum, it is easier to see them in relation to each other. The first, one-stop-shops, tends toward the embedded (existing entity) approach. The second, international platforms, tends toward the dedicated (new entity) approach. One-stop-shops are as embedded as they can be while still accommodating shared decision making. International platforms are as extenuated as they can be while still incorporating existing entity support. We have now gone full circle.

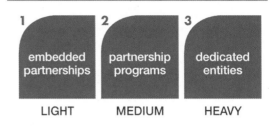

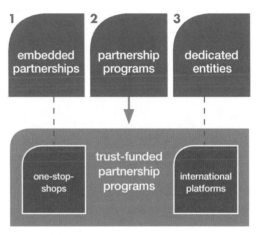

Conclusion

Under the broad rubric of international partnerships and programs, many collaborations do not rise to the level of structured partnerships. There is no intention here to preach the virtues of structure in the abstract, or position structure as a panacea. To the contrary, structuring too much is as great a pitfall as structuring too little. Many collaborations deserve a light touch through simple forms of engagement and documentation. It may well be overkill to sign binding agreements or adopt fully developed charters.

That said, certain things, like shared decision making, pooled fund flows, and allocated roles, commonly trigger structuring and design exercises. With the introduction of governing bodies, trust funds, and fiduciary responsibilities, partners enter structured partnership land, where it is incumbent upon them to choose their approach and then draw the lines and make the connections that build their structure. If one of the partners is a suitable supporting entity, chances are good that the middle approach—not too heavy, not too light, but just right—may point the international partners in the direction of international partnership programs.

On the structure of international partnership programs, read on.

4 INTERNATIONAL PARTNERSHIP PROGRAMS

Partnership programs: What a clunky label, hardly indicative of its fuller dimensions. At least it has the virtue of reflecting both the partnership and programmatic nature of the construct, leaving room for a very wide span of possibilities between having either more partnership or more program, or more or less of both. It is a big tent header that picks up many variations around a few quintessential elements.

The partnership programs we take up here are a specific subset of structured partnerships in the international arena. (>@ Typology—The Broader Landscape of Partnership Programs) International partnership programs are global, regional, local, and particularly prevalent in the development arena. They exist for virtually every conceivable development topic with virtually every type of development partner. Back when there were fewer such structures, the label mattered less, as did any lack of policy to regulate them or procedures to establish and monitor them. However, the enduring popularity of this approach, now a fixture in the international aid architecture toolkit, justifies more direct attention, if not more elegant terminology.

A Little History

It all started innocently enough. Along at least one trajectory, going back several decades, shareholders of MDBs saw increasing opportunities to provide additional funding for additional activities. These broad-based development banks were happy to augment their work program and supplement their budget, at the margin. Sometimes a donor wanted to prod in a particular direction, but these add-ons were also about trying new approaches or filling gaps, often small amounts with high impact potential. Over time, this feedback loop strengthened. Donors appreciated the ability to engage directly, not just as a group of shareholders once removed. Development institutions got used to opportunities to expand their engagement.

As these dynamics fed each other, trust funds became vehicles of choice around which shared decision making and centralized support could be positioned. Over time, participants got increasingly opportunistic, and programs got increasingly autonomous. Many were still derivative of the MDB's bread and butter activities, but others were increasingly distant from the core. Everything still had to fit into the supporting entity's work program, but much could be justified under its overarching development mandate. Although efforts to mainstream trust fund operations into the MDB's regular operations may have served as a corrective, that did not always happen with due attention to partnership dimensions. The focus has tended to be on the money. And so the trust fund business booms along while the partnership program part, its penumbra, is pulled along in the shadows.

Taken as a whole, trust-funded partnership programs have seen enough success to constitute major business lines for some international organizations. What once was a complementary piece has become a cottage industry characterized by dependency, both on the part of donors and their multilaterals. Donors, especially those who have scaled back their own country presence and implementation, need the institutional framework and reach of the multilaterals. Multilaterals, especially those that are scratching for funds in resource-constrained environments, need the relief from diminished revenue and squeezed budgets. Many of their core products and activities are now financed by trust-funded partnership programs, making the absence of this business line challenging to contemplate. What was once an add-on is now full on.

International partnership programs and their related trust funds have changed the way multilaterals do business. Among other things, they have expanded opportunities for impact and raised expectations for collaboration. With some ventures reaching into the billions of dollars and hundred-plus staff, this can mean big engagement with big impact. Even the smaller ones can be major multipliers by piloting or positioning projects that catalyze and leverage activities many times their size.

To realize the full benefits of international partnership programs, however, there is no one size fits all. Full potential calls for a varied palette that reflects diversity in size, subject, scope, composition, conditions, structures, implementation modes, and more. The pressure to standardize and

From trust funds to partnership programs: What was once an add-on is now full on.

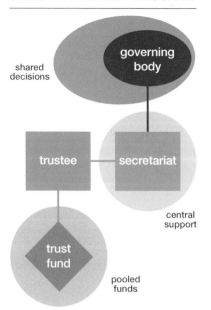

shared
decisions

central
support

pooled
funds

KEEP
CALM
AND
COLLECTIVIZE

contain this diversity bumps up against the need to customize for context and relevance. Likewise, international partners face pressure to stop the proliferation and consolidate, which begs the question of better partnering alternatives. (>@ Risk and Review—At the Front End) Meanwhile, pressure from participants, especially donors, to be more engaged chafes against the need for multilaterals to run their own businesses and manage their own risks (ironically, sometimes in the interest of the very shareholders who may be pressuring them). Partnership programs are not a slam dunk, but the opportunities and synergies have been enough to make them go forth and thrive.

The Quintessence

Partnership programs embody *collective action*. In international contexts, especially for international humanitarian and development efforts, both the "collective" and the "action" are critical to achieving results. Partnership programs connect the collective coming together (partnership) to the actions bearing results (program). They represent the structure that gives like-minded institutions a collaborative path for change and impact.

With the emphasis on *collectives*, partnership program structure is about convening and converging. This typically translates into the following key features:

- shared governance
- central support
- pooled funding

Beyond that, the permutations are practically infinite. Partnership programs can choose their geographic scope, from the whole world to a single country. They can involve participants of all stripes. They can address topics wherever there is a need and an interest. They can be strategic or operational, or both; big or small; heavy or light; high risk, low risk; long term, short term; effective, or not. They can be flush with funds or run on a shoestring. They can and usually do evolve over time.

Collectivizing

International partnership programs have both enduring advantages and challenges. Their premise is relatively simple—join forces by collectivizing elements—while their actual design can be multifaceted and their implementation complex. International partners not only have choices about what to collectivize, but also how much and how. It helps tremendously to map out where the partnership and programmatic integration points are, what is to be brought together under the partnership and program umbrella, and what is to be handled separately and independently. In defining connections and limits, however, there is more modularity than partners may realize.

Partners have decisions to make. They can be empowered to make better decisions when the individual dimensions are separated out and better understood.

So what does it mean to collectivize? Specifically for international partnership programs, collectivization can happen along many, or few, dimensions. Among the most fundamental integration points, six elements or "collectives" are listed here: (1) decisions are shared; (2) support functions are centralized; (3) funds are pooled; (4) activities are coordinated; (5) knowledge is combined; and (6) all of it is branded.

Let's take each one in turn.

———————————●———————————

1. one brand

2. shared decisions

3. central support

4. pooled funding

5. coordinated activities

6. combined knowledge

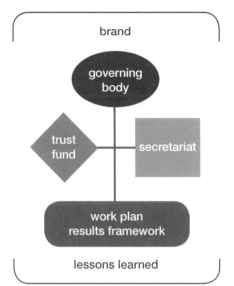

Shared Decision Making

In most partnership programs, shared decision making is where the collectivizing begins. A partnership is not a partnership without agreeing on common terms, and that framework is the foundation of the partnership collective. These are pre-partners making decisions about their status as partners. Once successfully tested in the founding phase of a partnership program, some form of shared decision making, or more broadly, shared governance (to include bodies that are consultative or advisory), typically continues throughout the life of the partnership program until the group collectively decides to disband.

Shared decision making is about decisions that are made together, multilaterally, not unilaterally. Partners are the sine qua non of partnering, and this is reflected in at least some version of a meeting of the "collective" minds. Active governance models have ongoing engagements that range from advisory to high-level strategy and oversight to operational micromanaging, and points in between. Under active shared governance, partners reserve some degree of rights for themselves to participate, rather than leaving all decisions to, for example, the trustee, secretariat, or other implementing entities.

The spectrum shown on the next page covers the types of partnering that we recently reviewed. (>@ Typology—The Even Broader Landscape of Structured Partnerships) Embedded partnerships (no shared governance) sit at the far left, while dedicated entity partnerships (corporate governance) sit on the far right. Everything in between belongs to partnership programs (shared governance), starting with one-stop-shops toward the left and culminating with international platforms toward the right.

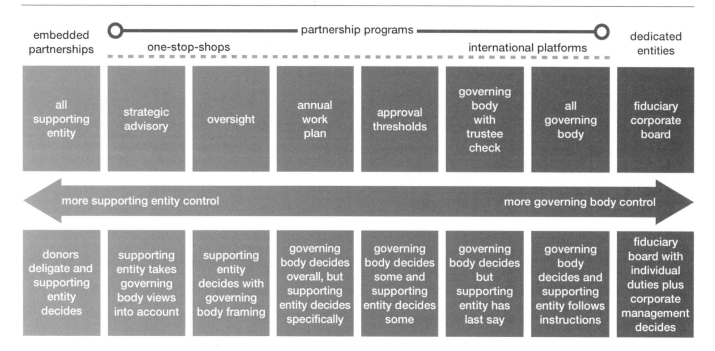

Governing Bodies

The most visible sign of shared governance is the governing body, through which partners convene both to benefit from each others' views and to reach common understandings and agreed positions. Sometimes this in itself is the gist of the partnership program—the opportunity to share and coordinate, without adding an array of partnership program–sponsored and branded activities. (>@ Typology—Coordination Partnerships) However, international partnership programs are usually more than just talk shops, since the "program" part offers a platform for implementation. With a programmatic focus, partners talk, but then also walk the talk as part of their coming together.

To be spelled out, then, is the relationship between the governing body and the program, which is another way of saying how far collective inputs (advice or decisions) reach into individual implementation responsibilities (trustee, secretariat, or implementing entity). This presents an interesting duality of a collective element (the governing body) interacting with an institutional element (the partnership program's supporting entity base). Between these two, the balance of engagement and division of responsibility deserve a seamless flow in both directions, linking program implementation across upstream and downstream. (>@ Structure—Bridging Action and Results)

Power Spectrum

Shared governance accordingly runs on a spectrum of more or less power for the governing body. Shared governance with shared decision making can empower governing body participants to shape or determine the path of the partnership program. How much control or influence is vested in the governing body is something to be agreed. Endorsing an annual strategy, for example, is a lesser order of magnitude than approving individual projects.

If the annual strategy is prepared by the secretariat, even more of the balance of control and influence may lie in the supporting entity. For some partnerships, this deference is desirable, as when partners prefer to leave the heavy lifting to their supporting entity. That can sit very well, especially when the supporting entity is considered a peer-to-peer partner in addition to providing support. For other partnerships, this deference is less well-suited, as when other partners have an agenda, worry about reputational risk, or want to ensure their imprimatur. Some partnership programs care more about upstream buy-in; others may happily delegate down. The end result is what the supporting entity is willing to accept in relation to what the other partners want.

Shared governance need not be heavy to be effective; it need not even be shared decision making. It can instead be consultative or advisory. Governing body participants that are relegated to advisors, rather than deciders, may have less heft, but can still make a difference. Even though no decision points are teed up, and no input is binding, the feedback generated through a consultative or advisory body is not likely to be ignored. At a minimum, convening a body already sends signals of inclusion and raises expectations of input. In particular, comments from donors, freighted as they are with the power of the purse, are likely to be heard.

As a result, the practical difference may not be that great between an advisory body that shares opinions and concerns and a decision-making body that operates by consensus, especially if content is largely supporting-entity driven, as is typically the case in one-stop-shops. More dispositive of the governing body's impact may be how often the body meets, how well the chair manages the dynamics, how strongly the secretariat drives the agenda, and how much the trustee maintains implementation control. In that sense, shared governance in international partnership programs can be more of an organic dynamic, largely between the governing body and the supporting entity.

Whatever the characterization of the governing body (decision-making or advisory), and whatever the support role of the supporting entity (trustee or secretariat), the determining factor may be the culture of the partnership. What are the politics of engagement? Who really has the upper hand? How attentive is the governing body, and how proactive is the supporting entity? Personalities may also shift the dynamic, as can bad experiences. Nonetheless, it is useful for partners to think about where they want to be on the power spectrum and what approach will get them results.

No Fiduciary Responsibility

It is important to understand that no matter how much power they hold, governing bodies of international partnership programs are still a far cry from governing bodies, like boards, of corporate entities. Corporate boards and equivalent bodies of incorporated entities are caught in the thicket of statutory requirements and legal jurisprudence of their domestic seats of incorporation. These include fiduciary responsibilities of individual representatives on the governing body of the corporate entity, with liability implications. (>@ Governing Bodies—Informal vs. Formal)

The cost of going against donor views can often be calculated.

There is nothing comparable for informal governing bodies that are convened in the international arena by an international organization supporting entity. Just the opposite, both the body and the participants are remarkably devoid of direct responsibility and liability even when they micromanage decision making. (>@ Fund Use Responsibility—Collective Responsibility) This alone is a good reason to avoid the label "board" for international partnership program governing bodies, where much of the point is separating upstream decision making from downstream implementation responsibility. The ability of governing bodies to have a collective say without being collectively on the hook is one of the major attractions of international partnership programs.

Central Support

Enter the secretariat. The corollary of shared governance is a focal point for administrative support. Partners can stay in the driver's seat while delegating logistics for convening and decision making to a dedicated function with more time and resources. Tasks like arranging meetings, distributing meeting materials, handling no objection processes, and running websites all lend themselves to delegating and outsourcing. While the chair or members could do it themselves, and in the occasional case rotate these responsibilities to share the burden, most international partnership programs with active governing bodies are happy to involve a secretariat for all active administration.

Strong Secretariats

"Secretariat" is used here as a catch-all term for administrative support without implying a large or formal apparatus. Whether collectivized support is provided by one person or one hundred, the point is that partners look to designated staff within a designated entity to support the partnership program. The idea is usually that partners take on substantive responsibilities, while secretariats take on administrative responsibilities; however, in practice that line can shift considerably. Many international partnership programs are run by their secretariats more than their governing bodies, depending on how much partners decide to defer (or supporting entities decide to give up). But even partnership programs with strong governing bodies may need strong secretariats, especially those with large, active programs. It is tempting to say that, as a rule of thumb, the stronger the secretariat, the more sustained the partnership program, if only because the secretariat has incentives to keep itself going. (>@ Risk and Review—At the Back End)

Even when the administrative center of the partnership program has a major role, however, the secretariat may not have a separate identity. In many cases, especially trust fund–centric cases, the secretariat role is wrapped into the trustee role, as a kind of trustee plus. This is common in one-stop-shops and conveniently keeps the secretariat functions more internalized within the supporting entity, more inward-facing than outward-facing.

Supporting Entities as Partners

Among the great synergies in international partnership programs is when the secretariat supporting entity doubles as a partner in the partnership

Having the supporting entity double as a partner is one of the great synergies.

program. The conjoining of partner status and support function in one and the same entity has clear benefits. Administrative support from a partner is usually more informed, engaged, and risk-aware. That said, it can also give rise to interesting dynamics. This can range from internal schizophrenia, when a secretariat tries to formalize contractual services with the governing body in which it participates (>@ Supporting Entities—Duality and Balance—Middle Ground?), to having a downstream secretariat seek equal status to donors while also being second rung on the fund flow hierarchy. (>@ Trust Funds—Recipients) As is always the case when the supporting entity plays multiple roles, it can also raise questions of conflicts of interest, for which the answer for international partnership programs is usually an appreciation of more synergies than conflicts. (>@ Synergistic Conflicts—Seeing and Seeking Synergies)

The value of an administrative center is especially great when partners place value in branding, like when they leverage a big name to mobilize funds or push advocacy. Then this administrative support is usually given major resources for communications, messaging, social media, and web presence—as encouragement to be heard above the din. Moreover, once a partnership program sets up a common support structure, it tends to benefit from this support in ways not even imagined. (>@ Custodial Effect)

Whether the secretariat is lean or abundant, or even absorbed into the trustee, a shared administrative platform is what holds the partnership program together and combines the partners with the program. The chance to lean on a well-tuned, resourceful, supporting entity to manage partnership program business—while also being a partner—is another major attraction of international partnership programs.

> The partnership program secretariat connects the partners with the program.

Pooled Funding

In the world of international partnership programs, in deference to the Great Moolah, pooled funding usually gets the most attention. Pooled funding through trust funds is a major industry and a main driver of international partnership programs. Often pooled funding is the very reason a governing body meets. In many of these cases, the governing body's primary raison d'etre is watching or weighing in on the use of the funds held in trust. The partnership brand is framed by the scope of the trust fund. The partnership results are generated by the trust fund. In such trust fund–centric partnership programs, it is easy to see why the funding vehicle looms front and center.

This is in many ways the tail wagging the dog. Rather than consider the partnership as a whole, supporting entities may promulgate scads of policies and procedures for trust funds, but have little comparable bandwidth for partnership dimensions. This does not mean relationships with funders and funding vehicles are unimportant, but that secretariat functions and governing bodies are important, too. Looking at things from the bottom up rather than top down—seeing the world from the funding lens rather than the partnership lens—tends to skew the view, like missing the forest for the trees.

Commingled Trust Funds

Pooled funding means all contributions are made into a common pool; they are commingled. (>@ Trust Funds—Contributions) Once part of the pool, the dollars from donor A are no longer trackable relative to all other donors in the pooled fund. All the dollars become fungible with each other. There is no way to say whether A's dollar paid for X project or B's dollar paid for Y. A and B both paid for X and Y. It gives no specific credit to a specific donor for a specific activity; everyone gets credit for all activities. Pooled funds are the ultimate melting pot.

Commingling is the opposite of tracking and the inverse of earmarking.

As a widespread form of commingled pools of funds, international trust funds are basically administered accounts that serve as money buckets. Each trust fund bucket has its set of terms, as agreed between the donor and the trustee. Sometimes terms are agreed for a single point of entry at the level of the main trustee account, and then trickle down to affect any subaccounts, transfers, or disbursements that flow therefrom. Sometimes the top level features multiple accounts (or windows), mostly subject to common terms but with some key fund use or other differences attached to the individual accounts, like regional restrictions (this window is for Africa only, the other one is global) or thematic restrictions (this window is for country health projects and the other is for global knowledge projects). This slicing and dicing depends primarily on what the donors want and what the trustee is willing and able to accept, often within system limitations and donor appetite for extra costs. For sure, more subdivisions and restrictions mean more complexity and transaction costs. (>@ Trust Funds—Accounts)

Availability of Funds

Restricted funds are less flexible than unrestricted funds. Donors may prefer the specificity of having their dollars go to their pet projects, but there is a lot to be said for keeping donor-driven subdivisions, like tracking, earmarking, and even preferencing, to a minimum. (>@ Trust Funds—Contributions— Tracking, Earmarking, and Preferencing) Keeping the entire pool commingled from the top means full availability of all funds for the full scope of the trust fund. In this way, amounts can be leveraged for scaled opportunities, priorities can shift as the world changes, partners can fully collaborate across the partnership's programmatic scope, recipients can be selected through more holistic, strategic considerations, and synergies can be maximized. For all these reasons and more, collectivized funding through collectively tended trust funds is yet another major attraction of international partnership programs.

Coordinated Activities

Now for the content. Among the aspects of a partnership program that can be collectivized are its activities and projects. Calling it a partnership "program" already implies that at least some content is collectivized, but what that is can vary. A collaboration partnership may have very little collectivized content, whereas one-stop-shop collectivized content is at least everything financed by the trust fund and possibly more. The program of a partnership can be basically anything the partners all agree to claim as theirs and attach their partnership name to, as long as the implementer and owner of the activity (usually one of the partners) also agrees. Visibly pulling activities of whatever range into one common work program that is identified as such is accordingly a decision that partners make. Often they back into the scope by virtue of the funding sources and vehicles they included as part of the partnership program.

Work Plans

Collectivizing in this context usually involves both content (like activities making up a common work program) and process (like agreeing on a common work program). Rather than rely on de facto or ex post accumulations of activities, an agreed common work program lets the governing body be deliberate about its choice of priorities and engagements. Typically it is the secretariat (or the trustee undertaking secretariat-type functions) that pulls together a proposed overview or itemization of activities for the coming year.

This document can include more or less detail; more to give donors more insights and influence, less to leave the supporting and implementing entities more discretion. This document can stay high level or show budgeted line items specifying who will undertake what. A tried and true approach is the "annual work plan" or "annual work plan and budget" that the secretariat positions with the governing body for approval, written so as to leave room for some adjustments over time, ideally without governing body micromanagement. Once reviewed and approved, everyone is on the same page in terms of priorities and expectations for implementation.

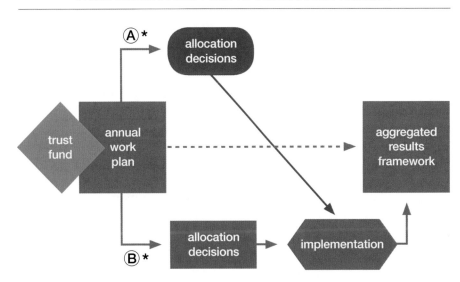

FROM COORDINATED PLAN TO COORDINATED RESULTS

* either (A) upstream decision making (like international platforms) or (B) downstream decision making (like one-stop-shops)

Results Frameworks

Assembling activities into a program-wide work plan is an ex ante collectivization. With an eye to the ex post, partnership programs can also collectivize content in a program-wide results framework. The two should obviously be aligned; the planned activities should be chosen to meet targeted results. Donor pressure to get value for money puts pressure on results. Hence results frameworks—collectivized expressions of what partners hope to achieve—are more and more common, not just for individual projects, but for the overall portfolio.

These meta-results frameworks—across a whole trust fund or the whole partnership program—can be notoriously hard to develop for partnership programs, especially if activities are dependent on proposals, and proposals are dependent on submissions, and all of that evolves on an ongoing, rolling basis that is dependent on funding availability. But even if the results framework remains high level and reflective of only a few performance indicators, partners that focus on results may nonetheless want the whole program to be measured across-the-board for outputs, outcomes, and ultimately, impact.

Combined Knowledge

The unsung hero in partnership program collectivization is knowledge. Information is power, and shared information that creates knowledge is powerful. This is all the more true in the information age, when the Internet, social media, news, and fake news all flood the world with content to the point that it is hard to absorb and discern. Partnership programs do not tend to set up information centers; they set up "knowledge" centers, and hope they will be transformative. In the same way that an Internet search can ring less true than word of mouth—those who tell you something directly out of their own experience are usually more real and trusted than what may appear online—an opportunity to either physically or virtually sit together around the development table and share, brainstorm, ruminate, and explore can be the ultimate prize when building a partnership program. This is about taking collectivized information and experience and making it collectivized knowledge.

In partnership programs, the potential benefits of shared information as inputs and shared reflection on the outputs are as immeasurable as they are unpredictable and serendipitous. This is especially true in the development arena. At the front end of the project cycle, the immensity of development challenges and scarcity of funding resources call for careful deliberation before proceeding with specific activities, ideally based on broadly informed views. At the back end, the emphasis on results puts a premium on measuring and evaluating what comes of a partnership program's efforts, or what could have, should have been done—and what to do next time.

Lessons Learned

Pausing to look back before looking forward can translate into valuable lessons learned. It takes concerted effort to capture these lessons—to understand shortcomings, imagine improvements, and try again. By gathering data, sharing information, and generating knowledge, partnership programs are at their healthiest when they build the great feedback loop from inputs to outputs to inputs again. Some would say development practitioners owe this kind of rigor to their taxpayers and beneficiaries.

Inclusion

In building knowledge, the days of going it alone are bygone. Solo ventures attract critics, whereas collaborative approaches create synergies. Experience has shown that it is generally better to bring in developing country voices than presume what the country wants. Experience has also shown that NGOs,

Sharing lessons learned means looking back before looking forward.

CSOs, and others can have their place in the debate. Their input can fortify approaches and impacts, and their absence comes at the risk of those who plow ahead.

In this age of inclusion, international partnership programs can become microcosms of all key stakeholders that partners want to hear from and align with. The allure of international platforms over one-stop-shops is the emphasis on inclusion over control. Admittedly (>@ Partners and People—Choosing Partners), horizontal platforms are messier than vertically integrated, hierarchical ones—that is history's experience with democracy as well. However, more collaborative inputs and outputs may more closely reflect the values we hold dear, especially for those whose ultimate goal is a better world.

One Brand

Which brings us to brand. A brand is both a name and a narrative, a label and a message. This lends itself to international initiatives seeking to coordinate and advocate; it seems a catchy brand is de rigueur for partnership programs. The alphabet soup of branded acronyms and abbreviations indicates that a pithy and (more or less) pronounceable name is key. If well chosen, the partnership program soon becomes known by its sound bite. Beginning with the name they choose, partners collectivize through their brand, and then it matters to everyone who and what is in and out. (>@ Typology—Trust-Funded Partnership Programs)

In the first instance, partners associate with a brand when becoming partners. Branding usually occurs in the chicken and egg phase, when prospective participants decide what they want to be while deciding whether they want to be part of it. Partners know that the choice of name can make a difference. In competitive funding environments, with no shortage of other initiatives, it pays to be visible—and that means distinguishing the partnership program, becoming known, being remembered, and garnering a following.

A brand is like an aura that emanates from the partnership program. It is not a tangible link like a funding agreement or the fund flows themselves, but rather an alter ego that lives on in social media, websites, halls and meeting rooms, the press, and word of mouth. If participants want their partnership program to have presence, then an amplified brand can extend their efforts from their inner workings to the outer realms of the brand's broadest reach. Just as in the private sector, the power of brand can play loudly for partnership programs in the international arena.

Communications

A brand projects the partnership program to others, and that works through communications. After the program head, the next hire in the secretariat is usually the communications person. In this day and age, a partnership program of any prominence is unimaginable without a website, Twitter account, online newsletter, blog, and all the other amplifying technology. The name may be great, but it only becomes a working brand if leveraged in media and messaging. The broader its reach, the stronger its identifying quality, and the more partners will care about what it stands for.

What's in a brand?

A name and a narrative.

To name a few:

ACBF	GGFR
AFFI	GIF
ALLFISH	GPE
ANSA	GPOBA
APOC	GPSA
ARTF	HANSHEP
CAFI	IFFIm
CGAP	IHP+
CGIAR	MAPS
CIF	PAF
CoST	PEF
EFA-FTI	PEFA
EITI	PMNCH
FCPF	PNoWB
FIRST	PPIAF
GAFSP	PROFISH
GAIN	PROFOR
GAVI	READ
GCFF	RUTA
GDLN	SDRF
GEF	SE4ALL
GFDRR	StAR
GFF	We-Fi

In that sense, a brand is also like an umbrella, gathering everything under its canopy. Everything that is the partnership name belongs to everyone that is the partnership. This is a one-size-fits-all choice; there are no modulations or halfway stations when it comes to brand, no way for one partner to be half-branded and another some other half. For all the modularity available in partnership programs, a brand invariably gives all partners exposure to all branded activities, everything under the canopy. Visibility in that sense comes with the good and the bad. Everyone gets credit for all the great things the partnership program is doing, but also, hopefully never, anything bad.

Content

A brand is therefore defined by the partnership program's content more than its name. A brand by itself rings hollow without content and is not sustainable without substance. That puts pressure on partnership program operations— to disburse funds, get projects going, and generate results. Branding accordingly works in tandem with collectivized activities and collectivized knowledge, first through internal sharing, leveraging experience, and creating buy-in, followed by external sharing. Some partnership programs are more project-based and others more knowledge-based, depending on what they seek to do, but virtually all seek to reach out. To resupply funds, be advocates, gain relevance, and contribute meaningfully to their particular missions, partnership programs are likely to channel their accomplishments through branded identities and branded platforms.

And More

The half dozen elements presented here are not an exhaustive list. Many other things can be collectivized, including operational aspects, like harmonized reporting formats, or risk aspects, like collectively agreed remedies procedures. Partners can also agree to common codes of conduct, like on conflicts of interest or private sector participation, or common standards, like accreditation requirements.

The point of collectivizing can also be manifold. It can be for the sake of efficiency: streamlining through commonly agreed approaches and ramped up with economies of scale. It can be for the sake of advocacy and legitimacy: for greater buy-in with strength in numbers and diversity. It can be a source of synergies, particularly when comparative advantages leverage each other, and the whole becomes greater than the sum of the parts. Collectivizing, as considered here, is more than simply cooperating or collaborating. It is a structural choice, a design linkage, based on partnership agreement and sustained as a partnership dimension.

What works well is that shared structure and centralized support set up the pre-conditions for more (or less) collectivizing to occur initially and over time. If partners agree, the partnership program can opt to take a common approach on any number of topics, as presented and approved, whether partners agree up front or establishment documents give partners the prerogative for the future. Once partners collect themselves, they can collect a whole lot more.

Conclusion

As the world pulls ever closer together, as we realize our futures lie in the well-being of others, and as we accept collective responsibility for our planet, it is no wonder that partnership programs proliferate in the international arena. In the search for venues where international coordination and inclusive collaboration can make a difference, international partnership programs offer effective platforms to convene partners and converge funds and activities. They do so one after another, responding to different contexts with different constellations, each to fit and adapt to their specific collective goals.

This is as it should be, except that needs are great and resources are scarce. To be effective, partners must do their utmost to be deliberate and diligent in their approaches. Sustainable, efficient, and impactful partnership programs do not grow on trees; they are built from the ground up. By focusing on structure and making thoughtful design choices, partners can use international partnership programs to create greater collaboration, economies of scale, synergies, and other multiplier effects. Leveraging collective behavior through international partnership programs takes—and makes—good business sense for international partners that want to make a difference.

International partnership programs take and make good business sense.

5 GOVERNING BODIES

The confluence of partner influence convening for:

1. collaboration
2. buy-in
3. legitimacy
4. advocacy
5. flexibility
6. sustainability

As defined here, it takes a governing body to be a partnership program—no governing body, no partnership program. The governing body is the manifestation of the partnership in the partnership program. It can be decision-making or advisory, central or peripheral, large or small, but it is the conduit by which partners can maintain coordinated input into ongoing operations. The governing body not only creates the confluence of partner influence but also leverages the collective for collaboration, buy-in, legitimacy, advocacy, flexibility, and sustainability.

Characteristics

It is up to the partners—who first must agree on who is a partner—to decide what kind of governing body they want, whether as a framing header, the main text, or just a footnote. Everyone, the supporting entity included, has a vested interest in the partnership program's agreed functions. From a functional point of view, the governing body normally positions itself in relation to the supporting entity, not in a stand-alone vacuum. The relative prominence of the governing body is usually either a direct inverse or direct compounding factor of the importance of the supporting entity. (>@ International Partnership Programs—Central Support)

The governing body can be instrumental in many ways, depending on how the partners choose to structure the relationships and how much control or influence they decide to reserve for themselves collectively through the governing body. It can be a platform for many things, including collective sharing, decision making, coordinating, and planning. It can give greater credibility to the partnership program through collective buy-in. It can fortify engagement for the long term, especially with an eye toward continued resource mobilization. And it can make changes over time to terms that it owns.

This last point is worth emphasizing. Governing bodies are not just decision-making instruments, but also amending instruments. If governing body members adopt a charter, they can amend it, thereby keeping their hands on the reins, steering the partnership program along twists and turns, rises and falls, and lessons learned. If properly positioned, governing bodies can be valuable tools for flexibility. (>@ Like Rock, Like Water—Like Water)

All of this and more is possible because, compared to partnership arrangements and structures under domestic law, most international partnership programs have a pretty open greenfield in which to pitch their stakes and build their structures. (>@ Partnering Internationally) If you are sitting as a representative on an international partnership program's governing body, or if you are the manager of such representatives, this chapter is for you. You have both the benefits and challenges of convening in international space.

Representative Governing Bodies

Governing bodies can be leveraged for charter amendments if they are sufficiently representative. Donor voices, in particular, expect to be heard. Their funds are at stake, under terms agreed in contribution agreements. This calls for any charter amendments to carry over to contribution agreements. However, that works only if all donor signatories have a say on the governing body, whether as direct representatives or through constituencies. (>@ Trade-Offs—The Horizontal Buy-In Spectrum) If any donors are outside the governing body, they will not like being disenfranchised by giving the governing body amending power over their contribution agreements. By contrast, giving all donors some form of representation on the governing body, direct or indirect, lets them comfortably accept automatic applicability of charter amendments, thereby obviating the need for signed amendments. (>@ Like Rock, Like Water)

Informal vs. Formal

One of the most valuable aspects of partnership programs in the international arena is that they can come into being without being established under domestic law. This means the partnership program itself is not governed by national or subnational rules and requirements. Often shorthanded as informal vs. formal, international partnership programs are considered informal, whereas incorporated entities are formal. Informal processes are used to establish a large variety of international partnership programs supported by international organizations, without being directly subject to formal, statutory categories and mechanisms of incorporation under domestic law. Put simply, international partnership programs do not need to be incorporated.

Relative to formal, incorporated ventures, informal partnership programs have informal governance arrangements, including informal governing bodies. Participation in these informal bodies is accordingly also informal. As the informal equivalent of corporate directors and officers, governing body participants are not boxed in with the usual prescribed responsibilities owed to formal, incorporated entities. "Informal" in this sense means outside the bounds of domestic laws and jurisprudence with the relative freedom to operate under less defined terms of applicable law in the international arena. (>@ Partnering Internationally—Applicable Law)

International partnership programs are simply created, and creatively at that.

Applicable Duties

Informal, international governing bodies of partnership programs do not feature the kinds of fiduciary duties that invariably attach to directors sitting on corporate boards of for-profit or non-profit incorporated entities. Corporate fiduciary duties are personal responsibilities to the incorporated entity, like the duty of care and the duty of loyalty. Individuals sitting on corporate boards are usually duty-bound to promote the interests of, and avoid harm to, the incorporated entity, with reasonable care and due diligence. For corporate entities, there can be no self-dealing by board members, like putting personal interests first or maneuvering personal benefits to the detriment of the incorporated entity. Consequences can be legal and even criminal. This does not apply in the same way to participants in informal governing bodies of international partnership programs.

That is not to suggest that participants in international partnership programs have no duties and should feel free to engage in self-dealing—not at all. However, the source of the prohibition is different, as is the emphasis on the individual and the attribution of personal responsibilities. In international partnership programs, the norm is for partners to convene as sovereigns, ministries, institutions, and organizations and to keep their separate legal personalities even within the partnership. Representatives attend meetings and make decisions not for themselves, but for the country or entity they represent. Usually they sit as national or international civil servants with a duty to their employer, their home base. In these cases, there is also no self-dealing, no place for personal interests over institutional interests, or for personal benefits to the institution's detriment. However, the relevant duties are not to the partnership program or its governing body, but rather to the actual partner, meaning the representative's home base.

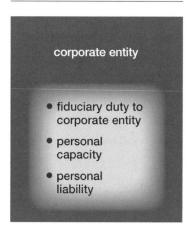

PARTNERSHIP PROGRAM GOVERNING BODY	DEDICATED ENTITY CORPORATE BOARD
international arena	corporate entity
• duty of loyalty to home base	• fiduciary duty to corporate entity
• institutional capacity	• personal capacity
• privileges & immunities	• personal liability

Convening as informal partners in international partnership programs, each participant comes in an institutional, rather than personal, capacity. Often this is implicit, not explicit, but no less true. Participants are usually duty-bound to their own entities, not the partnership as a whole. It is even likely that partner entities do not allow their representatives to act in their personal capacities. Even when sitting on governing bodies on their own time, the reasoning goes, individuals should be precluded from sitting in their personal capacities when the overlap with their professional responsibilities is so great that it cannot be separated from themselves. Under this view, national and international civil servants cannot simply check their institutional backdrops at the door and enter the meeting room without them.

Non-International Partners

International partnership program participation has become increasingly diverse over the years, and in many cases now includes NGOs, CSOs, academic institutions, private foundations, and even private sector companies. This can create asymmetrical participation, with apples, oranges, and potentially a whole cornucopia in the bowl. Differences can be as basic as the layers of bureaucracy. Representatives from smaller, focused entities, like local NGOs, are potentially more nimble than those from legacy multilaterals. Similarly, if everyone is expected to recuse themselves in cases of conflicts of interest, a representative of a large organization may not have the same overview as one of a smaller organization.

There can also be a major difference in the nature of the representation. Most international partners, including governments, participate as entities and send their institutional representatives, but other partners participate as individuals, in their personal capacity, and simply send themselves. A partner from an academic institution is likely to sit as an individual with an area of expertise, whereas an institutional partner, like an MDB, is partly there to send its legions of experts—the trustee representative for the trust fund, the task teams presenting projects for approval, the finance person for the finance and audit committee, the senior level manager to make decisions, and so on. This asymmetry of representation and resources can create imbalances of support and influence, perhaps appropriately so, but still something to consider in cases that mix institutional and personal representation. Even questions of attendance can poke the bear. A member sitting as an individual has no alternates and no choice but to send her- or himself, whereas institutional members can at least theoretically send alternates to wherever and whenever.

There are other ways international organizations, in particular, will never be like domestically incorporated entities, P&I being a major case in point. (>@ Supporting Entities—Basic Elements—Privileges and Immunities) Imagine a partnership program that enters into a partnership-wide confidentiality agreement with private sector companies, complete with indemnifications to hold harmless in case of breach. And now imagine that everyone at the partnership table has some form of protected immunity, except a private foundation that is also contributing funds. How does that feel? We can assume the uniquely exposed private foundation is not feeling the spirit of partnership at this point. Indeed, more generally, the private sector brings its own set of challenges when tapped as partners. (>@ Partners and People—Engaging the Private Sector)

These and other differences can create curious dynamics in governing body business that may need some managing and finessing. International partners that are mindful of these differences can create parameters and incentives to alleviate imbalances.

Differences in representation and resources can poke the bear.

Asymmetries may take assuaging.

Composition

Taken as a whole, participants will want to consider whether the governing body has what it takes to be effective in its business. Solid secretariat support is key, but the review starts with the governing body itself. Several factors are usually high on the list. Expertise in relevant areas—technical, political, financial, operational, depending on the governing body's roles and responsibilities—is an obvious area for attention. Diversity is perhaps less obvious, but increasingly valued, especially in development contexts where developing country voice and gender matter. For partnership programs that are looking for a broad view and widespread buy-in, that usually also spells inclusivity, which can be drawn from a combination of donors, beneficiaries, fiduciaries, supporting entities, and other key stakeholders at global and country levels.

Composition operates on two levels: first, **the governing body members and observers**, at the institutional level, and second, **their representatives**, at the designated individual level. We can address each in turn.

Members

Chicken or egg, the initial members are who they say they are. Maybe founding members invite others. Maybe a convening member asks others to self-select. Maybe all members are in place on day one or gradually join over time. There are many ways for members to come together, as long as partners agree.

As a term, "member" refers to governing body participation and usually overlaps with the term "partner." This book reserves the term "member" for decision-making participants in the governing body, while "observer" is a non-decision-making participant in the governing body. Partnership programs that create "partner" categories that are broader than governing body participation can get complex. An example might be "associate partners" who express their allegiance, but do not join the governing body. While not inherently problematic, since informal partnership programs have wide latitude to define their participants, a proliferation of labels can end up in a latticework of definitions and relationships. With each additional category of participant, questions of who is in and who is out, and how so, become harder to define, with potential implications for associational exposure and reputational risk.

Constituencies

Some governing bodies are quite laissez-faire with open membership categories, letting the mix land wherever it lands. A common example is that any donor to a multi-donor trust fund gets a member seat on the governing body, no matter whether two or twenty. Another example is that every member has open season on deciding how many representatives to seat at the table, whether one or a handful. Other governing bodies are more deliberate in defining their composition. Whether for discipline, oversight, or fairness, being clear on composition can be a step toward efficient proceedings.

Partnership regulation of the composition usually starts vis-à-vis its members, at the level of participating entities. This can involve dedicated seats for specific entities or types of entities, but it can also take a broader numerical approach. For example, a governing body that has an explicit goal of balanced representation by developed and developing countries—mostly reflecting donors and beneficiaries—could engineer a half-and-half result by defining two constituencies, each with a fixed and equal number of representatives. For another example, a partnership program for bolstering CSOs could have a governing body made up of three equal constituencies—donors, beneficiary countries, and CSOs.

Constituencies not only create balanced participation, but also cap the numbers. (>@ Trade-Offs—The Horizontal Buy-In Spectrum) This may not be necessary at inception, but can prove useful as the partnership program matures and grows. Anticipating this, the ability to shift from open membership to a constituency approach through a one-touch decision point as a charter amendment can spare partners a major headache. (>@ Like Rock, Like Water—Like Water)

The main challenge in setting up constituencies is to figure out who gets the fixed number of constituency seats. On the one hand, if the constituency is made up of partners that are on the governing body because of a specific partnership program role—like being donors to the trust fund—the number of participants may be finite enough that they can decide among themselves whether to simply rotate or rely on another approach, like who is contributing the most funds. Although these constituencies would normally have the prerogative to decide their seat allocations, it may still, as a matter of transparency, be good to have them share their allocation mechanisms with the rest of the governing body.

On the other hand, if a constituency is intended to bring in diversity beyond the immediate partners, the partnership program can look for a proxy method to make that decision. For example, if the category is CSOs, there may be an international platform with sufficiently broad participation that can be tasked with identifying a desired number of CSOs to act as governing body members, perhaps on an annual basis. Similarly, for private sector participation, deferring to a trade association to make the selection can constitute a level-playing-field approach. This would be far better than inviting one or the other favored company to the exclusion of its competitors. (>@ Partners and People—Engaging the Private Sector)

Making Constituencies Work

Partnership program participants may resist constituencies. They provide a high-level solution for the partnership, but at the cost of individual engagement and control. Non-participating partners have to feel comfortable deferring to other members participating on their behalf, and hope they will take their representative capacities to heart. It takes extra time and effort to canvass members of the constituency before a decision is made, and real-time meeting decisions can be encumbered by not having other constituency members in the room for direct input. On the one hand, the participants filling constituency seats need to feel a strong sense of responsibility to their other constituency members, and on the other hand, the non-participants left in the wings need to harbor a strong sense of trust. In that sense, constituencies that have natural connection points outside the partnership program (like countries in a region or members of an international network) often work better than ones that lack other integrating factors.

Observers

Observers are a common participant category in governing body meetings. They have one foot in the room and are visible, but not responsible. Observers can be invited one-off per meeting, as in the case of prospective donors being wooed, or they can be expected at every meeting, like the trustee and secretariat. The latter are standing observers, who are likely also active observers.

Standing observers are fixed positions on the governing body, dedicated to specific named entities, and usually written into the charter or equivalent constitutive document. As mentioned, the trustee and secretariat normally have standing observer seats in partnership programs where their roles are limited, like international platforms. Other standing observer seats might go to downstream fiduciaries or downstream beneficiaries, whose presence is helpful for collaboration and information flow, but whose downstream

Observers as:

1. standing observers
2. active observers
3. by-invitation observers

engagement might be considered a conflict of interest when it comes to allocating funds. Multiple downstream actors competing for funds may be treated differently in this respect from single countries in settings where country ownership dynamics are paramount. (>@ Synergistic Conflicts) Rather than resort to repeated recusals, observer status allows for input and influence without being part of the final decision. In consensus environments, this engagement is usually quite collegial. Standing observer seats might also go to key stakeholders or central international players relevant to the partnership program's focus—like the International Labour Organization for labor or the World Health Organization for health—whose presence is desired more for coordination and information flow than decision making.

Active observers is just a way of saying they are not only visible, but also vocal. Active observers generally have all the same rights of engagement as decision-making members, except for the final decision. In other words, active observers have everything except the veto. (>@ Decision Making) Charters usually do not identify observers as active, but rather let meeting culture evolve. However, if a distinction is relevant, the terms can be more precise and specify that some observers, normally the standing observers, are active—with rights to contribute at the table—while other observers, effectively non-active, may speak up only when invited. Such invitations to speak can come from the chair or the secretariat, depending on who is given the gatekeeper and coordination roles.

By-invitation observers round out governing body participation on an as-helpful basis. Most international partnership programs use their informal governing body status to be somewhat fluid in managing participation. The best way for prospective donors to be won over may be to have them experience a meeting, even though some prospective donors have been known to stay in prospective mode with the benefits of ad hoc attendance for quite some time. Other key stakeholders can be asked to present, perhaps participating in only part of a meeting, to collaborate on specific topics as they arise. A proactive secretariat and an engaged chair can stay alert to occasions for the governing body to field additional participants. Although opportunistic in approach, close collaboration between the secretariat and chair can ensure that this added fluidity still has purpose and order.

Supporting Entities

Supporting entity as:

1. chair
2. decision maker
3. observer
4. absent

How the supporting entity fits into the governing body is an important question for every partnership program. The choices are basically four-fold: taking the chair seat, being a decision-making member, being an observer, or not participating.

- *Chair*. As to be expected, the chair position usually plays out differently in one-stop-shops and international platforms:

  - In the one-stop-shop, full support model, it is the norm for supporting entities to chair the proceedings in a decision-making capacity, usually on the basis of consensus decision making. (>@ Decision Making) This allows for streamlined substantive input in close tandem with the secretariat, trustee, and all other supporting entity functions, a seamless soup-to-nuts approach fulfilling the full support potential that donors and others want from the one-stop-shop—very efficient, highly coordinated, and cohesive. In this model, the chair carries a decision-making role and articulates the consensus decisions for the record.

- In international platforms or other models where the supporting entity could agree to play a more limited, less substantive role, the result would be the opposite. In those cases, the chair position belongs to more substantively engaged decision-making members, which would not include the supporting entity. In some cases, however, a partnership program may position the supporting entity as a neutral, non-decision-making chair at the head of the table, more as a moderating, managing role. There is even room to let the supporting entity be a substantive chair in international platform contexts. (>@ Supporting Entities—Basic Elements—Risk Profile)

■ **Decision maker**. A decision-making supporting entity signals an overall substantive role, which again varies for one-stop-shops and international platforms:

- For one-stop-shops, or any model that puts critical mass reliance on the supporting entity to carry the weight of partnership program decisions and operations, the supporting entity is expected to be a decision maker, representing the secretariat, trustee, and any other roles, all in one. Although the supporting entity usually also steps up to the chair role, it may be enough for the supporting entity to have a decision-making role while leaving the chair position for others. Relinquishing or sharing the chair position in these situations is usually more political than substantive. Substantively, as long as decision making is based on consensus, the effective veto of the supporting entity remains. By inserting another member as the chair, however, the supporting entity may lose its ability to ensure seamless governance across all functions and has less control over governing body proceedings.

- For international programs, by contrast, the supporting entity is less likely to be a decision-making member of the governing body. That approach usually extends directly from the limited trustee and limited secretariat roles housed in that supporting entity, limited also with respect to decision making. However, sometimes the secretariat is not so limited. And sometimes the supporting entity is still valued as a vital partner. Although at first blush, a decision-making supporting entity might seem to undermine the limited trustee/limited secretariat functions, each role is its own. The supporting entity as an institution, as a partner, also has an interest in helping shape the direction of the partnership program and managing its own risk profile—and other partners may be fine with that. As with so much in partnership program design, this is a trade-off. Partners could agree to let the supporting entity partner be on a decision-making par with the other partners, in exchange for more complexity. Partners would understand and accept the supporting entity's multiple roles, as a substantive decision maker, limited secretariat, and limited trustee, all at the same time and under the same ultimate senior management. The supporting entity would need to believe it can handle these multiple roles in distinct and balanced fashion.

■ **Observer**. The supporting entity is basically never going to be an observer in a one-stop-shop; it is always going to have decision-making status

on the governing body. For international platforms, however, where the supporting entity's trustee and secretariat roles are limited, those two roles naturally gravitate to observer status. Indeed, these roles are so central to partnership program functioning that it is hard to imagine conducting governing body business without having them in the room. Each role is distinct, so that usually means two separate seats. As observers, they can participate and be responsive without becoming substantively responsible. The view tends to be that a supporting entity with substantive responsibility for decisions could hamper its efforts to limit secretariat and trustee roles to administrative and financial functions. It could also upend the level playing field vis-à-vis downstream fiduciaries. As noted earlier, however, whether a supporting entity could successfully have two limited roles (secretariat and trustee) together with one substantive role (decision maker) is a matter of both sensitive practice and willing perception.

▪ **Absent**. It is always possible for the supporting entity to be entirely absent from governing body proceedings. In light of the alternatives presented above, that would be a mistake.

Participation

Although partners usually join international partnership programs as entities, the partner that actually walks into the room, or gets on the phone, receives the email, reads the documentation, and does the legwork, is always a person, one or more. This applies to all functions within partnership programs, but is especially visible within the governing body, where the table tent card says Wakanda, but the name tag says T'Challa. So let's talk about the member's representative, at the individual level.

Choice of Representative

Partnership program design looks at structure from an entity point of view. In a governance context, members are usually entities. They are confirmed collectively at the beginning, agreed by everyone, but subsequent decisions about specific representatives are left to each of them individually. Partners clearly care who their other partners are, but they ultimately also end up caring who those partners' representatives are. In terms of ongoing partnership program operations, that is where the rubber hits the road.

In general, partnering entities control their own seats. That of course means making their own decisions about what to approve and what not to approve, but it also means deciding who sits in that seat—notwithstanding efforts to ensure diversity and balance. Who represents the governing body member can be a very consequential decision for that member, as well as the whole partnership program. People and personalities matter. (>@ Partners and People)

Different partnership programs pitch their desired representation at different levels—some want only high-level representatives, and may say so in the charter. Others want technical experts that are versed in the program's subject matter, or they might be more political in targeting who attends, like those closest to the purse strings. Continuity of participation is an obvious advantage, but that can be elusive if the right engagement is not secured. Opting for high-level representation, for example, can pose a scheduling headache. If different experts are needed at different times, continuity may also take a back seat to more focused inputs, especially when large member organizations with ranks of experts can swap out individuals to meet the needs.

During the organizational phase, partnership initiators may well send signals to prospective participants indicating their expectations for engagement,

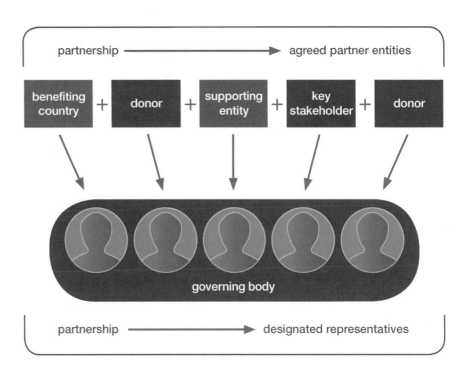

including how they view governing body participation. Sometimes this can be very clear, as when two-tiered governance positions a high-level strategic body with senior representatives over a working level, operations-minded body with more technical representatives. At other times, participation may evolve—perhaps higher level in the beginning for the opening éclat, trending to working level over time, or with increasing reliance on the secretariat as the partnership program gets down to business.

The number of meetings is also a clue. Meet more frequently, like quarterly or monthly, and that signals working level needs. Annual meetings, by contrast, may encourage more senior engagement. Roles and responsibilities of the governing body are another clue. Project-level, nitty gritty decision making usually calls for working level, hands-on, time-consuming activity at and between meetings. A strategic, oversight role—especially if advisory rather than decision making—affords governing body participants more spontaneous inputs, with less homework in between, arguably more suited to higher level participation. If participation is more about mobilizing resources or pursuing advocacy than about partnership program operations, the trustee and secretariat may basically do all the work, while more senior governing body participation primarily helps keep coffers lined and branding primed.

Who keeps the coffers lined and branding primed?

Status of Representative

Collectively, everyone benefits from good representatives, and everyone feels the effects of not so good ones. Individually, all representatives have an interest in knowing they are both well-placed and well-equipped to contribute to the governing body's business.

Being well-placed as a representative means having resonance back home, which suggests good institutional support and uptake. Representatives that

do not connect back to their own member organizations are likely to be lower impact for the partnership program and higher risk for their member organizations. In many ways, governing body representatives have a bridge role between the partnership program and their organizations, for information flow, coordination, decision making, visibility, and often funding. This bridge functions best if potential conflicts are managed, each member's goals are aligned with its representative's assignment, and the representative's terms of engagement are clear. This points to a close relationship between representatives and their managers.

Being well-equipped to make substantive contributions suggests that representatives have adequate knowledge and available resources. Representatives who do not understand the partnership program, their roles, or the relevant subject matter are a potential hazard. It takes only one member to block a consensus decision, which means any individual member can have an outsized role vis-à-vis the whole. At the same time that representatives are each entitled to their views, a partnership program governing body relies on a certain level of decorum and good will, plus competence. All partners contribute to the functioning of the whole in the guise of their representatives. (>@ Partners and People—Being a Good Partner)

Reinforcement

Given the importance of representatives, both to their members and the partnership program as a whole, it can be useful to consider ways to strengthen performance on all fronts: acting as individual participants, serving on behalf of the home entity, functioning as a bridge between the home entity and the partnership program, and contributing to the partnership program's work. Competence in undertaking the multidimensional role of a governing body participant does not usually come by osmosis, but instead deserves explicit grounding at home and in the partnership program.

Training

For the individual representative, help can come in the form of training. But is training really necessary? Governing body representatives can surely grasp

Governing body representatives:

1. acting as individual participants
2. serving on behalf of the home entity
3. being a bridge between the home entity and the partnership program
4. contributing to the partnership program's work

many concepts without needing more training, especially if they are seasoned staff of their member organizations and were chosen for their abilities. But yes—training can be valuable. No matter how expert in sector-specific knowledge, or even other partnerships, it is not obvious that an individual would intuit the functioning of a particular partnership program. That includes details about the specific roles and responsibilities of the governing body (especially relative to other partnership program functions), shared history, and agreed expectations other partners are drawing from or relying on, and perhaps other characteristics and quirks of the context. Moreover, the partnership program collectively and member organizations individually each have different interests within which individual representatives must position themselves.

This all speaks in favor of some form of orientation, like a workshop or packet of materials, that partnership programs can use to bring individual representatives on board. It also points to the value of continuous representation, rather than having new faces pop up too frequently. Member entities, too, can train their representatives about what matters to them, across all partnership program representations and with respect to specific cases. Overall, both the member entity and the partnership program as a whole, not to mention the actual representative, have an interest in giving that individual a leg up.

> It's not intuitive; training can convey the quirks of the context.

Terms of Reference

Additional help for individual representatives can come from terms of reference (TOR) generated by the home entity. They can be used to articulate clear linkages and expectations up the representative's management chain. Even if the governing body's roles and responsibilities are clearly laid out in a charter or equivalent document operating at the member level, the relationship of individual representatives to their own institutions could use additional clarifying.

Representative assignments are often handled quite informally by their member organizations; accordingly, they may miss important aspects. International partnership programs deserve a more systematic approach, if only to anticipate issues and strengthen the bridge between partnership engagement and home base. To fortify the span at both ends, staff representatives are encouraged to agree to specific TORs with their managers, potentially following institutionally prepared templates. In defining the relationship of staff representatives to their member organizations, relative to the partnership program, such TORs can underscore the institutional (as opposed to personal) nature of the representation. Given the minefield that this aspect presents when international partners participate in dedicated entity partnerships (>@ Partnering Internationally—Governing Body Ramifications), TORs can be similarly helpful for corporate board participation.

After anchoring the representative at home, the same can occur with the partnership program. Once a TOR is internally agreed between a staff member and relevant management, an appropriately redacted version can be shared externally with the partnership program. Depending on the sensitivities of the documents, it can be shared with the chair of the

Representative Terms of Reference

Topics like the Ten Terms below can be included in a governing body member's TOR for its designated individual representative (and potential alternates):

1 Recognizing that the staff person is serving in an institutional capacity for the organization

2 Identifying the supervising manager and clear reporting expectations

3 Positioning the representative's responsibilities in relation to the governing body's responsibilities and in relation to any other roles of the representative's member organization

4 Noting specific skills required for the representative to meet member responsibilities

5 Specifying the expected duration of the representative's position

6 Noting what the representative is expected to accomplish

7 Identifying what budget and other organizational support is available

8 Recognizing the minimum number of meetings expected to be attended by the representative and procedures for alternates if needed

9 Considering the implications of any staff rules on the representative's position, including conflicts of interest

10 Confirming that this is part of the organization's work program, and covered by P&I if applicable

governing body, the whole governing body, the secretariat, and even posted publicly on the partnership program's website. Internal terms should of course stay internal, but sharing one or the other point externally may help ensure common understandings and expectations.

Institutional Support

If an organization has numerous staff assigned as representatives on governing bodies of various international partnership programs, some additional steps can make for smoother sailing both at home and in those partnership programs:

- Developing clear and consistently applied processes for approving member participation in partnership program governing bodies and for assigning individual representatives

- Keeping an updated database that catalogues all of its representatives on governing bodies of partnership programs (and formal incorporated boards of dedicated entity partnerships)

- Attaching each individual TOR to this database as a condition of governing body representation

- Confirming that representation is on the basis of an existing charter or equivalent document of the partnership program

- Confirming that the partnership program's website contains current, transparent information about governance, including the charter, names of bodies, members, meeting minutes, relevant reports, and evaluations

Conclusion

Two concluding comments may be obvious:

First, given the open field that applicable law affords most international partnership programs and the innumerable options and alternatives, *clarity is key*. Clarity is a general theme when it comes to structured partnerships, but governing body participants have a special role in being clear. Starting with their own role in comprising the governing body, it is better for them to know what they are about, preferably before, not after, the partnership program is launched. If they constitute a decision-making body with oversight, they have both the prerogative and the responsibility to determine how much clarity, in terms of detail and precision, should exist for the partnership program overall. Is there a charter or equivalent document defining the whole? If so, does it say enough? Have shared terms been agreed by all relevant parties (not just by donors and the trustee in the contribution agreements)? Are there efficient procedures for amending to keep current over time? These questions are typically ultimately in the hands of the governing body.

Second, international partnership programs consist of partners that are usually entities convening institutionally, but their *representatives are individual people*. Having individuals sit at the nexus between their organizations and the partnership program inevitably results in dynamics (and maybe drama) that have real consequences. Ultimately, a governing body, and the people on it, can make or break a partnership program. With people in the room, engagement is organic. Participants are apt to respond to the atmosphere as much as the agenda. It may sound hokey, but convening like-minded partners, represented by compatible individuals, all acting respectfully as good citizens focused on a common goal, can also be key to governing body success.

With people in the room, engagement is organic.

6 SECRETARIATS

Secretariats—or coordination units, focal points, program hubs, or simply administrative staff; whatever you want to call them—are the glue that holds international partnership programs together. International partnership program participants will want to match their support structures to their ambitions. On the one hand, support comes at a cost, and that takes resources away from program activities. On the other hand, support can make things happen, allowing the partnership program to build a track record that enables more resource mobilization and more activities. Deciding how much support is desirable is in part seeking that *virtuous cycle* where support begets success and ultimately sustains itself. This is "just right"–sizing that even Goldilocks would like.

Options

In considering their administrative support options, particularly to connect participants and support the governing body, international partners have three main options:

1. **No dedicated support.** Partners can go light and forgo dedicated support, relying instead on each other. This most likely means a rotating function, where everyone takes a piece of the support responsibility, perhaps attached to a rotating chair position as convener of the group. This also most likely means the partnership program's purpose is to coordinate more than implement, likely without a dedicated, commingled funding source. (>@ Typology—Coordination Partnerships)

2. **Existing entity support.** Partners can piggyback, using existing infrastructure to provide dedicated support. Leaning on an existing legal entity to act as secretariat means getting a piece of a larger institution, which can be leveraged for the benefit of the partnership program. Common supporting entities are international organizations, like UN agencies or MDBs, or government ministries in the case of single-country partnership programs. Partnership programs with dedicated, identifiable administrative support structures fit this bill. (>@ Supporting Entities)

3. **Dedicated entity support.** Partners can go whole hog and create their own new dedicated, incorporated entity. In this case, management and staff of the entity are effectively the secretariat. However, starting new like this is only possible with sufficient secured funding over time, since this calls for not just a new partnership program but also a new legal entity. Partners can select their legal venue and shape their entity within that context, potentially as an international organization founded by member countries, but more likely as a domestically incorporated entity within the constraints of domestic requirements. (>@ Typology—Light to Heavy)

LIGHT

MEDIUM

HEAVY

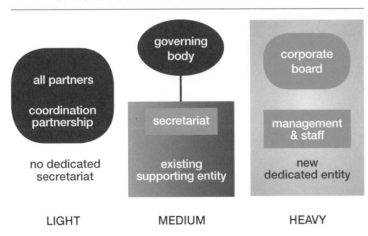

OPTIONS FOR SECRETARIAT INFRASTRUCTURE

Spectrum of Support Options

Light. Option one, the "light" variant, is often based on in-kind burden sharing with minimal to no dedicated administrative support function. It is similarly light on partnership-generated programming, since the "program" basically consists of partners convening and sharing. To put it another way, option one emphasizes partnership more than program. For most coordination partnerships, it is enough to informally or occasionally convene to, for example, coordinate respective downstream activities, consider lessons learned, or bolster a country's strategic compact, without needing daily secretariat support. This type of coordination and light collaboration can be productive for partners without having to add major resource mobilization or implementation activities, since each partner already has that at home.

Heavy. Option three, at the other end of the spectrum, is heavy. Creating, funding, and sustaining a new legal entity is a heavy lift. Before going ahead with incorporating a new entity:

- Partnership program participants should be convinced that ample fund flows are forthcoming over the long term, or else they risk having support costs overwhelm intended gains.
- They should believe that no other existing platform can adequately address their development or other concerns, or else they add to the proliferation of platforms.
- They should prioritize elements that a separate entity can bring—like independence, focus, a fresh start, political momentum—in ways that existing entities cannot.

Medium. For the average ambitious but not super-high-profile endeavor, option two is a reasonable choice. This is particularly true in the development arena, where multiple existing international organizations can provide support on a comprehensive and sustained basis. The range of possibilities within option two is significant. The right size and scope, tailored to the partnership program's desired profile, can usually be worked out. Whether a focal point of one individual staff person or a designated unit of a hundred staff or more, a dedicated secretariat-type function in an existing entity may offer a better combination of ease, efficiency, attention, cost, and calibration than options one and three allow.

Options one (light partnership infrastructure) and three (heavy partnership infrastructure) are straightforward. Option one is basically horizontally placed and relies on all the partners, while option three is vertically integrated and relies on a new entity. By contrast, option two (medium partnership infrastructure), embedding into an existing entity, is a hybrid mix that invites complexity. That is an option two challenge. It can take a while for partners to grasp how it works so they can make key business decisions about how they want it to work. This requires extra effort upfront to clarify roles and responsibilities, while also establishing expectations and limits; it also takes extra effort throughout to operate within agreed terms. There is enough here to dig deeper and study the workings of these embedded support units, also known as "inhouse secretariats."

Embedded, Inhouse Secretariats

Inhouse secretariats—the ones that are embedded in and part of existing, supporting legal entities—live in the twilight zone of partnership programs. They are both in and out, or somewhat in and somewhat out, serving the partnership program but still beholden to their home entity. This can make the lives of secretariat staff particularly tricky, and tricky for the lives of partners, too. While inhouse secretariats are a special subset of secretariats generally, they are the basis for most trust-funded partnership programs. Their complexities merit exposition and may carry lessons for other partnership configurations as well.

For starters, to whom do these inhouse secretariats belong— the supporting entity where they are housed or the partnership program they were created to serve? If the partnership program wants to direct and control the inhouse secretariat, can it? When presenting themselves, should inhouse secretariat staff put the name of the partnership program or the supporting entity on their business cards? The answers depend in part on the supporting entity's applicable policies and procedures, which may provide some direction on these fronts. It may also depend on how the partnership program is engaging the inhouse secretariat, whether more at arm's length as a hired provider of outsourced services or more integrally, as a partner first and a support function second. International partnership programs regularly favor the latter.

HYBRID IN + OUT

- secretariat focused outward
- secretariat embedded inward

Outsourcing specific functions to a contracted provider is a legal relationship based on deliverables. In this case, the administrative function is a paid-for service, rather than partner-provided support. This can work well, if the price is right and partners know what they want. A substantively engaged governing body that simply needs someone to take instructions and follow through can afford to outsource. In this way, participants get what they pay for and keep the terms at arm's length and enforceable.

For hybrid secretariats, however, the international community has an alternative through existing international organizations, especially in the development arena. Among others, the Bretton Woods family that emerged after World War II and its related progeny offer a range of candidates, including UN agencies, MDBs, and other IFIs, that can provide more all-around, substantive, and interconnected support—as a partner rather than a service provider. These support models are less contractual, less arms-length, less prescribed, and less enforceable, but more integrated and more comprehensive. This often means providing multiple support functions, like secretariat plus trustee plus implementation, which is a particularly synergistic combination. (>@ Typology—Introducing Two Mighty Oaks)

This abundance of supporting entity support makes for a supporting entity–centric approach with shared governance tacked on, rather than the other way around. These are truly "inhouse" secretariats where partnering guests come into the house—or, as shareholding members of the supporting entity, have already taken up residence.

Benefits

Several things make these embedded, inhouse secretariats particularly comfortable for international partnership programs:

1 ***Secretariat-Trustee Axis.*** First, the combination with the trustee function—administrative and financial management support functions together—can be immensely appealing and efficient. In fact, this secretariat-trustee combination is sometimes so integrated that partners see just the trustee without perceiving a separate, secretariat-type function. For trust-funded partnership programs that are trust fund–centric, like one-stop-shops, secretariat support is but a natural, almost inadvertent add-on, often not even separately named. This is especially true when the same entity carries responsibility for downstream implementation. In those cases, support may be so seamless that it is counterproductive to separate secretariat functions from fiduciary functions at the trustee and project levels.

2 ***Inside Track.*** Second, partners are especially close to the secretariat supporting entity when they sit on the supporting entity's board or are otherwise part of the institutional governance, as do the traditional donors that are also shareholders of MDBs or members of the UN. While it does not really work to have an outsourced, contracted relationship with an entity you are a part of, the reverse is also true; getting direct support from your own entity can work very well. Partnership program participants who have this inside track can do more to monitor and control the supporting entity than an outsourced relationship would ever allow.

3 ***Privileges and Immunities.*** Third, at least as important but less articulated, is the comfort of P&I. A number of international organizations can claim broad P&I, even if they may be increasingly at risk of being eroded. This protection means two things. First, partnership program activities that benefit from P&I—those performed by the protected supporting entity—can be undertaken in a protected zone. Second, there is operational complementarity when support functions carry the basic P&I that other partners, like national governments, also enjoy. Understandably, donors, recipients, and key stakeholders that are countries, or international organizations founded and run by member countries, may prefer to augment their own protected status by handing support functions to entities that have similar protections.

Challenges

Nothing is perfect. For all the benefits of leaning on existing multilateral institutions, there are also challenges:

1 **Established Operating Frameworks.** First, not surprisingly, is that piggybacking on existing entities means operating within existing frameworks—policies, procedures, practices, management, governance, and more. From the get-go, the relationship is heavily prescribed, staff are deeply embedded, and activities are duly constrained. This would hardly work if the existing entity were an unknown quantity, whereas it can work quite well if the existing entity is known and even governed by many of the partners.

2 **Supporting Entity Staff.** Second, part of what that entails is the status of secretariat staff. When secretariat staff are hired for or assigned to a secretariat unit within a supporting entity, they do not suddenly stop being supporting entity staff. Rather, this continuing staff relationship with the supporting entity—contractual, financial, operational—permeates the secretariat. Typically those staff persons also continue to have a duty of loyalty to their hiring organization, including a duty to inform managers, maintain supporting entity confidential information, behave within ethical boundaries, avoid besmirching the supporting entity's reputation, and whatever else pertains in the staff rules. In some cases, this even requires a sole and absolute loyalty to the supporting entity, which may be difficult to reconcile with the expectations of others in the partnership program. (>@ Partnering Internationally—Governing Body Ramifications) And it even carries over to seconded staff, who technically become supporting entity staff during the time of their secondment. (>@ Supporting Entities—Duality and Balance)

The solution to this conundrum is not to exempt secretariat staff from supporting entity rules. That would be throwing out the baby with the bath water and wreaking havoc with supporting entity privileges and protections. It is also not as easy as saying all interests of the supporting entity are the same as the interests of the partnership program (or more precisely, the combined interests of all other partners), so there are no conflicts of interest—although some might wish to believe it. If the partnership program is a good fit, then that is true most of the time, but not necessarily all of the time.

The better approach is to be open about the situation, transparent about the tensions, and clear about the implications. Disclose and manage. This starts with supporting entity staff and their managers, making sure they have an adequate understanding of this topic, and then continues with partnership program participants, making sure they have the same understanding. These baseline understandings, ideally established at the start, can help both individual staff members and the partnership as a whole.

Challenges:

1. established operating frameworks
2. supporting entity staff

Piggybacking on existing entities means operating within existing frameworks.

Working from Within

Some frictions are inevitable, as certain partners push for customizations and exceptions. At times, these frictions are the most pronounced coming from shareholder partners. This is, however, not how it should be. If shareholders of the supporting entity do not like how that entity is supporting partnership programs as a matter of its policies and procedures, a better answer is to make changes from the top, institutionally, directly to those policies and procedures—not from the bottom, partnership program by partnership program. Piecemeal and disjointed accommodations on a large scale can be a recipe for chaos. In the end, partnership program participants should not rely on an existing entity for secretariat support unless they are willing to go "inhouse" and all that entails.

Inhouse Secretariat Roles

Given the benefits and challenges, partners want to think carefully about the scope of the secretariat's role (or secretariat-type functions handled by the trustee) as they consider whether the embedded option two is the best fit. Inhouse secretariat support for most international partnership programs can be roughly divided into five broad, somewhat overlapping categories:

Secretariat support for:

1. consolidation
2. governance
3. legal entity
4. gatekeeping
5. implementation

1 Consolidation support—the glue that holds it all together and supports the brand

2 Governance support—functions that support governing body business

3 Legal entity support—formal legal entity status needed for contracting, hiring, and procuring

4 Gatekeeping support—screening control for all partners, including the supporting entity

5 Implementation support—responsibility for undertaking partnership activities

Consolidation Support

Consolidation support by the secretariat goes to the very core of the partnership program. It entails a number of functions that create coherence among partners and amplify the partnership program brand. This type of support is virtually indispensable for partnership programs with any type of visible identity, including for advocacy and resource mobilization purposes. The media component in particular, including dedicated websites, knowledge platforms, dissemination channels, and interactive engagement, has become increasingly important, as the Internet and social media offer ever-increasing opportunities to communicate and be visible. This core support also encompasses broad and abundant relationship building and nurturing among partners, prospective donors, and other stakeholders.

Governance Support

Governance support kicks in with shared governance, with the secretariat as the focal point for getting governing body business done. If there is a governing body, there is secretariat-type support. That said, secretariats can do a lot or a little, depending on how much the governing body does for itself and how much support the governing body wants and is willing to pay for. It also depends on what the supporting entity is willing and able to do, usually coming in as a partner and mindful of its own risk profile. As a general rule, secretariats are indispensable complements to governing bodies, basically making sure the trains run on time, luggage is properly stowed, and wheels are greased. This applies to both in-meeting and email decision making. If the secretariat is not teeing up agenda items, keeping meeting minutes, and managing no objection processes, decision points are bound to lack the clarity, legitimacy, and historical record needed for smooth operations. The secretariat is the alter ego to the governing body's ego, and the two go hand-in-hand. Given this close relationship, it is almost always advisable to give the secretariat a dedicated seat on the governing body, either as a decision-making member or a standing, active observer (>@ Governing Bodies—Composition—Supporting Entities)—in all likelihood, with other secretariat staff also roaming around to provide support as needed.

Legal Entity Support

It may be tempting to leave thoughts of legal entities to the lawyers. Don't. Legal entity status is an essential business component of international partnership programs because they do not have legal status of their own. Somewhere, somehow, there has to be a legal entity that lets the partnership program conduct basic business, basically anything that requires contracting. That includes hiring staff and consultants, procuring supplies, leasing office space, engaging a website server, purchasing a domain name, getting plane tickets, and so much more, all based on the legal entity's internal rules. One of the usual and crucial benefits of a secretariat is its legal entity status through the supporting entity. This is a non-issue for partnership programs that choose to be dedicated legal entities in their own right, but it is a major, usually unarticulated and unrecognized element of informal partnerships programs. (>@ Custodial Effect) Legal entity status can be part of an outsourced arrangement, and in some cases it is. Most common, however, is legal entity status through a supporting entity that is also a partner, whether this role comes through the trustee, as in one-stop-shops where the trustee integrates the secretariat, or a distinct secretariat.

Legal entity status is a business matter.

Gatekeeping Support

Gatekeeping is a clearing house role with teeth. Secretariats sitting at the central node of international partnership programs are superbly placed to manage in- and outflows vis-à-vis other elements of the partnership and the outside. Secretariats can do this normatively, passing substantive judgment on what comes and goes; or they can do so only administratively, screening on the basis of pre-set rules, requirements, criteria, or other articulated standards, in basically a compliance function. Perform due diligence on

Secretariat support can be the difference between high- and low-risk ventures.

prospective members or donors? Check project submissions against prescribed templates? Screen proposed charter amendments for compatibility with supporting entity policies? Whether these kinds of reviews tend more to the administrative or substantive is something the partners can decide. Either way, inserting secretariats as gatekeepers and compliance agents can be a valuable tool for partners, including supporting entities, to streamline processes, manage risk profiles, and keep things within bounds. While some partners may see the related procedures and delays as bureaucratic, this kind of support can be the difference between a high-risk and low-risk venture.

Implementation Support

Implementation support is more variable. Whether the secretariat role picks up downstream responsibility is a matter of both design and definitional choices. Some international partnership programs prefer to couple shared governance support and implementation roles in the secretariat, fully leveraging the secretariat supporting entity. When trust funds enter the scene, however, the secretariat may well cede the downstream role to others. In one-stop-shops, where partnership programs typically revolve around a single trust fund, or a single trustee with multiple trust funds, partners often think of downstream implementation as the trustee's responsibility, no secretariat needed (more a matter of perception and labeling). Other partnership programs draw a bright line and keep implementation downstream distinctly separate from trustee/secretariat support and upstream governance. Exhibit A for these scenarios is the typical international platform, where the trustee is limited and the secretariat is similarly held to a neutral, level playing field vis-à-vis multiple downstream fiduciaries that are vested with full downstream responsibility. An umbrella arrangement draws comparable lines, in this case combining multiple trust funds with multiple trustees and leaving the partnership program secretariat with a governance coordination role, rather than a project implementation role. (>@ Typology—Umbrella Arrangements)

Secretariat implementation:

1. as part of the trustee (some one-stop-shops)
2. as a full and distinct function
3. as a limited secretariat (some international platforms)

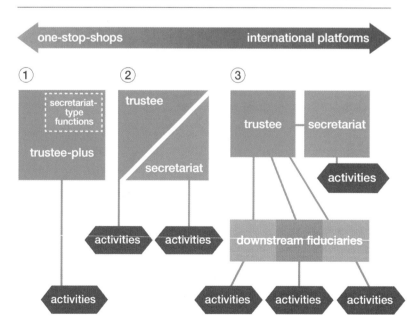

OPTIONS FOR SECRETARIAT IMPLEMENTATION SUPPORT

Secretariat Self-Restraint and Self-Support—Two more "roles" deserve (dis)honorable mention:

Ensuring Self-Restraint
As valiant as being the hero may sound, rescue mode is best avoided. In general, secretariats should not take on responsibilities assigned to others. A case in point, limited secretariats should not slip into substantive roles. (>@ Typology—International Platforms) Compilation, for example, stops short of a desk review. Substantive responsibility for another entity's funding requests or progress reports belongs with the other entity. The secretariat can coordinate, compile, and compliance check, all secondary roles that facilitate the work of the partnership program. It can even cajole. However, the secretariat cannot control and should not undertake what others are supposed to do.

Many a secretariat has jumped into rescue mode when another partner has failed to deliver. This may help in the short term, but is not a durable solution. It also makes the secretariat vulnerable. An ineffective rescue not only makes the secretariat responsible for the failure, but is ultra vires to boot—an illegitimate usurpation of power. That may backfire on any good intentions. It is usually better to openly recognize where implementation deficiencies lie and then work collectively within the partnership program to shift things around. The goal is always to keep clear lines of responsibility and accountability, even as they may adjust over time.

Ensuring Self-Support
What clearly belongs to the secretariat is conducting and managing its own operations, whatever the defined scope. This has both operational and budgetary dimensions, with the focus—as it should be—on the people.

- Budgetarily, the biggest secretariat line item is usually staff. Partners may not love the idea of paying for core support, but you get what you pay for. Whatever the agreed secretariat load, partnership programs that skimp on resources for secretariat staff can expect to get less overall—the opposite of a virtuous cycle. The reverse also applies. If funds are forthcoming, supporting entities should match agreed responsibilities with adequate staff and resources. What if the secretariat signs up for various responsibilities, but then the supporting entity limits secretariat staff through institution-wide hiring caps that impair partnership program operations? Both supporting entities and other partners need to understand and follow through with funds and resources for secretariats, or at least be open about limitations and discuss adjustments.
- Operationally, hiring decisions are normally the prerogative and responsibility of the secretariat supporting entity, whose human resources policies must prevail. Of course, those policies can leave room, if agreed, for the governing body to influence staff-related decisions, although this can get complicated, even if just for the secretariat head. The contractual, hiring relationship is with the supporting entity, including in relation to management, performance evaluations, benefits, termination, and any legal claims—legal aspects that an informal governing body cannot supplant. (>@ Supporting Entities)

So how does an embedded secretariat head mesh with the partnership program overall? Think of it as contractual, straight-line responsibility to internal (institutional) management complemented by dotted-line accountability to the external (shared) governing body. The secretariat head reports to the legal entity in the management sense and reports to the governing body in the information sense—not the other way around. A partnership program that tries to flip the equation is out of line. Whoever stands in the contractual shoes with staff cannot relinquish contractual obligations to a non-legal entity like a governing body. The supporting entity therefore needs to keep the final prerogative on human resources, including hiring, firing, and everything in between, while also staying mindful of the interests of the partnership program.

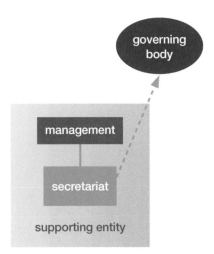

Lessons Learned

A word to the wise:

A partnership program is as stable as the secretariat; shifting sands make for slack foundations.

Partners may want to benefit from a few lessons learned when it comes to inhouse secretariats. Four come to mind:

1 *The "Secretariats Are Indispensable" Phenomenon.* It is hard to overstate how important secretariats are in keeping partnership programs together. (>@ Custodial Effect) Core support is not a favorite budget item, but a partnership program without a robust core is not much of a partnership program. Ironically, the same donors who need extensive coordinating, cajoling, and handholding by the secretariat often consider "lean" secretariats to be a badge of honor. This pressure to scale back support staff belies the critical role inhouse secretariats play in managing the wide collaboration and coordination needed to foster effective and sustained partnership consensus. Without swelling the ranks and spending more than merited, partnership program participants may want to focus more on value than cost when it comes to secretariat support.

2 *The "Secretariats Are Not Trustees" Perspective.* There are fundamental differences between trustee and secretariat roles. As explained, secretariat staff must be responsive to both the supporting entity and the views of external partners. Their responsibilities point both inward and outward. When inhouse secretariats are pulled heavily in the direction of the governing body, this outward attention becomes even more pronounced. The trustee, by contrast, acts only for the supporting entity, as a principal in its own right, not as an agent or on anyone else's behalf. This is because the trustee entity is contractually bound under fund flow agreements and liable for breach. With this liability potential, donors give full fiduciary responsibility to the trustee and remove themselves from the equation. A rule that trustee staff persons report directly to supporting entity management, rather than through the secretariat head, can avoid misaligned responsibilities that taint trustee operations with overbearing, one-off partner influences.

No messy middle.

3 *The "Secretariats Stay Clean" Caution.* Ideally, secretariats stay out of the messy middle. (>@ Ten Tried and True Tips—Be Clean) They know their roles and stick to them, not just vis-à-vis the trustee. They delineate and distinguish their roles vis-à-vis upstream and downstream participants as well. Call it too many cooks in the kitchen, but overlapping responsibilities are best avoided in partnership programs, secretariats included. The risk is having either too many or too few attend to matters. In this vein, joint secretariats across more than one supporting entity are not recommended. There once was a joint secretariat among seven entities, jointly including all seven of the partners; that could not go well. Even two is a recipe for muddied water, unless the responsibilities are clearly subdivided with no overlaps and no gaps—and that of course is not joint responsibility, but division of labor. Rotating secretariats are similarly prone to issues, especially when gaps arise from the lack of continuity.

4 **The "Secretariats Are Forever" Syndrome.** Secretariat staff may be tempted to perpetuate their own secretariat. If, for example, the secretariat head's position is paid for by the trust fund, something that would be in keeping with notions of full cost recovery, it might create a bias for keeping the trust fund—and partnership program—alive. Program management could then become motivated by personal staff interests more than institutional, donor, or development interests. For this, a rule that secretariat heads not be funded by partnership program trust funds could be one way to avoid conflicts of interest or incentives to prolong a trust fund for the wrong reasons.

Conclusion

At the end of the day, internally embedded functions, like the secretariat, must be reconciled with the broader partnership nature of the initiative. The supporting entity qua partner engages both as an outward looking partner and an inwardly obligated provider. Expectations set at the beginning should include an appreciation of the prevailing institutional—and secondary partnership—nature of secretariat support roles. This should then be defined with clarity and delineated with precision in the partnership program's constitutive establishment documents, like the charter.

Complex issues come with the territory, but so far they have proved worth the effort, as the embedded, inhouse secretariat model endures.

7 TRUST FUNDS

INTERNATIONAL
PARTNERSHIP
PROGRAM

the trust fund,
it's just a funding vehicle . . .

There is no partnership program without funding. Money makes the world go round, and that applies to international partnership programs, too. Among the most tried and true formulas for coupling international partnership programs with financial resources are trust funds administered by partnering international organizations. These funding vehicles are so popular and so effective that they easily overshadow the partnership elements, especially when the smell of money fills the room. This results in design decisions and management attention that take the trust fund perspective, at times at the cost of partnering considerations. Even in focusing on trust funds in this chapter, the intention is to flip the perspective, starting with the realization that trust funds are just funding vehicles. Important as trust funds are, the partnering around them and the programming funded by them is where the action comes alive and results arise. (>@ International Partnership Programs)

Accounts

At their most basic, international organization–administered trust funds are accounts. They contain funds that are managed by a so-called trustee. Money flows in and out. A contributor agrees to provide, and the trustee agrees to receive, funds for specified purposes under specified terms. These terms define the trust fund's operations and the trustee's promises to the contributor. If the trust fund involves shared decision making, like a governing body, that relationship is (or should be) spelled out as well. The trustee then manages and disburses the funds for the agreed purposes within the agreed terms.

Trust Funds in Relation to Partnership Programs

Many partnership programs include trust funds, and many trust funds are part of partnership programs, but not necessarily. A partnership program can have multiple trust funds or none. A trust fund can be part of a partnership program or not. When combined, the trust fund may be the center of gravity, orbited by an advisory or high-level, strategic governing body. But in many other cases, the governing body is at the center, with primary decision-making responsibility, fed by one or more trust funds and perhaps other funding sources.

Trust funds, as funding vehicles, are not to be confused with partnership programs. Trust funds feed into and support partnership programs, which consist of much more than their funding vehicles. In this world view, partnership programs embrace trust funds, instead of letting trust funds consume partnership programs. Partners that view partnership programs from a trust fund lens are encouraged to step back and see the forest for the trees. Rather than inverting the landscape by letting money define the collaboration, the view may be clearer—and more comprehensive—the other way around. In cases where there is more trust fund than partnership, this inversion may be exactly what is going on, but often enough it is appropriate to let the partnership program frame the vista. It is in any case good to test the lens first, before losing sight of what is important.

WIDEN THE LENS

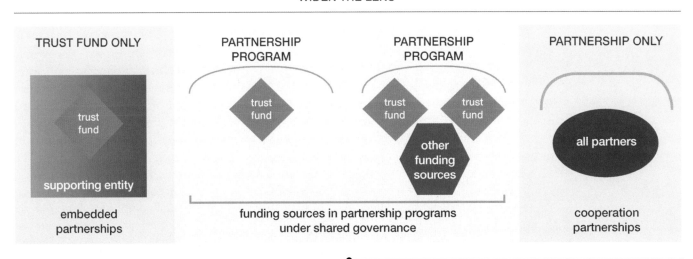

Since this is money, trust fund deposits invariably come with formal agreement terms. Fund flows are contractualized, typically through signed contribution agreements on the way in, and grant or transfer agreements on the way out. These agreements are usually bilateral, between the trustee and the contributor (upstream) or recipient (downstream), even when they pertain to multilateral efforts, like commingled pools of funds and collectively agreed work plans. (>@ International Partnership Programs—Collectivizing)

The main point of these contractualized terms is to attach fiduciary responsibilities to the funds. The trustee is entrusted with the funds, meaning the donor expects the trustee to follow through on the agreement terms— anything less is a case of breach. In this way, a trust fund is an account within a fiduciary framework. The trustee is the fiduciary, responsible for proper fund use as defined by the contractualized terms, and those agreed terms constitute the framework. Once signed, the trust fund terms attach to

$$ \$ \; + \; \text{trust fund} \; = \; \$ \; + \; \text{fiduciary responsibility} $$

contribution ⟶ use

any new funds contributed to the same trust fund, under the same or amended terms, and the trustee stays on the hook as defined over time.

Partnership programs that involve multi-donor trust funds collectivize their funding, in whole or in part, by establishing common accounts under common terms. Whatever goes into the common pool is commingled. That means the separate identity of each donor's contribution is lost. Every dollar (or every currency converted into the operating currency of the common account) is fungible with every other dollar; there is only one common currency for a commingled fund. With the commingled pool, an individual donor cannot say it uniquely funded a specific downstream activity. Instead, every donor effectively funds every activity funded by the trust fund. Every donor can lay claim to and get credit for all activities and all results, no matter how small the individual contribution. This gives all donors great visibility (in the sense of public recognition) for all things positive—and also reputational risk for all things negative.

Q: What is the color of trust fund money?

A: Fiduciary green.

Depending on the versatility of the trustee entity's back office systems, trust funds can also be set up with multiple accounts or pools that are top level accounts, without being conveyed through an initial, commingled account. In these cases, a donor can provide specific amounts to specific destination accounts, often referred to as windows. Normally this allows for financial tracking, whereby the donor can link specific funds to specific windows, thus ringfencing their use and avoiding direct association with other funds in other windows. On the positive side, this typically allows more donors to participate in a broadly framed trust fund because they can more narrowly target their own funding to reflect the specific purposes for which it has been approved. On the negative side, this can create a cumbersome patchwork of restricted funding, without the fungibility and flexibility that a main account with unrestricted funds allows. This not only puts a damper on core support funding, since donors usually find less glory in funding administrative overhead than visible downstream activities, but also increases logistics and transaction costs for separate recordkeeping, reporting, and other operations needed for multiple top level accounts. Restricted funds also undercut strategic, portfolio-wide approaches that benefit from shared inputs. (>@ Trade-Offs—The Central Harmonization Spectrum)

TRUST FUND ACCOUNT STRUCTURES

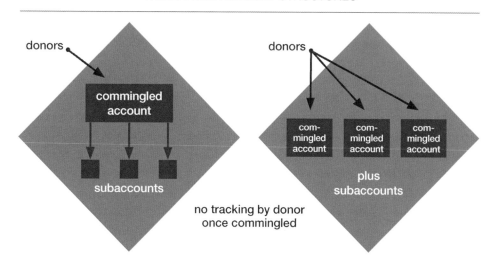

donors

commingled account

subaccounts

no tracking by donor once commingled

donors

com-mingled account

com-mingled account

com-mingled account

plus subaccounts

Trustees

Who exactly is this "trustee"? Come to find out, in international partnership programs, the trustee is not really a trustee, not as defined by any jurisprudence other than the rules of the international entity playing that role and the terms agreed with the donors. For that matter, trust fund agreements are not always agreements either, but sometimes "arrangements." Nor are trust funds "trust funds" in the doctrinaire sense.

As if the topic were not complex enough! Terminology can be deceptive, so it is worth looking under the hood. Although the term "trustee" is used liberally here and in practice, there is no direct connection to typical jurisprudential trust or trustee concepts, only an attenuated notion operating by analogy. Indeed, the international trustee is usually at pains to specify in the agreed legal terms that no other trust or fiduciary jurisprudence has any bearing on the trust fund.

Featuring the as-defined, as-agreed trustee.

If trust funds are accounts, trustees are the keepers of those accounts. Being a trustee is both a role, as manager of the funds, and a responsibility, on agreed terms. The trustee is necessarily embedded in a legal entity. Only this way can it enter into valid fund flow agreements with donors upstream and recipients downstream. At this juncture between the upstream and downstream, the trustee is also the fulcrum, legally and operationally transforming funds in to funds out, all for purposes of the partnership program, as agreed and decided by the partners.

The topic of trustee is meaty enough that a whole chapter is reserved for its variations on the theme, the first of three that delve more deeply into trust fund aspects. (>@ Trustee Types; Use of Funds; Fund Use Responsibility) There we take a closer look at full trustees compared to limited trustees, plus a closer look at the trustee entity that backs them.

Donors

Who uses international trust funds? The range of donors, also called contributors, or somewhat euphemistically "development partners" (aren't all other partnership program partners addressing development topics also development partners?), can be broad. Multilaterals who are in the trust fund business actively support hundreds of different donors. Most donors are countries that dispense official development aid (ODA) through their ministries, departments, and agencies. Private foundations, international organizations, and others contribute as well, although to a much lesser degree. In general, the bar to give funds is lower than the bar to receive funds. Partnership program participants like the color of money and may concede on various points if the price is right. For its part, the donor has but one primary obligation under a contribution agreement: to pay the funds when due. Most development aid donors are long-standing customers and do not have to meet the same kind of weighty function tests that tend to apply to downstream recipients, like the ability to properly manage or use funds. (>@ Trust Funds—Disbursements—Fiduciary Frameworks)

Nevertheless, international partnership program participants can be selective about who contributes funds. In recognizing this, partners are recognizing partnership dimensions around trust funds. The expectation of being like-minded is usually not overt, since self-selection generally works that way, except when it does not. Like-mindedness is especially important when donor status is a direct ticket to the governing body and decision-making functions. If donors are governing body participants that help steer the partnership program and carry veto power under consensus decision making, then hopefully those donors fit together enough to support shared objectives. (>@ Partners and People—Choosing Partners) In addition, since participants coming together under one header are also exposed to each other, donors—like all other partners—can affect the reputation of every other partner. (>@ International Partnership Programs—Collectivizing—One Brand)

While partnership programs can be selective about donors, the dynamic is usually the other way. Donors are most certainly selective about partnership programs. There is no shortage of competition for their funds; opportunities to contribute abound. As a result, they are usually quite deliberate and directed in their engagement, often providing funding within strategic frameworks and overarching mandates. They are apt to seek partnership program alignment with their homegrown agendas and ministry portfolios, typically also with their national political interests. They can do so by selecting well-matched partnership programs, influencing partnership programs into alignment, or catalyzing new endeavors around their ambitions and interests. Their ability to engage and shape may depend on the amounts they bring and the alliances they build, but almost always, traditional donors are not coy about their intentions and wear their donor role on their sleeves.

In this way, donors are usually the drivers of international partnership programs, often pushing for better results, higher standards, and innovative approaches. Partners, especially supporting entities, spend much of their time trying to crowd in more donors to contribute to the cause. Most of these donors are donors first and foremost, taking the donor view even as decision makers. Less frequently, donor roles are secondary or complementary to other factors. These combinations can add to partnership program complexity and at least three of them deserve some exploration.

Beneficiary Donors

Developing countries that are aid recipients or beneficiaries occasionally contribute small amounts to trust funds, like membership fees where everyone pays their allotted amount. (>@ Trade-Offs—The Horizontal Buy-In Spectrum) These developing country contributions in effect pay for low-budget seats on the governing body of the partnership program. Asking for contributions is one way, for example, to winnow down multiple beneficiary countries that want to participate in the governing body.

It is quite possible for some donors to contribute in the tens of millions (or more), while others contribute only in the tens of thousands, all to the same trust fund. From a legal perspective, if all are contributing to the same commingled pool, the amount of contribution makes no difference regarding rights and responsibilities, since all donors have the same common terms, unless donors all agree to some distinctions. Vis-à-vis the trustee in particular, all donors normally have the same rights and the trustee has the same obligations, no matter how large or small the contribution. If a contribution translates into a seat on the governing body, and the governing body makes consensus decisions, then even the lowest-paying donor has a full veto on anything to be decided.

Special donor types:

1. beneficiary
2. private sector
3. supporting entity

Things can get awkward if an entity that is contributing also ends up receiving. This is called "roundtripping," an apt label when money comes from and goes to the same entity, channeled through the commingled trust fund pool. For understandable reasons, roundtripping is normally not allowed—why put the trustee in the middle—but one could perhaps imagine scenarios where even this might be justified, as in the case of membership fees or if the trustee otherwise serves a beneficial, partnership-approved role in managing the beneficiary's own complementary funds.

Private Sector Donors

Donors from the for-profit private sector, or even some company-branded foundations, can also make things interesting. Private companies and their foundations with deep pockets may wish to contribute, for example, to international development efforts. And yet engagement by the private sector in internationally positioned trust funds is not that widespread. Corporate business interests—like maximizing profit and promoting shareholder gain—do not inherently dovetail with development objectives. Even when interests appear to overlap, it is still prudent to double check that the primary motives of prospective private sector participants are not, for example, whitewashing past bad behavior or getting good press coverage for marketing purposes. (>@ Partners and People—Engaging the Private Sector)

Supporting Entity Donors

In some cases, the trustee entity may also be a contributing entity, where the donor role is in addition to the trustee role. When a donor role is added to a support role, the participation of that entity becomes more substantive and potentially more complex. In a one-stop-shop setting, where the full trustee is already fully responsible, adding a donor role can be of little consequence from governance and responsibility perspectives. However, in a limited trustee setting, like international platforms, adding a donor role may be considered at odds with limits set on the responsibilities of the trustee. While the trustee seeks to stay in a financial management box, the donor part of the same entity has a substantive interest in the use of its own contributed funds, as well as all funds commingled with them. In other words, at the same time the trustee entity disavows any responsibility for downstream implementation, the donor part of that same entity has a keen interest in the downstream implementation.

And yet, these two roles—limited trustee and engaged donor—can coexist side-by-side in the same entity if properly set up. Most important for this juxtaposition is to achieve a clear separation of duties and clear lines of accountability, both within the trustee/donor entity and vis-à-vis the partnership program. For example, the governing body may seat a trustee representative as an observer and a separate donor representative as a decision maker, each from different parts of the same entity. Chinese walls or other internally imposed information barriers arguably do not help in that both roles converge in the same senior management that oversees participation as a whole, and—significantly—that participation converges across roles as an overall partner. With partner engagement as a matter for the whole institution (partner status is at the institutional level), we can expect such walls to end up porous at higher levels. However, as long as the individual roles and terms are clear, distinct, and transparent to all partners, the limited trustee can still seek to stay limited and (mostly) clean without having the additional donor contribution and governing body participation muddy the water. (>@ Governing Bodies—Supporting Entities)

Contributions

Contributions can come all at once upfront, or be dribbled out over time. They can be committed early for payment later, or just-in-time when ready to pay. Trustees are usually quite flexible when it comes to payment schedules, at least before signature. After signature, the payment schedule is usually treated as a commitment, at least from the trustee's perspective. Admittedly, some donors may see it differently, whether simply as a technical matter to avoid treaty implications regarding binding terms, or more consequentially if they choose not to pay, knowing payment will not be enforced. Donors should be aware, however, that partnership programs usually make implementation plans in reliance on specified amounts to be paid on specified due dates. In the best of circumstances, donors are willing and able to make multi-year commitments that allow for longer-term planning, and then stick to them.

Obligations to Pay

It is basically unheard of for an international trustee to sue a donor that fails to pay. Missed payment dates usually result in conversations that ultimately lead to resolutions, even if an obligation to pay goes away in the end. Trustees know they cannot afford a gap between downstream funding commitments and upstream funding availability. Transfer and grant agreements are normally limited to "available" trust fund balances to keep trustees from being directly liable. However, even with this legal protection, trustees realize that an inability to meet downstream obligations can pose serious reputational and other risks. Careful trustees put in controls, so as not to fall short.

In addition to downstream operational precautions, trustees usually also limit upstream fund allocations and project approvals to available funds. This means that if a proposal involves an amount greater than the available trust fund balance, net of other already committed amounts, that proposal cannot be approved until the balance exceeds the proposed amount. While available funds could be calculated to include contributions receivable— meaning amounts in the contribution agreement scheduled for future payment and not yet paid—the safer route is to limit funding availability to actual cash in the kitty. This choice of "basis of commitment"(BoC)—whether cash only or cash and receivables—is the basis upon which the trustee agrees to accept upstream allocations and downstream commitments. Ideally, all partners converge on an understanding of the BoC when the trust fund is first established. Cash BoC may limit cash flow and thereby constrain operations, but is playing it safe.

Another area of precaution centers around "conditional" or "qualified" contributions, meaning contributions receivable that are tagged with specified prior conditions or requirements. Well-meaning donors may want to leverage their contributions for certain behavior, or they may feel comfortable

Playing it safe with cash BoC.

committing funds subject to certain things still needing to happen. Maybe they insist on seeing a good progress report before advancing more funds; maybe they need parliamentary approval before following through on the payment. Some conditions are very substantive, subjective, and hard to meet. Others are formalities and more about chronology than content.

From a trustee perspective, conditional or qualified contributions are like throwing sand in the gears. The idea that funds are committed, but not really because they are "subject to," "conditional upon," or "qualified by," does not sit well with contractual relationships built on expectations. It also requires more nuanced recording and messaging by the trustee. Funds are maybe available, but not necessarily, with varying probabilities of payments, varying timelines, and so on. That is especially true if conditions are outside the trustee's control, like completion of a project phase or passage of legislation. From a trust fund accounting perspective, conditional commitments with remote chances of being fulfilled are unlikely to be recognized as receivables anyhow. Trustees can decide whether to accept conditional contributions in their agreements. If conditions are too remote, they may well prefer not to sign at all. They may instead say that donors can come back and sign when they are good and ready with their clean commitments.

Tracking, Earmarking, and Preferencing

Among the conditions for contributing is often an effort by individual donors to require funds to be used for specified purposes that are narrower than the overall scope of the trust fund. A donor may want to give funds, but only if they are used for, say, projects in Africa and nowhere else, even though the scope of the trust fund is global, or only for health sector projects in a trust fund with broader, country-wide scope. This amounts to restrictive funding, where individual donors want the use of their specific contributions to be subject to explicit restrictions in their bilateral contribution agreements. This disconnects in two ways: first, the donor wants a limit on use that does not exist in the commingled pool, and second, the donor will be associated with other projects outside of its restrictions that are funded by the commingled pool.

Efforts to attach fund use restrictions often arise because donors get their contributions from restricted pots of money back home, perhaps tagged to deal with refugee issues or natural disaster recovery, and have to pass those restrictions on. The issue may also arise when donors want to move the partnership program in a certain direction, push a certain agenda, or be identified with a certain type of activity. Whatever the reason, this can happen so often that the partnership program workplan ends up looking like a quilt of donor-designated activities, with little left over for strategic implementation and core support.

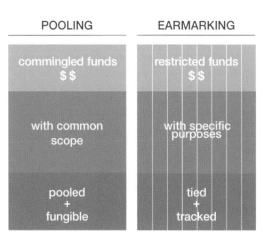

Problem No. 1: From a practical perspective, donor-driven fund use restrictions do not fit with pooled funding. When funds are commingled in multi-donor trust funds, and funds are fungible, there is no way to separately track what donor A's funds and donor B's funds are used for. In pooled funding from multiple donors, all funds fund all activities, and this means no earmarking for specific uses and no financial tracking by donor. All funds lose their donor-specific identity once they enter the commingled pool. As an alternative, we have seen that trust funds can (if the trustee is willing) be broken out into separate accounts already at the entry level to deposit contributions into more limited commingled pools. (>@ Trust Funds—Accounts) But this top-level segregation is a hard-line solution with loss of fungibility and other complications.

Problem No. 2: From a governance perspective, in trust-funded partnership programs with governing bodies that decide fund allocations on a multilateral basis, it is a mismatch for specific donors to dictate fund use on a unilateral basis. If the decision is in the hands of the governing body as a whole, it is neither in the hands of the specific donor nor the trustee. The trustee cannot sign a contribution agreement that allocates specific funds to specific activities if that conflicts with an agreed allocation process that involves shared decision making, whether at the work plan level or project level.

Softer approaches are available. In an attempt to manage earmarked funding requests, trustees and partnership programs have tried different techniques that go hand-in-hand and often give donors what they need:

- *Preferencing.* Many donors are satisfied with the inclusion of a "soft preference" in their contribution agreements that says the donor intends a certain fund use even if there is no trustee obligation to that end. This makes the donor's intentions visible and may be enough to satisfy requirements back home, especially if coupled with an informal understanding with the trustee or governing body that funds will in fact be allocated according to the donor's wishes.

- *Notional approach.* Many donors are also able to internally apply a "notional approach" that says but for their specific funds, certain activities would not have happened and are therefore directly attributable to their respective funding. The donor internally connects the dots between funds provided and activities undertaken. The idea behind this notionality is that it happens only at the donor's end. Nothing changes in the trust fund itself, nor in the contribution agreement or the trustee's behavior.

- *Granularity.* It also helps to ensure that there is sufficient granularity for visibility (1) in the proposal process, whether as individually presented projects or in defined work plans; and (2) in the reporting process to reflect the donor's specific area of fund use. This ex ante/ex post identification lets donors apply notionality that relates outcomes to their soft preferencing. In effect, donors can be persuaded by enough granularity in project descriptions and progress reports to evidence the use of their funds for their targeted purposes.

- *Timed contributions.* If a donor simply wants to be sure a particular project or subject area is funded, and if the trust fund contains a sufficient reserve of funds, the solution may be all in the timing. With an informal understanding, the governing body could be asked to approve a specific funding request, knowing the donor in question will sign for the funds and deposit them shortly thereafter. Once the funds are deposited, the trust fund is replenished back to its starting point.

Softer Tagging Alternatives Within Pooled Funding

1 Preferences, with non-binding contract clauses

2 Notional approach, funds in assumed first out

3 Granular ex ante proposals and ex post reporting

4 Timed contributions, after allocation decisions

These solutions can work in lieu of financially tracked earmarking in ways that may still enable contributions to multi-donor, commingled trust funds. If the alternatives are losing the funds or opening a series of single-donor trust funds—a bucket per donor—then these techniques are certainly worth trying.

Motivations to Contribute

Donors can have many different motivations for contributing to a partnership program trust fund. In the international development arena, trust funds let donors hand the development work to someone else, like an MDB, effectively passing on the responsibility for implementation along with their funds. Even if the trustee is not the actual implementer—instead acting as a pass-through (limited trustee) for others—the trust fund is still the first step in an arrangement to undertake the donor's intended use. As the insertion point for fund flows, the trust fund leverages the trustee and any subsequent recipients for and on behalf of the donor.

To be clear, however, this is not simply about outsourcing, and the international trustee is usually more than a service provider. The trustee contractually agrees to perform in a particular manner, with various obligations back to the donor, but is normally not bound to provide specific deliverables or prescribed outcomes. An international trust fund is not intended to be a procurement contract or a performance guarantee. Indeed, trustees should guard against such characterizations. Despite all the parameters around fund use, and all the emphasis on results, a trust fund donor is not buying results. Even if funds are intended to finance specific outputs, donors are not buying specific levels of quality or guaranteed outcomes. Donors normally do not get their money back for results that are unsatisfactory or did not happen.

Partly at play is the importance of distinguishing between proper fund use (as contracted) and "proper" results (not contracted), which in part reflects the contractual/structural nature of international partnership programs. (>@ Structure—Connecting Fund Flows and Decision Flows) Proper fund use (eligible expenditures) can be required, audited, and refunded if misused. By contrast, results arise from a host of factors, many of which are out of the trustee's and/or recipient's control. (>@ Fund Use Responsibility—Implementation Responsibility)

This is especially true in development contexts. Development initiatives intentionally go into settings that are challenging, with low capacity, limited experience, insufficient resources, and even fragile or conflict-affected environments. In addition, a number of trustee or fiduciary entities, like some MDBs, put a premium on country ownership, capacity building, and local implementation in ways that amplify the challenges. Fund use in these settings is already at risk, hence the robust supervision built into trustee and downstream fiduciary roles. On top of that, fund use is frequently a matter of experimentation, when partners pilot new approaches that may or may not produce hoped-for results. These cases are not just at risk, but understood to be beyond assurances, more than what a trustee can promise to deliver.

That is not to say donors should lower their expectations and standards. Over time, the ability of the trustee to use funds in an effective manner—both to handle funds responsibly and deliver on donor expectations—becomes a track

International trust funds are not procurement contracts or performance guarantees.

Visibility

"Visibility" is an important theme for donors. For many donors—especially traditional donors that provide ODA and are under scrutiny ranging from taxpayers to NGOs—it is not enough to do good, but also to be seen to do good. If a trust fund affords good visibility, it can be an incentive to contribute; if visibility is poor, it can be a deterrent. The first step to good visibility is getting good results, and that is the point of all international trust funds. However, the second step can be as important: getting credit for good results. Donors look for explicit reference to their participation in the partnership program, the trust fund, the funded projects, and the project results. Even though partners come together as a collective, the partnership program name need not mask their individual contributions. Even though donors contribute to commingled pools, the trust fund need not obscure their identities as individual contributors. Collectivizing can be self-effacing, but it can also be self-magnifying. Effective partnership programs learn to mobilize resources by amplifying each donor's efforts as part of a greater whole, keeping the individual donor visible—with appropriate bylines in publications, quotations in press releases, taglines of flags and logos, references in speeches, and other forms of recognition—while also giving credit to each donor for all of the achievements across the whole common pool and consolidated program. It is fair for partners to take collective credit for individual contributions, since it took the whole to make it happen—and it is sustainable, effective, and impactful when good visibility enables more good results. (>@ Trust Funds—Accounts)

record that influences whether contributions keep flowing. With no guarantee of satisfactory performance and no legal recourse for poor performance, donors vote with their purse. With many competing funding options, that is a stronger feedback loop than any contractual or legal remedies.

Two recipient types:

1. beneficiary
2. fiduciary

Recipients

With respect to trust fund recipients, it is worth separating fiduciary recipients from other downstream recipients. International partnership programs rely heavily on fiduciary functions as part of their structure. For trust funds, the fiduciary can be either direct (a first level full trustee) or indirect (a second level fiduciary under a first level limited trustee). This makes for two-tier and three-tier options, generally corresponding to one-stop-shops and international platforms. Virtually always, international trust funds operate with fiduciaries from top to bottom, from the receipt of funds to their use. Cases of trustees disbursing to nonfiduciary, unsupervised beneficiaries (also known as "direct access") are by far the exception and, as can be expected, challenging. (>@ Use of Funds—Role of the Fiduciary)

In the hierarchy of fund flows (upstream to downstream), fiduciary recipients are always above beneficiary recipients. Funds are used either directly by a fiduciary entity or under

full trustee

* → beneficiary recipient

one-stop-shops

hybrid trustee

* → beneficiary recipient

* → fiduciary recipient

* → beneficiary recipient

combination

limited trustee

fiduciary recipient

* → beneficiary recipient

international platforms

* fiduciary relationship

fiduciary supervision. This means implementation (fund use) is always either by the fiduciary itself or a subsequent recipient, if there is one, which amounts to four basic possibilities for implementation:

1. Full trustee implements

2. Beneficiary recipient implements under full-trustee supervision

3. Fiduciary recipient implements

4. Beneficiary recipient implements under fiduciary-recipient supervision

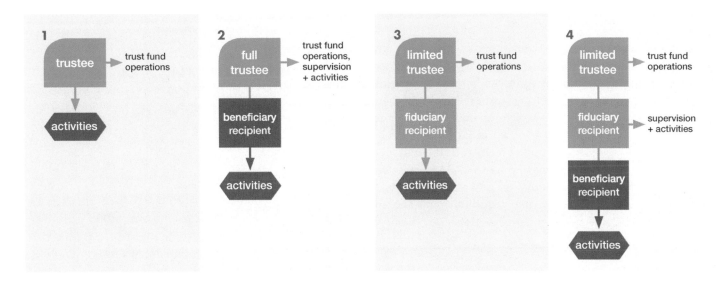

Beneficiary Recipients

In general, recipients of international trust funds can be as varied as donors. However, like donors, most recipients are countries acting through their ministries and agencies. The difference between these two groups of countries is, of course, that donors have money to give and beneficiaries have needs to fill. This usually divides between developed and developing countries, or high vs. middle/low-income countries, with some countries transitioning from list to list over time.

Beneficiary recipients are most frequently countries, but can also be NGOs, CSOs, academic institutions, and others that meet requisite financial management and other standards. Some beneficiary recipients are the actual beneficiaries; some are implementing for the benefit of other beneficiaries; but in both cases they are not doing stand-alone implementation. Instead they are implementing under fiduciary supervision. As noted, it is the unusual international trust fund that skips the fiduciary layer and allows beneficiary recipients to supervise themselves.

Beneficiary recipients sometimes leap the trust fund hierarchy and participate upstream. They can be part of the governing body, sitting at the table as recipients or beneficiaries, or even as donors paying membership fees. This particularly happens when partners want to effectuate country voice and country ownership. That usually means donors put their money where their mouth is, by using trust fund resources to pay the way for beneficiary participation. Once invited to the table, however, country beneficiaries typically join as decision makers, and no distinction is made from a governance perspective. In a consensus decision setting, every decision-making member—donor, recipient, or otherwise—has an equal voice, which is to say an equal veto. (>@ Decision Making—Consensus)

But what about bias? Is there no conflict of interest when a beneficiary plays both upstream and downstream? A beneficiary on the program-shaping, fund-allocating body must be like the fox in the hen house, no? While there may be cases where a seated developing country has an unfair advantage over other developing countries, or is questionably able to channel benefits to itself, most partnership programs see more synergies than conflicts between the upstream and downstream. In fact, in many cases, partners want the recipient country to have a voice and influence downstream activities. (>@ Synergistic Conflicts) If partners see the benefits, are aware of the dynamics, and focus on substantive merits in project selection, then being more inclusive around the table can be hugely beneficial for the partnership and the results.

Country Voice, Country Priorities

One case in particular lends itself to connecting upstream and downstream dimensions through the governing body: country-focused partnership programs, with the country as the main focus and recipient under one or more trust funds. (>@ Typology—Umbrella Arrangements) A single-country partnership program concentrates on country strategies and priorities in seeking to bolster country efforts. Here the country is already integral. There are no competing country recipients; the bias is built-in. Having that country join the decision making—and in many cases also run the secretariat and chair the governing body—is consistent with this country-centric approach. Instead of raising inappropriate conflicts of interest, this model promotes valuable development synergies. (>@ Synergistic Conflicts)

Fiduciary Recipients

Tried and true fiduciary recipients are usually the same entities as tried and true international trustees: international organizations like MDBs, other IFIs, and UN agencies. They receive funds both directly for implementation in supporting entity capacities, as trustee or secretariat, or indirectly as downstream fiduciaries one tier below.

As with trustees, fiduciary recipients use funds both for fund management operations and their own activity implementation. The dividing line between fund management and activity implementation is not always clear—for example, is commissioned security for local supervisory staff support part of general overhead or a specific funded activity?—nor does it necessarily matter, as long as budget terms are clear, expenditure categories are well-defined, and the amount is funded. The point is cost recovery, or using trust fund resources to pay for trust fund costs, rather than dipping into the fiduciary's own funds.

As far as activity implementation, the general approach is for implementation to follow a fiduciary entity's "comparative advantage"—doing what each entity is especially good at. In some cases, that means fiduciary implementation in a stand-alone approach without further disbursements. Some trust funds are fiduciary (trustee or downstream fiduciary) implementation only. This applies especially if trust fund objectives play to knowledge generation, international coordination, standard setting, advocacy, humanitarian aid, and other areas where international organizations are well-positioned. In other cases, fiduciary implementation is more limited, primarily as a way to supplement and support implementation by the downstream recipients that carry the lion's share of the partnership program's work program. These trust funds are geared to primary use further downstream—which brings us to the subject of transfers and grants.

Disbursements

In a typical trust fund, funds flow in, commingle, and flow out. The trustee pivots from the contributions upstream to disbursements downstream, keeping track of both and managing the balance in between. Downstream fund flows can be either transfers to fiduciaries or grants to beneficiaries. While common usage of "transfers" and "grants" may be somewhat interchangeable, they can have specific meanings in international trust fund contexts that reflect two different relationships to the trustee.

- **Transfer** usually denotes a clean break between trustee and recipient in that both funds and fiduciary responsibility are passed down (by the limited trustee).

- **Grant** usually denotes a continuing, subordinate relationship between trustee and recipient in that funds are passed down while the trustee retains supervisory responsibility (as the full trustee). Although "grant" in the accounting sense also broadly means any disbursement from a trust fund, this narrower, full-trustee distinction is helpful from legal and implementation perspectives.

- In addition, **internally used** funds may be absorbed by the trustee to cover its own costs or passed to other parts of the trustee entity, like the secretariat or implementing units, for their use within the same supporting entity.

Both transfers and grants include the notion of an arm's-length flow of funds, from one legal entity to another, usually on the basis of a negotiated and binding legal agreement. Failure to use the transferred or granted funds for the specified purposes in accordance with the specified terms constitutes breach and can give rise to claims of refunds or other remedies, like suspension of future tranches.

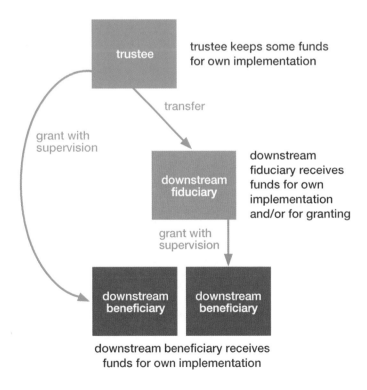

Transfers to Downstream Fiduciaries

Fiduciary recipients receive transfers from a trustee, basically one fiduciary to another. Transfers are seen as less hierarchical and more horizontal; peer to peer. Rather than end up with a dominant-subordinate relationship, the trustee simply takes itself out of the equation when transferring funds, thereby also transferring itself out and the recipient in. Transfers usually occur within agreed terms that rely on the institutional framework of the transferee, with policies and procedures robust enough to meet donor-driven fiduciary/fund use standards. These standards may be articulated, but are often just subsumed in the actual selection of downstream fiduciaries eligible to receive funds. Transfers can also be precursors to grants, when downstream fiduciaries follow up with ongranted funds to beneficiary recipients.

Grants to Downstream Beneficiaries

Beneficiary recipients receive grants from fiduciaries, either directly from trustees or tiered through subsequent downstream fiduciaries. "Grants" in this sense passes funds and implementation responsibility, but not fiduciary responsibility. Fiduciary responsibility stays with the grantor and is operationalized through ongoing supervision and monitoring. Downstream grants can be for many different kinds of activities, including investments, deliverables, outputs, and other project endeavors, pure cash transfers to targeted groups, budget support of a more general nature, core support of entities to pay for staff and other administrative expenses, and other variations. Multiple grants can be combined from different funding sources to support the same activity or project. Grants can also be coupled with loans, guarantees, or other financing mechanisms, in cofinanced or parallel-financed arrangements. They can come in very small or very large amounts, paid all at once or tranched over time, sometimes as automatic payouts and other times paid only if certain milestones or triggers are met. The variety in grant making generally covers the gamut of efforts where cash can be used and not repaid.

For both transfers and grants, the vast majority of internationally positioned trust funds flow in one direction only. Trust funds get money from upstream donors and give money to downstream recipients, usually with no expectations of repayment—basically just free cash. That said, most trust fund arrangements expect investment income from unused balances, actual unused funds at the end of a project, and refunds of misused funds to migrate back up to the trustee. With multi-donor trust funds, these amounts are usually reabsorbed by the trust fund for reallocation and further use.

Fiduciary Frameworks

In the grant modality, the beneficiary recipient uses the funds within a fiduciary framework, either that of the trustee or subsequent downstream fiduciary. That is in the nature of trust funds, where donors want assurances that funds are used for their intended purposes and effective results. MDBs and other fiduciary regulars have particularly robust approaches to trust fund grant making, with lots of attention both ex ante and ex post.

This before-and-after apparatus is much of what donors pay for when they engage in internationally positioned trust funds. The cost is not neglibible—and it comes at the cost of actual development—but donors who use taxpayer money and undertake development efforts under the scrutiny of national and international NGOs, CSOs, and others, including their own public, are under pressure to demonstrate proper and effective use of public funds. In trust funds, that pressure gets passed right down the fund flow hierarchy. Financial reporting, audits, and progress reporting, on the recipient side, are matched

Transfer over: peer-to-peer

Grant down: with supervision

Fiduciary Front to Back

Ex ante: Before funds are released, and even before funds are allocated, recipients and project terms usually undergo intensive scrutiny by the fiduciary entity. This typically includes assessments of compliance with minimum standards, especially economic and social safeguards, procurement rules, anti-corruption measures, and financial management processes and controls. This can also include iterative levels of expert peer review and internal management approval. This necessarily includes coordinating with the recipient, as a signatory party to the negotiated grant agreement, and potentially other stakeholders, including bilateral donors with related initiatives. Part of donors entrusting their funds to trust funds is the expectation that these downstream fund use packages will be well-cooked and well-coordinated before funds are released and used.

Ex post: After funds are disbursed and as funds are being used, the fiduciary entity remains on the hook. Fund use is not the end of the story, but needs to be reported and confirmed. This exercise involves comparing the terms agreed upfront, including with respect to safeguards, procurement, and other standards, to the actual use. The grant recipient, with implementation responsibility, has to regularly report on how funds were used, including through outside audits, and what was achieved (or not). Meanwhile, the fiduciary entity has to check and make sure that how funds were used and what was achieved are in line with what was agreed. This backend role falls under the broad headers of monitoring and supervision from a fund use perspective, and monitoring and evaluation (M&E) from a results perspective, effectively making international trust funds a trust-but-verify instrument.

by desk reviews, project missions, site visits, and the like on the trustee/fiduciary side. Partnership programs may further supplement project reviews with portfolio-level mid-term reviews or independent evaluations every few years, for a rigorous, systematic, results-based fiduciary framework.

Taking this kind of front-to-back fiduciary approach is an especially good fit for MDBs and other institutions that combine financial management with technical expertise and country reach. When it comes to development aid, in particular, this all-in-one cumulation of support functions—whether two-tier in one-stop-shops, or three-tier in international platforms, or some other combination or variation—can give donors a seamless set of fiduciary and operational touchpoints, both at the central and country levels, where centralized and decentralized staff of the trustee and other fiduciary entities pitch in as designated and defined.

Trust

Trust funds for international partners are both about financial management and proper fund use and about results and effective impact. Partnership program participants are always on the lookout for that sweet spot between comprehensive frameworks and cumbersome bureaucracies. Trust funds are apparently well-regarded in that space and considered worth the extra cost and effort.

Is that also because of trust? Much has been said about the *funds* part of trust funds, but not about the *trust.* And yet, there is plenty of trust to go around. One might even say reliance on trust is especially pronouced in the international arena. Donors trust their trustees and other fiduciaries to behave

as expected, fiduciaries trust their downstream recipients before they verify, trustees trust that donors will pay up, and supporting entities trust the other partners with their reputations.

Although fund flows are framed by contracts and subject to detailed terms, most of the parties involved in international partnership programs—sovereign governments and international organizations established by those same governments—interact in a context and culture that are based more on handshakes and diplomacy than litigiousness. The chances that a breach on either side will result in legal claims are slim to nil. Trustees are not going to sue donors if payments are late or null. Donors will either get trustee cooperation or walk.

That said, as part of a more general trend, the trust in trust funds is perhaps less strong than it used to be. In an era of scarce resources, donors are putting more scrutiny on trust fund operations and raising greater expectations for trust fund results. Some of the "trust but verify" that fiduciaries conduct downstream is now being performed by donors on their fiduciaries as well. In an era of fragmentation, participants are becoming more varied, including ones that are not buffered by protections like P&I. These participants are more likely to take contracts at their word and may more readily sue others if they can be sued themselves.

And yet, it still takes a lot of trust—and shared vision and good will—to pull off an international trust-funded partnership program. As long as these initiatives bring together like-minded partners with shared values and confirmed objectives, trust may still have its place in these trust funds. (>@ Partners and People—Choosing Partners)

The international trust fund is a trust-but-verify instrument.

Conclusion

Trust funds are drivers of international partnership programs, but also deflectors. A decision by donor countries to commingle their funds for a common purpose has resulted in many an international partnership program. In being the impetus, however, that same trust fund can swallow the whole and detract from the partnership itself. With due attention to the trust fund, appreciating its centrality and essentiality, it is nonetheless important to see the trust fund in relation to all other partnering elements. Ultimately, this means seeing the trust fund as a funding vehicle and an account, and then widening the lens toward the partnership program as a whole.

Many international partnership programs have no trust funds and accordingly manage with lighter footprints. But many, many partnership programs have trust funds, thereby significantly adding to their infrastructure. Being a trust-funded partnership program takes much more delineating and connecting, across donors, trustees, recipients, and all the related fund and decision flows. For trust-funded partnership programs, putting trust funds in context and positioning them as part of the whole is key to partnership program design.

Trust funds are both drivers and deflectors.

PART 2

BUSINESS CONSIDERATIONS

In this Part, we address aspects that can help partners—as organizations and individuals—make business decisions.

1 Ten Tried and True Tips
Clear, clean, modular, flexible, comprehensive, balanced, contextual, ready, aware, and simple—these are watchwords for designing international partnership programs.

2 Structure
Different ways of seeing structure make for more informed choices: upstream/downstream, bilateral/multilateral, contractual/structural, follow the power/follow the money, and more.

3 Trade-Offs
Trade-offs abound. Examples like the horizontal buy-in spectrum, the central harmonization spectrum, and the vertical continuity spectrum reveal how structural choices can manage and maximize trade-offs.

4 Risk and Review
How partners see and assess partnering opportunities and risks, from start to finish, affects the stability and effectiveness of their engagement in international partnership programs.

5 Partners and People
We come as partners—institutions structurally and people operationally—and convene and collectivize organically. Remembering this can help us manage our partnering dynamics.

1 TEN TRIED AND TRUE TIPS

Be clear.

Be clean.

Be modular.

Be flexible.

Be comprehensive.

Be balanced.

Be contextual.

Be ready.

Be (a)ware.

Keep it simple.

Some things come up over and over again, and some lessons are worth learning. There is a lot to keep in mind, but gravitating toward a few basic precepts can help stabilize the journey. To be or not to be, this list distills key *be*-haviors to benefit partners.

1. Be clear.

A solid partnership foundation rests on common understandings and expectations. When a partnership program is built in the open vista of the international arena, that shared basis is all the more important. It takes the spoken and written word to establish positions, test assumptions, make choices, and, in the end, agree. The very process of structuring partnership programs is one of the best assurances that everyone is on board for compatible reasons. *A few extra words now can mean fewer surprises later.* Being clear also helps avoid gaps. By mapping out roles, it is easier to see whether roles and responsibilities are all covered. For transitions in fund flows and decision flows, it is better to be clear at the start than to have partners shuffle and drop the baton. Prospective partners can embrace the charter drafting process as a way to articulate, shape, and own their partnership program.

1

2. Be clean.

In the partnership world, this is called *avoiding the messy middle*, especially when it comes to roles and responsibilities. After being clear, being clean means avoiding overlaps and overflow; no churn or spillage. After everyone is clear which base they are on—as in, "Is this a decision point for the governing body or the secretariat?"—players can stick to their plates—as in, "Sorry, governing body, we are just an administrative secretariat, you make the decisions." For all the encouragement to collaborate, and all the emphasis on collectivizing, this need to draw lines may seem paradoxical. However, with some responsibilities, particularly those regarding fund use, teamwork is baton work. Getting the team to the finish line in part means taking roles and responsibilities in separate lanes, each on its own.

2

3. Be modular.

Being clear and clean opens the door to being modular. By separating out roles and allocating responsibilities, delineating and connecting, the structure comes into view. On the one hand, *roles are described as distinct from each other*. On the other hand, *roles are described in relation to each other*. Being modular includes the ability to pin responsibility onto the entity taking the ownership, as confirmed by others relying on that ownership. Being clear, clean, and modular together allows partners to match accountability with authority, which means the assignment of responsibilities is given commensurate decision making and influence. Modularity can firm up the structure and fix things into place without becoming too rigid. If modular roles are defined, they can be mixed and matched, or stacked, like rocks in a cairn. By pivoting on modularity, international partnership programs can be both *stacked and solid*.

3

4. Be flexible.

International partnership programs use structure to become stable, but need flexibility to stay stable. Circumstances, priorities, and even partners change. Predictably, a successful partnership program grows and expands, learns and matures. Partnership programs experience funding highs and lows, personnel changes for the good and bad, political winds, and attention trends. Smoothly navigating all this requires *a combination of stability and fluidity*. When partnership programs anticipate change, they can embed ways to avoid putting form over substance and getting stuck in structure. For example, if the governing body is given the power to amend the charter with direct effect on related agreements, like contribution agreements, then governing body members can make decisions without any additional steps. This approach puts partners as people at the center without getting bogged down in formalities.

4

5. Be comprehensive.

International partnership programs usually reside **within the four corners of their partnership documents**, like adopted charters and signed contribution agreements. Most international partnership programs do not intend to be governed by national laws, and there is relatively little other legal jurisprudence that reaches into their structural and design details. It is up to the partners to articulate their material terms of engagement—their understandings, intentions, and expectations. Curiously, many an informal governing body has convened without an agreed written statement by which the partners say why they are there, how they do business, and what they are each responsible for (or not). And yet, the statement need not be overly extensive or even signed for partners to share a common view. Taking the trouble to spell out core and comprehensive partnership terms upfront may well avoid trouble later.

6. Be balanced.

At inception, international partnership programs are inherently a series of trade-offs, and that can become quite a balancing act. Over time, with many participants in play, a partnership program can get out of kilter. The seesaw of efficiency vs. inclusivity, due diligence vs. speedy disbursement, and other tensions can whipsaw the partners if not well-managed. The teeter-totter of keeping everyone happy and engaged despite big differences in contribution size or hierarchical funding relationships can take **good will, good humor, and good measure** to keep from tipping over. A partnership program needs enough common ground and balanced interests to get off the ground. Over time, active balancing can help partners avoid and weather future imbalances.

7. Be contextual.

Context matters, and what works best depends on all manner of things. International partnership programs need to be conceived and operate within their specific circumstances. This includes **the right amount of standardization vs. customization— basically contextualization**—that balances the pushes and pulls of these two poles. Every partner has its checklist and wish list, especially donors who carry the power of the purse. Nevertheless, these requirements and requests must be integrated with the well-developed operating frameworks of the chosen supporting entities. At the same time, all partners are seeking to match collective structures and interests with their own institutional parameters in the search for common denominators. Accordingly, contextualization also includes **the right amount of harmonization vs. individualization**. Case-by-case, the cacophony of interests and circumstances needs to be orchestrated into an agreed scope and structure that settles snugly into its context.

8. Be ready.

The degree of readiness at inception can determine the later success of an initiative. There is no single answer to when an international partnership program is ready to go live. As with all else this, too, depends on the context. Opportunity costs of starting later get weighed against birthing risks of starting earlier. In part, readiness is a trade-off—*detail and diligence vs. closure and commencement*—with an appropriate balance to be struck. Sometime down the road can be too late to make easy adjustments, especially if flexibility for change is unanticipated. Readiness can also be measured by the amount of common ground established among partners. What constitutes **critical mass is what it takes to make the center hold**. Despite this common sense, it is not uncommon to see partners jump the gun—including when they skirt issues early on, use vague language to mask differences, stay high level to avoid challenges, or rush ahead for a big public relations splash and political win, details to come later. Partners ideally put in the effort to reach a broad and deep enough consensus for a solid start.

9. Be (a)ware.

Once roles and responsibilities are clean, clear, and comprehensive, and structures are flexible, balanced, and contextual, it is important to stay aware of these dynamics as operations proceed. Putting things on paper is just the first step; putting them into practice also matters. Partnership documents should be easy to access, read, and absorb, which is another way of saying they are and should be operative. They are not abstract texts or theoretical notions but working terms that parties rely on for closure and thereafter as well. Therefore **beware of encroaching daylight between the evolving partnership program and its originally agreed terms**. Watch that the trustee and secretariat do not get caught between universes, where agreements say one thing, adopted documents say another, and practice is yet something else. Nor is it a good idea for any function to slip into rescue mode, even if all's well that ends well, since it may not. Partners are encouraged to put into print what they intend to practice, and then put into practice what they print.

10. Keep it simple.

This is so important that it makes the top ten both as a Take-Away and a Tried and True Tip. It may be hard to tell from the vast amount of detail in this book that **simple is golden**—for every scenario, there are at least three alternatives, and for every suggestion, it depends on many things. But writing comprehensively to cover all the bases is very different from taking a particular initiative and making it work. Notwithstanding the huge range of options presented page for page here, they are not all needed or neutral. This is not like throwing spaghetti against the wall and seeing if it sticks. Every time a choice is made, it should be carefully considered in relation to other choices and circumstances. Every time a feature is added, there should be a clear reason why, and that reason should justify the added complexity and cost. For example, a trust fund with windows, multiple trust funds, two-tier governing bodies, separate trustee and secretariat entities, multiple downstream fiduciaries, minimum pay-to-play funding requirements, all these things do not keep it simple. They may be right for the particular partnership program, but partners need to know why they are helpful and be up for the extra effort they require. Knowing that complexity is accretive and can add up every which way, it is worth taking the simpler option wherever available and working toward simple everywhere else.

2 STRUCTURE

In international partnership programs, structure matters, and that's the point of this book. Partners convene around an international challenge, bringing their agendas and technical expertise, ready to go, full speed ahead. The road is clear, the vision on the horizon, but they still have to find a way to travel together. Whether in a cart or a double-decker bus, they need to pick the driver, get comfortable for the long haul, figure out who is paying for gas, agree on the route, and observe a few speed limits. If not, they may spend more time changing tires and backtracking than they would have wanted. It is mostly better to work out the basics before embarking, rather than freestyling it en route.

Anything more than a loose network involves structure: who is doing what (roles), who is on the hook for what (responsibilities), and how they relate to each other (relationships). In international partnership programs, some structures are very simple, some very complex, but they all combine decision flows and fund flows in a series of defined engagements. In the international arena, this can involve a whole array of possible set-ups. Each international partnership program is different, depending on the participants, politics, sector, setting, and more. Each partnership program grows and matures, adapting to changing environments and lessons learned.

Taking Context into Account

The variety and creativity of international partnership programs is potent if responsive to each individual context. There is no substitute for taking context into account, for creating fit-for-purpose structures with flexibility over time. The institutional parameters of some partners may impose some constraints, but by and large, this is an arena for business calls. There is rarely one right way of doing things, and partners almost always have options and need to make choices, often around trade-offs between competing objectives. (>@ Trade-Offs)

International partnership programs are widespread, particularly in international development, and yet the practice of designing them is widely unappreciated. Team leaders with deep knowledge in their subject areas, multiple academic degrees, and many years of experience—true experts in their fields—are suddenly confronted with the task of making a partnership program happen and are somehow presumed to intuit how to get there. Rest assured, it is not intuitive. There are as many ways for things to go awry as there are for them to go right. And yet, most pitfalls can be anticipated and avoided, or at least approached with eyes wide open.

Teams may not realize that *how* they partner is as important as *why* they partner. How a partnership program is structured determines whether it will be effective, sustainable, and impactful. Teams that have the vision and technical expertise also need the design and governance know-how. This lets them realize the benefits of shared governance, central support structures, pooled funding with harmonized approaches, coordinated activities, combined knowledge, and one brand, all hallmarks of healthy international partnership programs. (>@ International Partnership Programs—Collectivizing) Structure embeds clearly agreed expectations and commitments that are based on clearly articulated roles and responsibilities, with clear mechanisms for change, so as to enable enduring, adaptable, and successful partnership programs. (>@ Like Rock, Like Water)

Designing structure can be pie in the sky, but there are ways to make structure more concrete (pun intended). Knowing what the partnership program is for and visualizing what it is about can enable clear delineating and connecting, which is how structure works. Doing that all in context then actually lets the structure work.

Bridging Action and Results

Partnership program structure is needed for collective action to produce results, bridging one to the other. Effective structure is the *coupling of partnership design with program content*, while structure for its own sake is just another layer

clearly agreed
expectations and
commitments

+

clearly articulated
roles and
responsibilities

+

clear mechanisms
for change

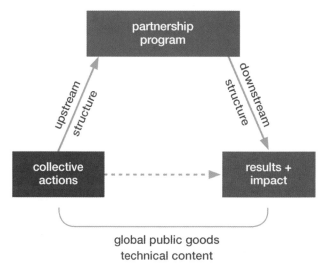

global public goods
technical content

of bureaucracy. When geared to specific needs and objectives, structure can give direction, impetus, buy-in, and consequence. With a fit-for-purpose structure, operations can become efficient and results timely. The point is for structure to work for the partners, not make partners work for the structure.

Upstream/Downstream

A useful way to think about international partnership program structure—especially for trust-funded partnership programs—is to look at the upstream and downstream. This division works from a horizontal axis across the administrative functions—in other words, upstream and downstream of the trustee and secretariat. This vertical, up-down dynamic is driven by fund flows, from donor to recipient, and trust-funded partnership programs are usually conceptualized this way. In this book, most diagrams showing international partnership programs start from this horizontal axis and up-down division. The currency of this perspective, with support functions in the center, is perhaps not surprising. It is indeed the trustee and secretariat, through the supporting entity, who are typically at the originating crux of the structure—crafting establishment documents, like charters and contribution agreements, for all of the partners, including themselves. In radiating up and down off the supporting entity, the support functions naturally reflect their own central vantage points.

The basic visualization of trust-funded partnership programs goes like this:

- **Upstream.** This is the arena of donors and decision makers, where the money comes in, where allocations are determined, and where the hierarchy begins. In effect, the trustee looks up to the donors to receive fund flows, and the secretariat looks up to the governing body to receive decision flows—money and instructions that determine what happens downstream.

- **Center.** At the center of this up-down view of the world sit the trustee and secretariat, commonly part of the same supporting entity. They are the pivot for flows in and out. They are the solder that connects the pieces, the center that holds.

- **Downstream.** This is the arena of supervisors, implementers, and beneficiaries, where the money goes out, funds are used, and results are generated. The trustee flows funds and obligations down to recipients, and the secretariat serves as the conduit to distribute results, reports, and lessons learned, generally bringing all of the partnership program activities together into a branded, messaged whole.

The Up-and-Down Dynamic of Trust-Funded Partnership Programs

Upstream is the realm of funding decisions.
Prominently, there are individual decisions on the part of donors to contribute funding to the international partnership program. There may also be collective decisions by the governing body about how that funding gets used for the partnership program. On the one hand, donors play on both bases and often exert the power of the purse in linking fund flows to decision flows. On the other hand, donors subjugate their unilateral rights to the collective when giving other members of the governing body a decision-making say over their respective funds or deferring to a centrally placed trustee or secretariat.

Downstream is the realm of fund responsibility.
Prominently, there is individual responsibility on the part of fiduciaries and grantees for specific implementation. There may also be collective responsibility on the part of the governing body for oversight and overall direction. (>@ Fund Use Responsibility) In a typical partnership program with a decision-making governing body, the governing body "owns" the partnership writ large, and the implementing entities own the projects on the ground.

Mediating all of this are the trustee and secretariat, on the support axis, who have to connect the dots and keep things aligned. That includes common terms for pooled funds and common views based on consensus decisions. This necessarily requires navigating and maneuvering; communicating, clarifying, and coordinating; pushing back, promoting, and persuading; all in the course of an ordinary day.

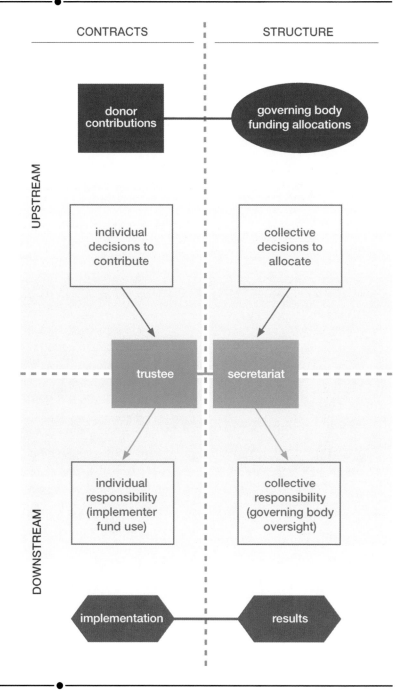

These upstream and downstream flows are a fascinating mix of individual and collective actions that underscore the importance of the administrative center. The interplay between the individual and collective is a large part of the careful calibration that takes place in international partnership programs. A flourishing partnership program is a testament to the organizational skills of the trustee and secretariat in balancing the partners' individual instincts with collective interests. Clearly, this trapeze act does not happen by itself. (>@ International Partnership Programs—Collectivizing)

Connecting Fund Flows and Decision Flows

Now watch how this works in trust-funded partnership programs:

- The individual elements follow fund flows, and the collective elements follow decision flows.
- The individual elements relate to agreements, specifically bilateral agreements, and the collective elements relate to adopted documents, the constitutive, partnership documents.
- There is a logic to it all.

Bilateral/Multilateral

Following the hierarchy of fund flows, from the donor to the trustee to the recipient, the usual approach is to enter into bilateral agreements with the trustee—on the one hand, connecting upstream to each donor with a contribution agreement and, on the other hand, connecting downstream to each recipient with a grant agreement (when the full trustee retains fiduciary responsibility) or a transfer agreement (when a downstream fiduciary takes on fiduciary responsibility from the limited trustee). Donors agree to specific, bilateral funding terms with the trustee, like the contribution amounts and payment schedules. These bespoke aspects do not need to involve other partners, as long as other aspects result in common terms that apply to the common pool of funds. The trustee in turn agrees to aligned terms with the recipient, flowing the upstream terms down and adding project-specific terms, again without needing other partners to be involved, as long as project terms reflect the relevant parameters set by the contribution agreements and, potentially, the governing body. This makes for a pretty efficient set of agreements, involving only those who need to be involved. This also makes for great reliance on the trustee to keep it all synchronized.

You may be wondering: How does all this bilateralism fit into the partnership program? Aren't partnership programs supposed to be multilateral? For sure, this series of bilateral fund flow agreements is not much of a partnership program by itself. So there is more. Framing around and crossing over into these fund flows are collectively established terms, and these color the way funds are received and disbursed by the trustee. For international partnership programs, four primary multilateral elements can be identified, some or all of which may apply in specific cases, some not:

1. The charter, or its equivalent, as the centerpiece that defines the governing framework for the partnership program
2. The common terms across all contribution agreements, which work in tandem with the charter
3. Other framing documents and decisions of the governing body that can be added or adjusted over time
4. Specific fund allocation decisions if they are within the governing body's scope

The governing body is an obvious source of multilateralism for the partnership. Both the trustee and secretariat also play significant roles in keeping the collective terms intact within the bilateral terms. Upstream-downstream is not just a visual tool. It also reflects a wonderful synergy in that

> The trustee links funding elements to partnership elements.
>
> The secretariat links partnership elements to funding elements.

trustee-secretariat axis. The trustee is the direct link from funding elements to partnership elements, and the secretariat in turn links partnership elements to funding elements. Could it be more neatly laid out and positioned?

Contractual/Structural

To make it even more interesting, and to put it another way, this interweaving of fund flow agreements and partnership documents ends up combining both contractual and structural aspects of trust-funded partnership programs. Fund flow agreements are always signed and are generally expected to carry legally binding terms. By contrast, partnership documents, like charters, are typically adopted and both the result and enabler of organic decisions (the proverbial chicken or egg). It is at the administrative center, through cooperation of the trustee and secretariat, that the two elements, con-

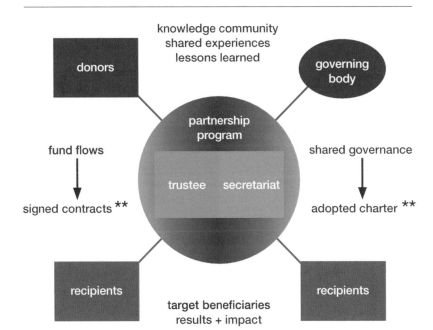

tractual and structural, are married into one, forming a web of relationships that build on each other. Whether expressed in contracts or through structure, emanating from agreements or bodies, it all combines into a comprehensive partnership package, hopefully on terms that are in synch and in support of each other.

Collectivizing

At this point you may be asking yourself, what goes where? Which aspects are agreed bilaterally and which ones multilaterally? If fund flows are viewed as the starting point in the defining hierarchy of trust-funded partnership programs—not an unfair view, taking into account the power of the purse—bilateral terms are the default, except as otherwise collectivized. More generally, collectivization is the crux of partnership. How much partners agree to partner depends on how much they choose to collectivize. Taking a closer look, there are numerous aspects that can be collectivized, each to varying degrees. (>@ International Partnership Programs—Collectivizing)

International partnership programs—especially in the development arena—emerge where pressures, needs, and goals are best relieved and furthered by internationally collectivized efforts. The specific items being collectivized are typically decisions (governing bodies), support (secretariats), money (trust funds), activities (work plans, results frameworks), information and knowledge (websites, lessons learned), and name (brand). When partnership program participants establish dedicated governance mechanisms, organize

Collectivization is the crux of partnership.

dedicated support, and receive dedicated funding (all without creating a new dedicated legal entity), they can in turn identify:

- a defined coterie of participants for inclusion and buy-in;

- a planned set of activities for results;

- a central legal entity for support;

- a financial manager for coordinated funding;

- an articulated message for advocacy;

- a robust system for knowledge generation and distribution with an ongoing feedback loop; and

- a shared label, the valued "brand name" that encompasses everything in the partnership program and belongs to all the partners.

International partnership programs that revolve around a single trust fund have a relatively easy time creating a tight and coherent center, all emanating, as it were, from the trust fund. By contrast, structuring around multiple trust funds (especially if they have different trustees) and other funding sources, requires extra effort to make the connections, since funding vehicles are by nature separate and delineated. Nonetheless, combining more than one trust fund, or other funding sources, under an overarching governing apparatus—like a common governing body, supported by a single secretariat—can be an effective partnership program approach. This is especially true in single country settings. (>@ Typology—The Broader Landscape of Partnership Programs—Umbrella Arrangements)

Potentially challenging are collaborations that add multiple downstream entities as upstream partners. Potential conflicts of interest are the least of it; indeed, they can be valuable synergies. (>@ Synergistic Conflicts) However, each downstream partner, including especially fiduciary partners, are separate legal entities with separate interests, rules, and requirements. These can, at times, be hard to reconcile for collective purposes. For these scenarios, the governing body (including donors) for the overall partnership program needs to adequately recognize and accommodate the institutional frameworks and legal personalities, including boards, of each downstream entity, while also creating space for harmonization and coordination. It is not a given that the interests of each entity will dovetail with the interests of the overall partnership program, or that incentives will drive toward collaboration more than competition. That has to be promoted and engineered.

PULLING IT TOGETHER

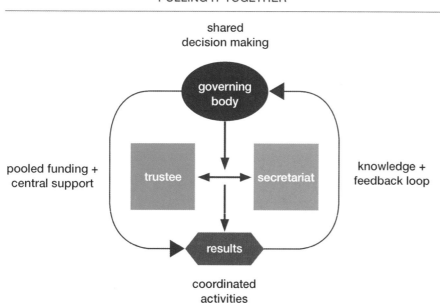

shared
decision making

governing
body

pooled funding +
central support

trustee ←→ secretariat

knowledge +
feedback loop

results

coordinated
activities

Fortunately for all of these cases, there is no one formula for international partnering. With enough common purpose and ample good will, the right degree of collectivizing on the right aspects for each specific case can be found, especially if given room to adjust over time. (>@ Like Rock, Like Water) As long as partners know where they are headed, they can map out the common ground and connecting structures that collectivize in fortifying ways.

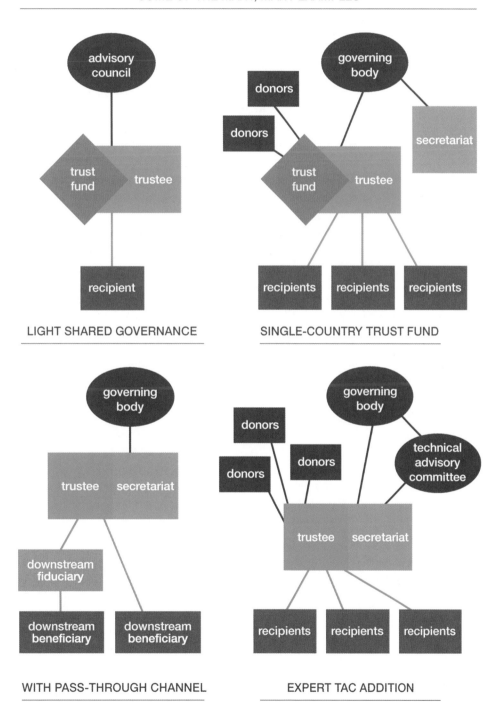

SOME OF THE MANY, MANY EXAMPLES

LIGHT SHARED GOVERNANCE

SINGLE-COUNTRY TRUST FUND

WITH PASS-THROUGH CHANNEL

EXPERT TAC ADDITION

Whiteboarding

One of the ways to zero in on structure is to whiteboard it—visualizing by drawing the picture, positioning the main elements, and connecting the dots. International partnership program diagrams—like many in this book—show up as an array of lines and links between entities, bodies, and functions as they track roles, responsibilities, and relationships. As indicated, the conventional way to show partnership programs starts with the horizontal axis: putting the trustee and secretariat at the center, and then working the upstream and downstream. This means populating upstream elements, like donors and governing bodies, along with downstream elements, like downstream fiduciaries and downstream beneficiaries, all anchored by central support functions, like the secretariat and trustee, in the middle.

Follow the power, follow the money.

As to lines and links, try the cliché "follow the power, follow the money." How do decisions flow? How do funds flow? Most partnership program diagrams do not distinguish between these two flows, but rather mix and match them both, making it hard to know the actual nature of the line or link. Money flows are more likely to show up because they are tangible, flanked by signed agreements. But other relationships show up, too, and often those flow in two directions, with instructions one way (down) and support, funding proposals, and reporting the other way (up). When only money is involved, a dollar sign next to the line can be helpful. When something else is involved, that can also be nuanced visually; for example, by using a dotted line or a line with arrows at one or both ends.

Most of the time, diagrams not only fail to be precise about fund flows and decision flows, they also do not distinguish between agreement links and structural relationships. This is usually one and the same omission, given the links between funds and signed agreements vs. decisions and decision makers. Fund flows invariably ride on agreements, since contributions always come with at least some terms for their use. Decision flows are another matter. They ride

---

Decision Flows and Fund Flows

Follow the power: Generally, this considers who makes what decisions for whose follow-up. Shared governance residing in a governing body can show up as a solid line for decisions or a dotted line for advice. For a decision-making governing body, a solid line typically flows from the body to the trustee or secretariat, who then acts on the decisions, either by direct implementation or transfer of information. For an advisory body, a dotted line from the governing body can signal that decision making resides in the trustee or secretariat (viz. the supporting entity). Ultimately, the trustee or secretariat may look like a hub-and-spoke system, reflecting its central conduit role for decision making, action, and information flows.

Follow the money: Here the question is who is getting funds from whom. Multi-donor trust funds link up separate funding streams from multiple donors into a centralized pool of funds and from there can be disbursed in multiple directions as well—flows converging upstream and fanning out downstream in relation to a central point, the trustee and trust fund. Flanking dollar signs (or other currency symbols) can show that these linking lines are fund flows. The trustee may also look like a hub-and-spoke system, reflecting its central conduit role for funding in and out.

Position the nexus: Between the two hubs, there is also a line across the secretariat-trustee axis, the girding nexus of partnership program support, which fortifies functions, connects flows, promotes synchronization, and creates synergies.

Diagram Detail

The lack of precision in partnership program diagrams in part boils down to TMI—too much information. Even in this book, most diagrams do not belabor whether lines are power, money, or something else. Most of them do not show arrows pointing every which way. Nor do they make much of straight vs. dotted lines to distinguish relationships. And only sometimes do they label money lines with dollar signs. That may be seen as a shortcoming, but it is also meant to spare the viewer an overflow of details when images are already cluttered. Let's just say that diagrams of international partnership programs can be fit-for-purpose, too, like the partnership programs themselves. It is good to have options for conveying nuanced information, but ultimately the level of detail can match the need for precision and the capacity for absorption. Glossing over some of the details in diagrams—ideally with an informed awareness—is sometimes part of keeping it simple.

---

on structure, emanating more than transferring. Decision makers are people and organic, while money is fixed and inanimate. In the same way, adopted documents can be living, breathing variants of signed agreements. And so, too, the lines and links for decisions, decision makers, and their governing bodies reflect more dynamic relationships and responsibilities, as opposed to the more staid status of account balances, wire transfers, and bookkeeping.

An international partnership program can have multiple funding sources, and it can also have various governing and implementing elements. Some partnership programs are more modular, more sliced and diced, more complex and layered. When whiteboarding the diagram—visualizing the lines and links—the point is to see the connections and the delineations. At root, structuring a partnership program is all about creating connections and delineating roles.

Of course, not everything shows up in these diagrams. While primary decision and fund flows are usually shown, other aspects are not. The level of detail can vary, along with determinations of what constitutes structure. For example, the provision of financial and activity reports is rarely explicit, probably because that is considered operational, not structural. Similarly, trust funds rank as structural elements, but websites do not. Every partnership program diagram is different, depending on what elements and relationships are of particular importance.

Whiteboarded renditions are in any case selective depictions, almost caricatures, of the more complex interplays of rights, responsibilities, and relationships in partnership programs. While these structural diagrams can be helpful in orienting partners and others to the essential elements and their interactions, they will never do justice to all the details. They are necessarily incomplete and easily misleading; accordingly, their use should be judicious. This includes avoiding them in legal agreements, where they are no substitute for clear agreement text.

> Create connections,
> delineate roles.

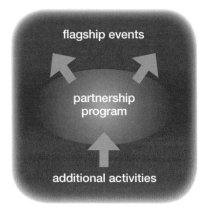

Broader Context

International partnership program structure is usually thought of as the internal governance of the partnership program—who runs the partnership program and how. This internal plumbing does not, however, operate in a vacuum. It occurs in a larger context. Considerations of structure can stretch beyond internal governance to other elements that affect how the partnership program functions. Structure in this broader sense includes ways for the partnership program to leverage outside factors and magnify its reach. Messaging factors, like brands, websites, and social media, are always essential, but structural extensions can also include diverse resources or activities that are brought into the fold or events that draw in more people—including in ways that reinforce and amplify each other. (>@ Typology—Trust-Funded Partnership Programs)

Resource Mobilization

Although this book is primarily about international partnership programs, the importance of funding—and, accordingly, the attention given trust funds and fund flows—is unavoidable. Funds are *primus inter pares* when it comes to partnership programs. And since funds don't just grow on trees, resource mobilization can be one of the most crucial aspects of running a partnership program. Resource mobilization is both a threshold exercise and an enduring element, carrying through the life cycle of every partnership program. Many a partnership program started because there was a donor champion. Most partnership programs end (if they ever do) because the funds run out.

International partnership programs are in the public interest and run on public funds; they are not-for-profit, even if they are not incorporated as such. They can be revenue generating, but for purposes of furthering the public interest. As with so much else that the supporting entity influences, the legal standing of an international partnership program is directly affected by the legal status of the supporting entity. If the supporting entity is an international organization with a mandate to operate for the public good (in the case of MDBs, for example, economic development), then that will be a major defining parameter for the partnership program. (>@ Partnering Internationally—Applicable Law)

Resource mobilization stands or falls on the partnership program's content—what it stands for, what it expects to achieve, what results it generates. Even back when traditional sovereign donors had easier funds to spend, the onus was on the program to prove itself. Nowadays, partnership programs are in constant competition for scarce resources, as herds of business teams court the usual suspects with deep pockets, each team seeking to persuade the respective ministry, agency, or foundation that its challenge is the most dire and pressing and its solution is the most effective and innovative. In a marketplace of ideas, there is no shortage of development and other initiatives ready and able to take someone's financial aid.

Partnership program funding is structural in the sense that some funds are easier to absorb than others—which is to say, certain kinds of funding streams and funding vehicles are especially attractive and user-friendly. By this measure, internationally administered trust funds are king. Their widespread use in international partnership programs speaks to their appeal, particularly for donors, upon which funding relies.

> ■ *On the one hand, donors position themselves in the mix.* Trust funds let donors impose an upfront degree of specificity about what their funds can finance, and donors then retain a direct, backend link to take credit for results. In between, donors on governing bodies can position themselves as ongoing decision makers (or advisors), by which they participate in allocation decisions over time, as funds become available.

> ■ *On the other hand, donors take themselves out of the mix.* Trust funds hand fiduciary responsibilities to trustees or other fiduciary recipients with robust operating procedures. Implementation then belongs either to fiduciary entities or downstream beneficiaries. Even collective decision making does not break through these arm's-length separations from donors. Instead, donors can redirect responsibility, let go, and rely on others for implementation and supervision.

On balance, this makes for an appreciated combination for donors to both keep and give control, within a spectrum of options. This two-tone relationship of donors to their partnership program is within a structural framework that keeps resources mobilized.

There are other ways to provide funding to international partnership programs, some more or less direct or integrated. For example, donors can contribute to supporting entities straight up, in ways that effectively get absorbed into their internal budgets. This can involve smaller amounts in the form of membership fees or larger amounts in direct contributions. Donors can also provide funding streams alongside partnership program activities, whether cofinanced, parallel financed, or some other bilateral but coordinated modality. Partnership programs can also be more or less structured in their resource mobilization efforts. Replenishment exercises, for example, can be structural add-ons that use public pledging and related peer pressure to great effect.

It may not take much for an international partnership program to recognize a particular funding stream or vehicle as part of its work program. This can be a mere decision point of the governing body. In trust-funded partnership programs, the tendency is to gravitate around the trust fund, but there is no reason the governing body cannot lay claim to a broader spectrum of activities as part of the partnership program, as long as everyone is okay with the inclusion. This works especially well if the funder or implementer is considered a partner, in which case it can be a win-win for both the originator and the other partners. For example, a private foundation that sits on the governing body as a donor to the partnership program's trust fund can additionally offer to associate its own related grantmaking activities with the partnership program brand, and the governing body can agree. When additional activities are included under the partnership umbrella, the originator gets the branded imprimatur, and all partners get the credit.

Flagship Events

International partnership programs can broaden their reach and magnify their impact by including more activities, but they can also do more by including more people. Structure in this sense is more than governance, and inclusion does not stop with governing bodies and fiduciary elements. Structure can also involve events. Serving visibility, advocacy, networking, resource mobilization, and knowledge functions, any number of events organized or sponsored in the name of a partnership program can be instrumental in meeting partnership program objectives. The combination of branding, messaging, and events can be a powerful amplifier of the partnership program's purpose.

The value of events may be obvious, and indeed, some partnership programs make events the heart of their work program. Less acknowledged, however, is the way in which events can complement the governance of the partnership program—as an extension of its structure. Many a partnership program that has wrestled with the trade-offs between inclusion and efficiency (>@ Trade-Offs—The Horizontal Buy-In Spectrum) has discovered the annual stakeholders forum, high-level convention, thematic conference, or the like as a way to help strike the balance.

A major partnership program event, put on with the express purpose of bringing many more like-minded or interested individuals and institutions under the tent, can create inclusion without creating more bodies or formal structures. These events can be invitation-only or wide open; they can be one-off or annual; they can be pitched at the ministerial level for political inroads or broadly for advocacy and knowledge sharing; they can be linked to other partnership program activities or meetings or be stand-alone. There is plenty of variety. No matter the set-up, thinking of events as an extension of structure, especially if they bundle branding, messaging, and mobilizing, can maximize trade-offs and results. More than just expanding partnership program portfolios, flagship events can leverage interest, involvement, connections, and even resources (like the replenishment exercises in the prior section) as additional pillars of partnership programs.

> **Think of events as extensions of structure.**

———————————————●———————————————

Events, Not Bodies

International partnership programs that prefer light governance structures have the option of convening through events, rather than governing bodies. The difference is structural. Events have no members to keep track of and no minutes to record and keep. If donors and other partners feel adequately informed and heard without having to be a body, they can simply meet to share information and views. If the governing body is meant to be advisory, why not reconfigure the body as an annual event, thereby serving the purpose while sparing some of the formality, logistics, and cost?

———————————————●———————————————

Conclusion

A book on structuring international partnership programs would be incomplete without a chapter on structure. In the international arena, this is largely what the partners create when they establish partnership programs. Sometimes the partnership program elements are so numerous and diffuse that it is hard to know where the center lies, and harder yet to know what's in and what's out. This, too, is the job of structure: to give identity to the partnership program, defining what is connected to and part of the shared space and overarching brand.

Everything in these pages is ultimately about how things connect to each other. As a corporate and commercial lawyer in my early days, I took comfort in knowing that, despite all the legalese, despite clause upon clause, every contract was ultimately about real relationships—and so it is with partnership programs. At their heart, international partnership programs are about how we interact, as individuals, as entities, through bodies and funding vehicles, under signed agreements and adopted documents—but always as we relate and connect. For those who are visual thinkers, this is a playground. For those who prefer the written word, this is prose and poetry, complete with plot lines.

Structuring international partnership programs is an active endeavor from start to finish. We can build structure to get things going and make things happen. We can keep it malleable more than fixed, stay contextual more than abstract, think ahead and long term, and make sure that form follows function, all so that people—both partners and beneficiaries—remain the focus.

Through their structure, international partnership programs have all the potential to respond to our collective instincts and make a global difference.

Partnership works best if it works for all partners.

Structure works best if it fits the context.

3 TRADE-OFFS

An important thing to accept about international partnership programs is that they are products of trade-offs. On many fronts, getting more of one thing can mean getting less of another. This is not entirely a zero-sum world, but in at least some respects, partnership programs present a series of tensions and conflicts, where it is hard to have it all. Understanding the pinches and pulls is the first step to making informed trade-offs. The goal is to maximize desirable aspects while minimizing challenges. When trade-offs cannot be avoided, they can be assessed and managed for all-around benefit.

As veritable balancing acts, international partnership programs have to reconcile the opposing interests and conflicting ambitions of many partners. While many design decisions pit trade-offs along various spectra, a closer look can sometimes reveal workarounds that alleviate direct tensions and conflicts. With a little ingenuity and packaging, workarounds may be able to maximize objectives even when those objectives are at odds.

Inclusion of these features is sometimes in the drafting, sometimes in the presentation, sometimes in the structuring—wherever the leeway lies. Sometimes there are ways to bend the arrangement to reach the goal. Particularly where common partnership terms and individual partner requirements collide, a partner may be able to temper its requirements and the partnership may be able to accommodate specific particularities, all for the sake of inclusive participation.

Three Common Spectra

● 1. Horizontal
● 2. Central
○ 3. Vertical

By way of example, there are at least three major axes worth mentioning in the realm of trade-offs common to international partnership programs. Each can be understood as a spectrum ranging from one objective to another, with inverse relationships between the two ends. Partnership programs can find themselves at some point along the spectrum, with more of one and less of the other, and possibly more of both, depending on the kinds of accommodations that can be made. To state the obvious, it is better to be open and deliberate about these trade-offs from the start than discover imbalances in requirements and expectations later, when imbalances are harder to fix.

Even so, most partnership programs reflect a constant managing of competing interests and impulses. After a certain balance is embedded in the establishment documents, the need to balance continues as partners weigh opportunities and actions. Discipline around this equilibrium rests significantly with the secretariat, as a support center that routes information and tees up decisions for the governing body. Choices in how to prepare and present issues, and even the personalities of the secretariat head and staff, can have considerable bearing on how effectively the partnership program navigates its trade-offs over time.

The three axes presented here reflect horizontal, central, and vertical planes: (1) the horizontal "buy-in" spectrum of stakeholder inclusion vs. governing efficiency; (2) the central "harmonization" spectrum of common terms vs. individual needs; and (3) the vertical "continuity" spectrum of global-level engagement vs. country-level impacts. Let's drill down on each.

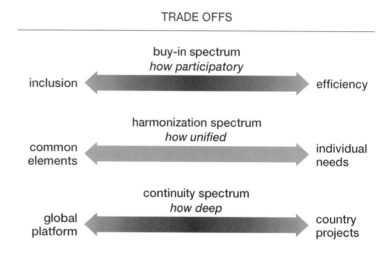

TRADE OFFS

buy-in spectrum
how participatory
inclusion ←——————————→ efficiency

harmonization spectrum
how unified
common elements ←——————————→ individual needs

continuity spectrum
how deep
global platform ←——————————→ country projects

The Horizontal Buy-In Spectrum

The buy-in spectrum asks how broadly participatory the partnership program is, horizontally across partners. The range is between more inclusive vs. more efficient, and the center of attention is the governing body. In designing partnership programs, key decision points involve the size and composition of governing body membership. This includes, for example, questions about the degree of direct and indirect representation, decision making and observer participation, and donor, recipient, and other stakeholder roles. These are among the many variables that can be adjusted to reach the optimal balance of engagement from a governing body point of view, even in deciding whether to have multiple governing bodies.

Inclusion vs. Efficiency

As a general matter, international partnership programs are concerned about inclusion, and partners spend time thinking about whom to include. Partnership programs are by nature invitation-only affairs, even if all agree the invitation is open to anyone (like a donor) who self-selects. The degree of openness of partnership membership is an explicit decision point, usually made by all those who are already "in" as members.

A primary limiting factor to the spirit of inclusivity is efficiency. It's the familiar axiom: The more people around the table, the less efficient the decision making. With more people, there are more voices to hear, more views to accommodate, more costs of attendance, and more personalities to absorb. In the same vein, if membership is too ad hoc, with new people coming every time, this flexible generosity can undercut continuity of information and impede development of a shared meeting culture. It can also detrimentally affect like-mindedness. (>@ Partners and People—Choosing Partners) If bad enough, the wheels of decision making can slow to a grind, or run off the rails.

So how many is too many, how few is not enough? When does more become inefficient and when does less leave out key players? In its most elemental form this is a numbers game, although how the numbers stack up also reflects choices about who has how many representatives. On the high side, most governing bodies of international partnership programs try not to go above two dozen decision makers, and above thirty is usually considered unwieldy. Very large partnership programs (read: big money) may go larger on the governing body, but that usually adds to the formality of the proceedings. On the low side—especially for trust-funded partnership programs—most governing bodies at the very least seat donors with the trustee and then think about whether to add anyone else.

The overall trend for international partnership programs is toward inclusion. For one, there is more sensitivity about including beneficiary views. In a development context, that increasingly means augmenting developing country voice as a way to promote country priorities and country ownership, as well as building country capacity. This can translate into downstream recipients sitting at the same decision-making table as upstream donors, a juxtaposition that is more about synergy than conflict. (>@ Synergistic Conflicts) For another, there are many more players in the international arena, with NGOs, CSOs, private foundations, and others populating the scene. Sometimes it is easier to include heavy hitters or topic-specific activists at the table for buy-in rather than leave them out and have to contend with their criticism. Then again, including them can be inadvisable if it impairs like-minded decision making. (>@ Decision Making—Consensus)

Workarounds

Whatever the calculus in the specific case, when numbers are challenged, partners have a number of options. Ten Tricks are collected here:

1. Constituencies
2. Rotating seats
3. Observers
4. Additional bodies
5. Association representation
6. Limiting members
7. Quotas
8. Minimum thresholds
9. Fees
10. Events

1. **Constituencies**—Partners that fit into a particular grouping—for example, "all donors," "European donors," "private foundations," or "NGOs"—can be aggregated into constituencies. A constituency is like a delegation where every member is represented but only some are seated. The constituency is entitled to a fixed number of governing body seats, usually one or just a few. Those seated members have direct representation at the table, while all the others have indirect representation through them. Constituencies typically decide among themselves how to select their seated members, although preferably with transparency to the rest of the governing body on the methodology. This can be based on simple rotation, highest donor contribution, or some other status aspect. Because the representatives of seated constituency members participate in the governing body on behalf of the whole constituency, everyone in the constituency is represented. Those seated members and their designated representatives should not accept the role without a willingness to coordinate with and be mindful of the other constituency members on whose behalf they hold the seat.

1

2. **Rotating seats**—Two or more partners can take turns sitting at the governing body table, meeting by meeting, year to year, or for some agreed time period. If the seated partner is additionally expected to reflect the views of the unseated, rotating partners, that is effectively a constituency.

2

3. **Observers**—In addition to decision makers, there is room for observers. They attend the governing body meeting, but without deciding. They are sometimes able to speak, depending on the will of the partners. (>@ Governing Bodies—Observers) Observer positions can serve crucial coordination functions, without swelling the ranks of decision makers. Information can usefully flow both ways, with observers both informing members and being informed by them. In international platforms, each of the trustee, secretariat, and downstream fiduciaries typically join as observers to keep a level playing field and avoid perceptions of decision-making bias. (>@ Typology—International Platforms) These are usually standing observer positions, with an expectation that representatives attend every meeting. Ad hoc observers, like prospective donors and others who might be interested in membership, can also attend as observers at specific meetings, as invited, typically within the prerogative of the chair or secretariat head.

3

4. **Additional bodies**—Too many participants on the governing body can also lead to a secondary body that serves a specific purpose. Although this secondary body likely has no decision-making powers, or only those delegated specifically and narrowly from the main governing body, it can still serve a valuable function in supporting governing body decisions. The idea is to match the nature of the participants and scope of expertise with the types of advice, screening, or decisions provided by this additional group, like getting private sector feedback and buy-in through a private sector council or tapping sector or scientific expertise through a technical advisory committee. (>@ Partners and People—Crowding In Expertise) When creating a secondary body, it is also worth thinking about two things: (1) clear delineation of functions or responsibilities vis-à-vis the main governing body and other functions; and (2) adequate linkages between multiple bodies and functions to keep things aligned and smooth. Links could include having a governing body representative regularly attend secondary body meetings and having the same secretariat support both bodies, in both cases to bridge the bodies.

4

5. *Association representation*—Another way to bring down the numbers is representation through organizations that already collectivize a particular category of participant. A regional association could, for example, seat members that bring in a certain voice without, however, a monolithic perspective across representatives. Trade associations are particularly useful ways to bring in the private sector in that trade association representatives come from different companies and take turns to avoid the "unfair advantage" problem vis-à-vis competitors. (>@ Partners and People—Engaging the Private Sector) This kind of representation differs from constituencies in that any one representative is not bound to represent the views of other association members. Like constituencies, however, association representation can spare partnership programs the politics of choosing one entity over another, leaving that task to the association.

6. *Limiting members*—It is, of course, also possible to simply put a cap on participation, whether first come, first served, or using some other criterion. However, this is usually too arbitrary and blunt an approach to be useful. Key participants may be left out simply because their timing is off. Potential partners—especially donors—may decide not to participate if they cannot be part of the shared governance. As a particular issue with trust-funded partnership programs, failure to include all donors on the governing body also jeopardizes the ability to use that body to amend the charter or equivalent document, leaving amendment processes to arduous signing exercises. (>@ Like Rock, Like Water—Like Water) In general, however, relying on abstract numbers is a shortchanging shortcut that puts form ahead of function and rarely ends up in fit-for-purpose design.

7. *Quotas*—Quotas are a way to set caps on participation with regard to specific groupings. Group by group, some can be limited while others can stay unlimited. For example, a governing body might be open to as many donors as wish to join (and they will naturally pay their way to attend meetings), but only a set number of developing countries (who need financial support from the partnership program to attend). Fixing the developing country quota raises the question of how the few lucky participants are to be chosen, something that then needs additional thought. Presented like this, however, it is also clear that quotas can work both ways—limiting too many and boosting too few. In this example, the issue may be not enough countries, or only enough funding to pay for a few. A boosting quota could be part of contextualized design if the clear purpose is to overcome a deficit, rather than position a number in the abstract. (Quotas can also be set for governing body decision making by specifying a minimum number of members that need to be present for a decision to be valid, but that is a different topic.)

8. **Minimum thresholds**—This one is specific to donors, who are otherwise the most obvious governing body candidates in trust-funded partnership programs. The minimum threshold approach still lets donors self-select but is based on a price per seat that can motivate higher contributions. Some partnership programs prefer this put-your-money-where-your-mouth-is approach since it puts a value on the privilege of contributing to governance while also creating incentives for donors to take their role seriously and step up their game. This can work well if the minimum threshold gets the most dedicated donors on board. What works less well, however, is having two classes of donors, when some have governance roles and others don't. This forces charter changes to go through signing exercises because the governing body cannot speak for donors who are not represented. Two alternatives can avoid this discrepancy: (1) either the same minimum threshold is applied to both contributions and governance participation, thereby preserving one class of donors; or (2) all donors below the minimum threshold still have the right to link up with governing body donors into constituencies, thereby giving all donors representation, whether direct or indirect. More generally, however, minimum thresholds can be crass in their singular focus on funding amounts rather than expertise or other value donors bring, including buy-in, balance, diversity, and voice.

9. **Fees**—Tiered minimum thresholds by category of participant are in effect fees. This is basically the price of participation. Sometimes they are called membership fees, as the cost of entry for everyone, not just donors. Membership fees reflect the view that every participant benefits from the partnership platform, so all should be willing to pay their share of support costs (core support). Usually structured on a pay-what-is-affordable basis, a fair share, they also work both ways, like quotas—setting minimums for those who can pay more, and boosting requirements for those who would not otherwise pay. Donor "fees" are typically much higher, for example, than those for academic institutions, which are still typically higher than for developing countries. At the extreme, partnership programs may have a half a dozen or more categories of participants with graduated fees. Although membership fees are well-intentioned, they can feel inflexible, as when partners join halfway through a funding period or want to make in-kind contributions that then result in waiver requests and one-off deviations here and there. Partnership-wide fee structures can also be awkward for beneficiary partners, like developing country governments, if those fees are paid into trust funds that effectively roundtrip their payments into their own downstream projects. (>@ Trust Funds—Recipients)

10. **Events**—Another way to increase inclusion without curbing efficiency is through events rather than bodies. (>@ Structure—Broader Context) Examples include an annual stakeholders gathering, a high-level meeting, or any convening that opens the tent for interested, usually like-minded folks to attend. Such an event can serve several purposes, including information sharing, activity coordination, lessons learned, and advocacy, all designed to move the partnership agenda forward with greater traction, political heft, resource mobilization, and visibility. Events are not expected to have governance functions—no decision points, no members, no minutes—although they are often planned back-to-back with governing body meetings for efficiency and may inform or be informed by other partnership program functions.

8

9

10

At the end of the day, in addition to sizing the governing body to conduct business efficiently, international partnership programs usually look for diversity—including geographic, gender, and other qualities—as well as like-mindedness in their participants. If the governing body makes decisions through consensus, as is recommended (>@ Decision Making), the governing body needs to be capable of consensus. (>@ Partners and People—Choosing Partners) Inclusion need not always come at the cost of efficiency but can instead become a force for efficiency if partners are convened accordingly.

The Central Harmonization Spectrum

The harmonization spectrum asks how unified the partnership terms are, which is to say, how much is centralized and based on a common partnering or programmatic framework. The range is between common terms vs. individual positions, and the center of attention is on partnership operations. In designing partnership programs, efficiencies and synergies can be leveraged through common elements and common approaches. This includes, for example, commingled funding pools like trust funds, standardized reporting formats for easy aggregation of information, and acceptance of partnership-wide protocols on topics of common interest, like conflicts of interest, disclosure, and remedies, preferably without policy overlays that impede downstream fiduciaries and implementers (>@ Custodial Effect—Eyes Wide Open).

The degree of harmonization can depend in large part on the purpose of the partnership program and whether having more commonalities—or "collectives" (>@ International Partnership Programs—Collectivizing)—is important for the partnership program's goals. In some cases, coming together to agree on certain global standards and common approaches is the whole point. In other cases, coming together to pool funds and scale operations, while respecting and leveraging individual implementation channels, may be the point. And then there are those partnership programs where partners convene to share information and compare experiences, nothing more. The spirit of the partnership program is reflected in whether the emphasis is on a strong center and multilateral approaches or on individuality and unilateral approaches.

As a general matter, partnership programs are about what partners can do together. What holds the partnership together is what the partners agree on and what they bring under the partnership umbrella, under their common brand. Not everything has to be harmonized for partners to have a solid and effective partnership. What to collectivize and how far to go are decision points that affect how the partners view each other, how outsiders view the partnership, and how effective the partnership program can be.

Harmonization vs. Individualization

The primary limiting factor to the spirit of harmonization is the span of individual requests and requirements that partners bring to the table. The risks go both ways. On the one hand, too much accommodation and you end up with a bunch of rules racked with exceptions, or no rules at all. The less

> Somewhere between the swiss cheese of overaccommodation and the chop suey of underaccommodation.

coherence, the harder it is for the center to stay centered. On the other hand, too little accommodation and you end up without common denominators. With less granularity of fit, you also lose a strong center.

While collectivizing and harmonizing move the partnership program toward the lowest common denominators, even one partner's inability to do something can kick the number up and become limiting for all partners. For example, if one donor to a commingled trust fund says it cannot accept an arbitration clause in the contribution agreement because it is legally prohibited from pre-agreeing to agree, then all donors to that trust fund are left without arbitration in the agreements, even if everyone else wants it. That is because, for a commingled pool of funds, recourse vis-à-vis the trustee should be the same across all donors, both for feasible operations and fairness.

The harmonization pressure points may be less about what partners want and more about what they need, often because of their internal statutory and policy environments. Each partner has its institutional setting, which enables more or less latitude in taking on partnership terms. Some partners are mature in their approach to international partnership programs, having recognized the value of multilateral engagements and worked to develop policy environments that facilitate their multilateral participation. Others may be less accustomed to international collaboration and more rigid in their ability to compromise and harmonize.

Partners without conducive policy environments can make it difficult for all other partners to collaborate on common terms. Partnership programs usually try to accommodate what partners need, but at a certain point, partners and supporting entities may have to decide whether an individual partner's requirements or resistance to common terms create too high a barrier to be sustained. Then it may be up to the partner to accommodate, rather than the other way around—and that may mean choosing to take it or leave it. Compatibility and commonality are still bottom lines for international partnership programs.

On the spectrum of possibilities, partners regularly give up autonomy for harmony. Unless partners feel like they can accomplish more together than individually—that all partners together are more than the sum of each separately—there may be little interest in making these sacrifices and joining up. Partnership programs can take hard work and make for hard choices, so they also take dedication to the common cause. There will still be limits to how much individual partners can agree to or take on, but fortunately, many areas of collaboration also leave room for individualization.

> Compatibility and commonality are bottom lines.

Unrestricted vs. Restricted Funds

A good example of this trade-off is the handling of commingled contributions in trust-funded partnership programs. In a commingled pool, donors cannot track their individual contributions apart from all other contributions. (>@ Trust Funds—Accounts) Dollars (or other operating currencies) are fungible, and once deposited, their specific provenances no longer attach. This can be a challenge for donors when they supply funds from budgets tied to specific purposes, like projects in Africa only. If the trust fund scope is global, that would be a disconnect since the funds could also support Asia. Here we have the trade-off from a partnership program perspective:

The upside of a commingled pool that is broadly deployable with more versatility of use but creates a one-size-fits-all for donors that may limit contributions	VS.	The downside of carved out, donor-defined categories that are strategically and operationally less responsive, less adaptable, and less scalable but are tailor-made for individual donors and can facilitate contributions

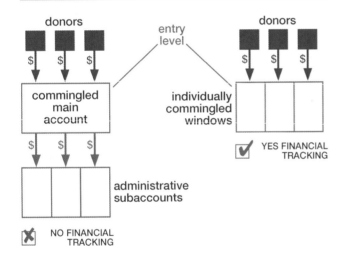

UNRESTRICTED VS. RESTRICTED FUNDS

This tension is commonly referred to as "unrestricted" vs. "restricted" funds. Unrestricted funds are as diversely deployable as the fund description is broad, which from a programmatic perspective gives valuable flexibility to a trust-funded partnership program in allocating funds over time. Unrestricted vs. restricted funds are on the spectrum of common terms vs. individual requirements. A fully harmonized approach features all unrestricted funds, universally available for all defined purposes. An individualized, swiss cheese approach pokes holes in the unrestricted pool by tagging or "earmarking" specific amounts from specific donors for specific purposes.

Covering Core Support

Particularly important is that unrestricted funds pay for what is known as "core support." Core support is basically administrative support, including staff, supplies, space, communications, overhead, and more—things that every partnership program needs to function as a partnership and a program. No partnership program can survive without at least some funding for core support, although amounts vary in relation to, for example, how much "center" the partners want, how much administrative support the governing body needs, how complex the structure and processes are, how much partners contribute in-kind, and how broadly the supporting entity is being engaged.

Core support is usually that non-sexy line item no one particularly wants to fund, but everyone should. International partnership programs that do not have trust funds or other dedicated funding vehicles may have a harder time ensuring core support. But even those with trust funds need to keep core funding in view—whether hived off the top as a small, uniform percentage when funds come in, or covered by unrestricted funds once in the pool.

Since commingled funds cannot be earmarked (>@ International Partnership Programs—Pooled Funding), donors are left with three primary options to attach their specified expectations for use to their specific contributions (>@ Trust Funds—Contributions—Tracking, Earmarking, and Preferencing):

1 Depositing funds into segregated accounts within the same trust fund

2 Depositing funds into separate trust funds

3 Depositing funds into a commingled account with soft preferencing

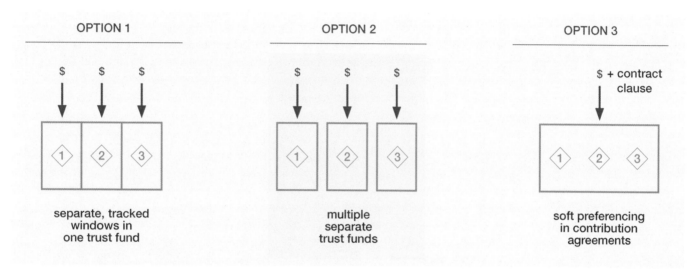

No matter how donors are allowed to restrict fund use, whether hard divisions (options 1 and 2) or soft preferencing (option 3), donor tagging divvies up the kitty in ways that limit downstream implementation. With restricted funding, individual donors make their unilateral views prevail over partnership views. Effectively removing their funds from the unrestricted, centrally allocated pool, they use the partnership program as a vehicle for their own agendas. Partnership programs as a whole need to decide whether this kind of engagement works for everyone in the partnership.

For some partnership programs this is a problem; for others it works fine. Some partnership programs have broad tolerance for hard-bucketed or soft-tagged funding, especially if the reservoir of core support remains ample. In high-restriction cases, the partnership program may pull together multiple funding streams, including bilateral donor-recipient grants and multiple single-donor trust funds, rather than a single, broadly cumulating multi-donor trust fund. A collection of single-donor trust funds is essentially an admission that more money through financial tracking—trust fund by trust fund—is worth the price of segregation. It makes for more transaction costs and less fungibility but can still become a strong collaborative platform under an overarching governing body. (>@ Typology—The Broader Landscape of Partnership Programs—Umbrella Arrangements) However, this type of multi-trust-fund route—rather than a multi-donor-in-one-trust-fund route—inevitably has a ripple effect on how harmonized the partnership program becomes overall, and how much else is treated multilaterally vs. unilaterally.

The Vertical Continuity Spectrum

The continuity spectrum asks at what level partnership program engagement spans, how deeply it connects and how vertically it operates in terms of activities and impact. The range is between global and country, international and local, and the center of attention is on linkages. In designing partnership programs, key decision points turn on country-level elements that are brought into international or regional partnership settings and the manner in which the global and local are aligned.

Global-to-Country

The global-to-country span includes both upstream and downstream aspects with respect to both ends of the spectrum. For example:

- On the upstream, this includes the degree of global vs. country focus as a matter of strategy and work plan, as well as the number of recipients and other downstream stakeholders on the governing body.

- On the downstream, this picks up the role of country-level activities in shaping the portfolio, including the use of pilots for scalable projects, the generation of lessons learned, and the achievement of results that feed into advocacy and more resource mobilization.

Both partnership governance (upstream) and program activities (downstream) are part of the partnership program's implementation, and both can be global and local. Given that international partnership programs are already international in nature, the question in each case becomes how much and how well the local is connected to the international. The global-to-country span reflects many variables that make up what the partnership program stands for and is seeking to achieve. The key question is not the relative proportion of the two, but to what extent global and local engagements, as relevant to partnership program objectives, are linked and leveraged off each other.

On upstream governance, partnership programs can infuse their platforms with local voice and direction, as when country consent is mandated for grant agreements, or country participants are included in the governing body. In some cases, partnership governance can spread across two tiers, an international body (the main governing body) coupled with a country-level apparatus (like a local, country-led coordination group, or one per country) that provides input, advice, or even makes specific decisions on country-level projects, along with other coordination of local activities and support to the partnership program's work. The degree of global/country engagement, and the degree of connection between the two, represent explicit decision points for partners.

On downstream activities, most international partnership program activities are global-local. Their work plans are usually combinations of global efforts

GLOBAL

stakeholder coordination
advocacy and awareness raising
knowledge platforms
standard setting
lessons learned

LOCAL

country coordination
country assessments and strategies
project operations
technical assistance and capacity building
pilots

mutually

reinforcing

that are directed to the broader international community, and country efforts that are directed to specific recipients and beneficiaries. Global endeavors include standard setting, information dissemination, advocacy, knowledge platforms, and stakeholder coordination. These tend to be softer shaping and influencing activities in comparison with more tangible country interventions. Direct beneficiary support at the country level is often in the form of grants or technical assistance and covers the range from project financing to capacity building, and much in between.

Feedback Loops

International partnership programs can successfully play on both global and country bases. These partnership programs recognize the value of bringing (1) country voice into strategies and decisions; and (2) global coordination into country implementation. They also recognize the value of global experience and standards in country implementation and the value of country experience and perspectives in global follow-through. Among other things, this allows for a great feedback loop that links ex ante planning with ex post analysis. Whatever the partnership program does in global and country arenas can cross-pollinate for future activities.

MUTUALLY REINFORCING FEEDBACK LOOP

This is the ideal scenario, where the global/international and the local/country aspects inform each other. However, that often takes effort, especially in development partnerships. A case in point is when partners seek to bring developing country voice into global governance. Other partners, especially donors, have to reach out to developing country participants, both because of limited resources (for example, paying for meeting attendance) and limited capacity (for example, having experienced staff available to attend). Deciding to upstream beneficiary country elements—rather than simply leaving beneficiaries at the end of the fund flow food chain— usually calls for deliberate steps initiated by partners.

TWO-TIER GLOBAL-COUNTRY STRUCTURE EXAMPLE

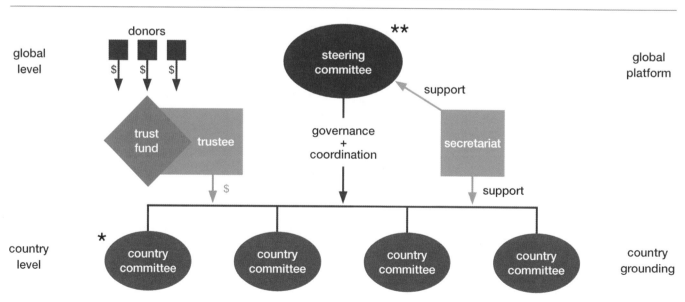

★ government ministries, local donor reps, NGO, CSOs, secretariat

★★ global level equivalents

Resources

In this respect, and more broadly, one of the limiting factors in reinforcing global and country linkages is resources. A finite element is budget: How much funding does the partnership program have and what is the relative mix of global and country engagement it can support? Decisions about where to put the emphasis can be baked into the mission of the partnership program or can evolve over time, as partners realize what is missing and work to add it in.

A likely indicator of strong global efforts linked with strong country efforts is the nature of the supporting entity. As with so much else, the choice of supporting entity can make the difference here, too. An international organization with deep country reach, like an MDB, embodies the linkages a partnership program might seek. By latching onto this breadth and depth across dozens of offices and hundreds of staff, partners can tap into extensive and long-standing resources and relationships. Partners may look for many things in their supporting entity, like a strong fiduciary track record and a robust operating framework, but expert staff on the ground and excellent relations with local government officials also rank as top benefits.

Impact

Ultimately, the question for partners is what mix of global and local can have the most impact. That depends on what partners want to achieve with their partnering effort, what gap they want to fill, what challenge they want to address. If bilateral efforts are already hard at work, there may be less need for an internationally convened venue. However, an international partnership program may be just the thing to coordinate otherwise disparate bilateral country interventions. If country challenges are not getting the attention they need, an international initiative can rally forces on a global scale, creating momentum for the country cause.

Indeed, global initiatives typically get their traction from country grounding, especially when addressing development topics. This is where international partnership programs get *real-life, data-driven, evidence-based understandings* of the issues and how they accomplish *real-life, sustainable, and impactful change* where it matters. Global platforms with country grounding—where international participation meets local impact—is where international partnership programs make their difference.

As it turns out, this vertical spectrum is not so much a trade-off as a matter of keeping both elements in view. Neither need come at the cost of the other, and both can be mutually reinforcing. The key is finding the right mix, with the right engagement, that reflects the values and goals of each international partnership program.

Global platform
+
country grounding:

Where international engagement meets local impact.

Conclusion

Trade-offs in international partnership programs are sometimes hard to spot. They may look like problems, conflicts, or differences when in fact they are choices that require balancing, more of one, less of another, or alternatives that maximize both. Balancing starts with taking topics head-on, having the discussions and negotiations that prioritize, compromise, and ultimately reach a point of maximized equilibrium. Balancing continues with ways to stay flexible and adjust over time, perhaps through principles, procedures, and periodic reviews, rather than fixed rules and static requirements.

This is the eyes-wide-open and on-your-toes approach to partnering—staying alert to where the blinders are and where the shoes pinch, while also being able to accommodate and adjust as needed and agreed. To this end, it helps to understand that managing trade-offs is part and parcel of making international partnership programs work.

4 RISK AND REVIEW

After so much terminology, typology, and taxonomy, plus more on dualities, dichotomies, and methodologies, we can take a time-out for some business basics. This chapter is a grab bag of topics on risks to consider and reviews to conduct when engaging in the business of international partnership programs. Mostly common sense, but offered as words to the wise, the thoughts here may help partners organize their approach to partnering.

Sizing Up Risk

Like virtually everything in international partnership programs, risk is contextual and depends on the specific circumstances. Risks can come from action or inaction; they can accompany opportunities or arise from lack of opportunity. Risks can be external, and outside the partners' control, but risks can also be internal, often of the partners' own making. The failure to ensure common ground through an agreed charter, the avoidance of hard topics like free riders or dwindling resources, and the neglect of other topics like applicable governing law—these and more can be sleeping dogs that come back to bite.

There is not room here to describe the full range of risks that could face international partnership programs. For one, risks run the gamut, including the unknown unknowns. For another, risks can be compounded when they are multi-dimensional, multi-issue, or multi-country, often with multiplier effects when risk begets risk. Then, too, one person's risk may be another person's benefit, as when the ability to condition contribution payments is less risky for the donor, but riskier for the beneficiary that may not receive needed funds or has trouble planning. Risk appetites can also vary significantly; not everyone sees risk the same way. A one-stop-shop supporting entity with exposure across all fronts of the partnership program is likely to have a heightened sensitivity to risk compared to partners that have delegated practically all responsibility to the supporting entity. There are also many kinds of risk. Here are a few of the common variants:

- implementation risks (failing to meet stated goals or causing harm)

- legal risks (from other partners or third parties, culminating in liability and remedies)

- fiduciary risks (exceeding available funds, misused or missing funds, and refunds)

- associational risks (connected through a common endeavor under one defining brand)

- catch-all reputational risks (vulnerable to external criticism; perceptions count)

1. implementation risks
2. legal risks
3. fiduciary risks
4. associational risks
5. reputational risks

Among the most common pitfalls in a partnership program is to focus on funding over partnership, something that by now may be sounding like a broken record. But here it is again, with risk implications. Money talks, which can easily mean partners see themselves establishing funding vehicles rather than creating partnership programs. In this context, donors may be given more weight than governing bodies, fund flows may matter more than decision flows, and supporting entity policies and processes may revolve around trust funds, not partnerships. With too much of a trust fund optic, partnering aspects can be at risk of not being well-understood, well-established, well-articulated, well-implemented, or all of the above.

This is passing strange, considering how much exposure partners have to the partnership program as a whole. Partners may be happy to take collective credit if something goes well, but tend to give less thought to the risk of collective detriment if something goes wrong. And then when something does go wrong, as it clearly can, partners are at pains to distance themselves under terms that may be muddy or lacking altogether. For organizations that participate in many partnership programs, particularly supporting entities, this neglect can become cumulative and chronic. Risk is certainly in the offing when staff are unclear about who is doing what and how, when results go every which way, and when bad precedent leads to bad practice.

Own Your Own Risk Review

An important piece of advice for international partnership program risk is this: Every partner needs to assess its own. Is a decision-making seat better than an observer seat for us? Do the fiduciaries in place meet our institutional standards? What level of engagement is needed from us to match our objectives? And so on. Partners each need to think about their own priorities and pressure points, and check in on them. Complete reliance on the supporting entity or other partners is misplaced when every risk profile is uniquely dependent on individual characteristics. Risk: It depends on *your* assessment.

Partners who are in it together also owe it to each other to address risk together. The ability to anticipate international partnership program risks collectively gives partners the ability to acknowledge and potentially manage those risks before they do real damage. Although risk assessment and tolerance have individual institutional underpinnings, risk identification and risk management can be powerful collective exercises. Even when partners, particularly donors, pass off responsibilities to others in the partnership program, they may still want to collectively signal the level of risk the partnership program as a whole is willing to bear. What is the risk common denominator? Is it high risk or low risk? How much risk is okay to get the job done? How much cost is justified to mitigate risk? Gathering a shared view of acceptable risk can be especially important when partnership programs focus on fragile or conflict-affected settings, where risk is built into the very nature of the endeavor.

At the end of the day, partners may choose to be more risk aware than risk averse. They may realize that some risks can be mitigated and managed, while the risks of inattention and inaction may be riskier yet.

> You can choose to be more risk aware than risk averse.

At the Front End

Business decisions look to maximize the good and minimize the bad. At the start of a venture, when everyone is in collaboration mode, thoughts tend to the positive and energies gear toward closure. This may not feel like the moment to dwell on problems or pitfalls, especially if they are merely potential or hypothetical. Without turning negative, however, there is still room to think about risk and do the review. On things that matter, partners can kick the tires and do some test runs before embarking on the journey.

Proliferation

The first tire to kick is the concept. A great idea is not enough basis to start an international partnership program. Even the simplest of partnership programs takes time, energy, and cost to build and maintain. Complex ones are exponentially more resource-intensive. The more sui generis and as-negotiated an international partnership program is, the more time, energy, cost—and expertise—it takes to build and run. In a world of limited resources and bottomless need, the use of all these things is worth justifying and assuring before going ahead with the endeavor.

Prospective partners should each make sure the new initiative aligns with their strategies and priorities. They should confirm the availability of their own capable staff to play their respective roles. And they should believe the opportunity is worth all the cost and diverted effort. Indeed, partners should be confident that the benefits of their new venture will amply exceed costs, including, particularly, benefits on the ground, where it matters most.

Even if that all checks out in the affirmative, prospective partners also need to consider the new initiative in the larger landscape.

- Does the new initiative fit with other existing initiatives?
- Is it adding value, or is it just competing with other efforts, redirecting funds and attention?
- How can this new effort link and leverage with other engagements and instruments?

Overlap and competition are particularly chronic in international aid architecture, and proliferating platforms do not necessarily help the cause.

Partners can ask themselves: Which is the greater effect of the proposed international partnership program—an exacerbation of already fragmented international efforts or a consolidation of international resources to fill an underserved need? It is worth taking a good, long moment to consider whether and how the new international endeavor fits with other endeavors before throttling full speed ahead.

Life Cycle

Part of taking a moment for the broad view is taking the long view. Pause to think about life cycle. Even if everything is good to go and falling into place now, how does it look for the future?

Most of an international partnership program's lifespan is in its ongoing operations. At steps along the way, there are existential events, starting with birth and continuing with other milestones that affect the very essence of the endeavor. As a matter of upfront risk and review, consider this short list:

Reality Check

- As the foundation is being built, is the partnership program primed to be sustainable, efficient, and impactful over time?

- At any point in time, is the partnership program where it wants to be and headed in the right direction?

1 Establishment: Has enough common ground been established to launch?

2 Operations: Is it clear who has responsibility for what?

3 Resource mobilization: Are there sufficient prospects for sustained funding?

4 Review: Will there be periodic checks, like a midterm review or independent evaluation?

5 Modifications: Is there a flexible mechanism for considering and adopting change?

6 Exit: What is the envisioned endgame, or is this open-ended, indefinite?

establishment launch ▸ operations ▸ resource mobilization ▸ review ▸ modifications ▸ ops ▸ resource mobilization ▸ etc. ▸ exit termination

Some perspective and comfort on each of these fronts is not misplaced at the start. An emerging partnership program can be a work in progress for some time to come, but total fluidity on some key points at the start may never gel once things get going. Transparency and awareness about what is open can at least set placeholders for future attention. Partners may need immediate clarity on some aspects, but may be willing to wait on others if the path to addressing them is clear.

Institutional Factors

When setting out on a partnership path, each partner is likely to feel pressures and pulls as it seeks to align its interests and ambitions with others—both at individual and institutional levels. While individual teams are focused on their individual initiatives, it is up to the institutional entity they come from to take a portfolio-wide perspective, both across partnership program engagements and relative to other business operations. The balance between bespoke engagements (designed for maximized effect) and institutional parameters (derived from policy, practice, or guidance) is a constant work in progress, as organic as the partnership programs themselves.

Contextualization vs. Customization

Maybe you are in a supporting entity that likes to partner but resists customization. Or maybe you are in a donor agency that likes to partner, but needs specific features and clauses to do so. These two tendencies are obviously at odds. Establishing a partnership program is often an extenuated exercise of managing these two dynamics down to a common denominator.

Efforts to minimize customization on the part of supporting entities, in their trustee, secretariat, and potentially other roles, is understandable and mostly laudable. Efficiency would be elusive if there were not some amount of standardization in supporting entity operations. However, allergic reactions to customization are not laudable. Just like any business that responds to its environment—its markets, customers, product lines, and targets— international partnership programs are similarly situated in their specific contexts. It is, for example, not possible to set up a trust-funded partnership program without specifying the unique objectives, scope of activities, and allowable use of funds. Similarly, unless the platform becomes an embedded partnership where all decision making is left to the supporting entity (>@ Typology—Light to Heavy), then shared governance terms also need tailored attention as to who is involved, on what aspects, and using what modes.

KEEP CALM AND CONTEXTUALIZE

Call this customization if you want, but it is actually contextualization in a way that is normal and necessary. Can there be parameters and guidelines for how this is done? Absolutely. Can supporting entities prescribe set governance models and pre-defined structures? Good luck. Models can be helpful to a degree, as examples and starting points, but prescribed formats tend to trip up on their terms. The value of pre-defined, off-the-shelf models may depend on the level of micromanaged detail. High-level prescriptions, with ample room for contextualization, can be useful guiding frameworks that embed institutional policies and lessons learned. However, if this book seeks to demonstrate anything, it is the ultimate lesson that international partnership programs benefit from sound business choices and deserve to be fit-for-purpose—something abstract standardization cannot do.

Do donors and other partners sometimes have to cool their heels? Yes. There is no way trustees, secretariats, and downstream fiduciaries can effectively support partnership programs if supporting entities are not able to follow their standard policies and procedures, thus creating some coherence within partnership program support functions and mapping support operations onto their internal management and control systems. In a way that may feel self-defeating to donors and other partners, it is actually in everyone's interest to pay due respect and give adequate room to the inner workings and risk profiles of their chosen supporting entities. And, at the same time, it is in everyone's interest to match partnership program design and structure to the partners and program at hand.

It is all in the balance and ultimately as negotiated. The fine lines between excess customization or standardization and necessary contextualization may always be a work in progress. Engagement in an international partnership program presumes a desire to go collective, which optimistically includes an ambition to reflect all partners in the whole with comfortably maximized common ground. Why convene an international partnership program unless it is fit-for-purpose enough to make a maximized difference?

excess customization → strain on supporting entities

necessary contextualization → maximized impact

excess standardization → strain on donors and others

Business Management

Most international partnership program participants are not one-timers. As ministries and organizations, they seek each other out time and again in the comfort of long-standing relationships and long-established track records. New partners join the scene, and some participate one-off, but the core partners are usually old-timers for whom participation in partnership programs is a business line. This is especially true of supporting entities, whose staff and resources can support hundreds of partnering ventures at a time, with assigned individuals in the thousands and assigned resources in the millions (or more). It is also true of traditional donors and customary country recipients, who are long-term players in the international partnership program ecosystem.

Some partners are savvy and understand the primacy of partnering elements in what they do. Some are so focused on funds coming and going, or so busy with other things, that they may neglect the partnership part of what they do. For individual representatives, when this happens, it is hard to be a "good" partner without strong organizational backing.

Addressing partnership engagement is not much different than addressing other business aspects. It starts with recognizing engagement in international partnership programs as a business area in its own right rather than operating by analogy or under the radar. That includes seeing this not as an extension of trust funds but the other way around. Staff need to know what policy environment applies, what matters to the mother ship, what is allowed and what is not, and where to get expert guidance if questions or issues arise, specifically with respect to partnering aspects.

Ten Tasks

Is your organization on the ball with respect to international partnership program engagements? From a business perspective, here are Ten Tasks posed as queries to gauge the internal workings:

1   Is there an internal business process for vetting engagements in partnership programs?

2   Are there clear avenues for considering deviations, waivers, and high-risk scenarios?

3   Do these processes include service standards with reasonable turnaround?

4   Are relevant units, like those dealing with donor relations and external partners, involved?

5   Do sponsoring business teams engage well with central policy units? And vice versa?

6   Is there a central location to get guidance on how to handle partnership aspects?

7   Is there pipeline visibility for emerging initiatives, including for internal coordination?

8   Is data being collected to monitor engagements, including as they evolve?

9   When the proper vetting/business process is not applied, is there follow-up?

10 Is someone keeping track of partnership program changes over time?

To set up robust institutional frameworks for engaging in international partnership programs, partners can consider instituting the following steps (if they haven't already):

1. **Clear business framework.** Institutionally, it is important to establish clear and visible principles or other parameters to be owned by the assigned business leadership. A high-level policy with additional, more detailed guidance may be a good combination to address the many variations inherent in partnering. This can be about content, including aspects that are definitional (for example, what kinds of initiatives need to go through vetting processes), technical (what substantive standards should be met), and operational (what baseline parameters need observing and what types of implementation are considered good practice). This can also be about process, including with respect to vetting (for example, who reviews, who clears), supervising (who is collecting data, who is accountable), and reporting (how often, to whom).

2. **Streamlined business systems.** Clear and efficient internal business systems for considering partnership program initiatives are ideally well-aligned with other operations and systems. An easy-access, web-based portal can be used to input key information (data tabulation) for the purposes of both review and reporting. Approvals can be provided and priorities can be set with visibility of initiatives across the board. Partnership programs can be monitored over time, with heightened attention to high-risk endeavors. Issues can be gauged systematically to develop preventive measures and track successful remediation.

3. **Central compliance function.** With a business framework and supporting systems in place, a support unit or specific individuals can be given the responsibility and prerogative to keep track of partnership program requests and operations, answer questions of implementation and interpretation, direct business teams to relevant guidelines and standards, and help manage risks for the institution.

4. **Center of experience/expertise.** As part of the compliance function or separately—which may depend on your view of conflicts vs. synergies (>@ Synergistic Conflicts)—a unit or specific individuals with deep experience on partnership programs can be an advisory resource on an as-needed basis. Sponsoring teams that are technical experts in their fields usually do not have partnership program structure and design expertise. With a central advisory resource, these teams can engage more smoothly, while managing institutional pressure points and hot buttons more effectively, and still keeping an eye on the overall well-being and reputational risk of the partnership program. A central resource can do wonders to help sponsoring teams and their institutions be "good" partners, both internally and externally.

5. **Pipeline visibility.** It can be very useful to track partnership program initiatives in their early, conceptual stages through the same web-based portal used for vetting more developed initiatives. Early visibility gives opportunities for coordination and, if needed, course correction. It is easier to shape and manage opportunities sooner, before staff start raising external expectations with other partners, than later, when options are out of the bag. Once expectations are set, they are harder to revise or reverse.

6. **If applicable, an inhouse secretariat support team.** Supporting entities can go further and designate a focal point specifically to support inhouse secretariats (whether the role is made part of or separated from trustee functions). Inhouse secretariats can raise tricky issues (>@ Secretariats; >@ Supporting Entities; >@ Custodial Effect), with broad exposure to reputational risk and liability. This can be true at any time during the ongoing life cycle, as partnership programs evolve and mature in adding partners, changing direction, restructuring, spinning off, and whatever else can come a partnership program's way. Expertise is most helpful if it is mindful of the supporting entity's rules and authorizing environment, while also panoramic enough to pick up cross-fertilized experiences and lessons learned.

Business management:

1. Clear business framework
2. Streamlined business systems
3. Central compliance function
4. Center of experience/ expertise
5. Pipeline visibility
6. Inhouse secretariat support team

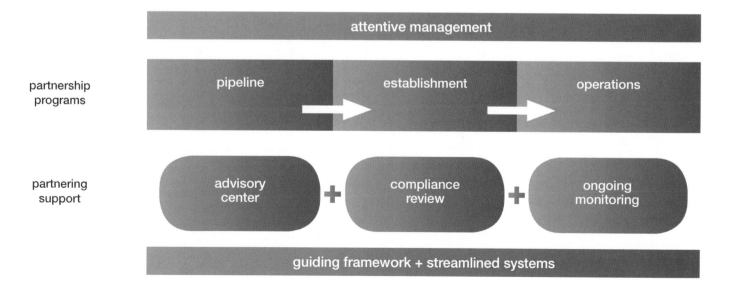

Risk Innovation

Risk is not a dirty word.

All partners have risk appetites and risk profiles to consider. That can mean risk avoidance and mitigation, but it can also mean opportunity. Part of bringing comparative advantages to the table is figuring out who is best positioned to bear what risks. Supporting entities, in particular, are usually well-equipped to deal with operational risks, but are also more acutely aware of reputational, associational, and other risks.

Standard operating frameworks of supporting entities—especially trustees and other fiduciaries with contractual obligations—and secretariats with broad partnership exposure often skew toward being risk averse. Some of that is accretive, in managing reputation and risk from lessons learned (sometimes painfully), while some of that is just about positing worst-case scenarios. Despite the valuable intent to be protective, however, there are common shortcomings.

First, supporting entities often shortcut into one-size-fits-all risk analysis. Standard formats for risk analysis easily become check-the-box drills. If the risk assessment template has categories—like strategic effectiveness, stakeholder support, financial soundness, and operational efficiency—teams may just do the rote requirement with one item per category, rather than put in thoughtful effort to pre-empt issues, tensions, missteps, and adverse side effects. Second, in trust-funded partnership programs, risk exercises often take a trust fund lens rather than a partnership program one. Both partnership risk and opportunity can get obscured with such a myopic view.

On the program level, operationally, glossed-over and inattentive risk analysis not only misses potential pitfalls but also misses opportunities for greater contextualizing. Partners that are purportedly on the lookout for innovation—every partnership program wants to be known as "innovative"—can adapt risk appetites when circumstances merit. In some cases, it could be okay to acknowledge from the start that a particular endeavor is high risk, that the normal fiduciary standards may not be met, or that implementation may lead to failure, and yet everyone is still on board to proceed. In other words, it need not be taboo to agree to go "high risk" and say so, for all or part of an international partnership program, especially if the potential benefits merit the potential risks, or if taking the risks is still better than not acting at all.

As an example, consider a grantmaking facility that lightens the transaction processing and supervisory load for smaller grant amounts. The goal would be increased efficiency and lower costs, with the understanding that this is also higher risk. If partners can feel free to stake out a risk-accepting position from the start, putting themselves and everyone else on notice that they are embarking on a higher-than-usual-risk partnership program, they can leave more room for error or failure, plus adjustments over time, while still reaping the benefits. This could be an innovative conversation, an innovative approach, an innovative implementation—attuned to the circumstances—relative to more standard, overmanaged, and undercontextualized approaches.

Many international partnership programs, especially in humanitarian and development contexts, are drawn to risk, like efforts geared toward conflict-affected areas, or are inherently risky, like efforts in low-capacity contexts. It is not possible to be the emergency provider, the lender of last resort, or the

Risks are contextual, like everything else about international partnership programs.

first mover in tackling challenges without stepping into risk. The P&I protected zone of some international partners, like the UN or MDB-supporting entities, is an opportunity to embrace risk in a way few other actors can. Without cutting corners or being reckless, partners in international partnership programs have unusual opportunities to face risk head on—doing the analysis, aligning the comparative advantages, and deliberately designing structures and relationships around risk.

Indeed, the more attention given to risk as an area for opportunity and optimization, international collaboration and innovation, the more international partners may realize that there is room to approach risk earlier and better. Embracing risk through greater attention to prevention, preparation, and ultimately risk mitigation can be a key element to positioning partnership program efforts and activities. International partnership programs can be designed to embed direct approaches to risk innovation and mitigation in their decision making and implementation arrangements.

> **Embrace project and other risks through greater attention to prevention, preparation, and ultimately risk mitigation.**

───────────────────────●───────────────────────

Risk vs. Risk

I have been in many a meeting where the risk review was lopsided. As colleagues zeroed in on a particular risk and made decisions to avoid it, they did not look long enough to realize that their solution opened the door to other risks. It's a bit like getting a gun to ward off the bears, but forgetting that having a gun in the house also has risks. The fact is, we rarely have the luxury to address risks in isolation. Business decisions tend to balance risks, weighing one against another, picking the lesser of two, or managing mitigations on multiple fronts.

A classic partnership decision is whether to go all in and take control or to keep one's distance and avoid responsibility. In a partnership program, which is riskier? It is a double-edged sword, with risk in either direction. Control brings responsibility, which carries direct exposure and the risk of failure, whereas lack of control coupled with partnership exposure carries the risk of someone else's failure. Often the risk most shunned is reputational risk. Given that partners are associated with each other, is there more reputational risk in being more or less engaged?

The answer, as usual, depends on the circumstances. A supporting entity's instinct may be to go all in, especially in a one-stop-shop, where it is already deep in the mix. Operating at the nexus of the partnership program, its best chance to manage reputational risk and ensure positive outcomes may be to take it on. Distancing itself from a small piece of the partnership program may afford little risk mitigation when it is already so wholly identified with the whole.

By contrast, a limited trustee, whose very positioning is based on a disavowal of responsibility, is a different case. Already boxed into a corner, it is apt to stay there, rather than invite more responsibility and reputational exposure. It may well conclude that its safest course is to say "It wasn't me, I wasn't responsible"—at least if the lines of responsibility that were drawn are clear and clean.

A concrete example is accreditation processes for downstream fiduciaries. The one-stop-shop full trustee is likely to say, "I need to be involved in setting the standards and confirming they have been met," so as to say this is less risky than leaving it completely to others. The international platform limited trustee is just as likely to say, "I need to stay out of it, the job of deciding and applying standards is the governing body's responsibility, not mine; I am just here to take instructions and transfer funds." And yet, even the limited trustee needs to realize that this kind of risk avoidance may result in subpar recipients to whom it has to transfer funds, with an unavoidable association and at least some reputational risk. It should only accept that kind of exposure if it has confidence the other partners will diligently undertake the accreditation. And it should recognize that if it steps up as a partner, not just a service provider, those dividing lines are not necessarily bright lines.

It is in the nature of partnership that association brings exposure. This is always a backdrop against which other partnership program risks—and their risk mitigations—are to be considered. (>@ Supporting Entities – Risk Profile)

───────────────────────●───────────────────────

At the Back End

When teaching Partnership Programs 101, my true/false quiz asks: "Are partnership programs forever?" That is only mildly tongue in cheek. It is the rare international partnership program that defines its end at the beginning, and even rarer for partners to hold themselves to it when they do. International partnership programs are notoriously silent on exits, whether for departing partners or dissolving partnership programs. As with remedies, choice of law, and anything else that projects discontent, exit questions on whether, when, and how are usually not addressed until the time comes.

Among other things, partners intuit that informal partnership programs allow for casual exits. There may be some reputational risk in the mix, but no one assumes a legal impediment to leaving, even to the point of donors pulling funds that have been promised but not yet committed or conveyed (committed funds are not so easily pulled back, and conveyed funds may be irretrievable). It can get messy at times, but no one is in an unequivocal position to enforce participation one way or the other. International partner participation is legally informal and basically voluntary by nature.

By contrast, international partnership programs, as collectives, are basically perpetual by nature. When partners establish secretariats, and when those secretariats are populated by staff, and those staff are there to please the partners, it is easy to find a self-perpetuating loop that feeds itself. Staff do not usually work themselves out of a job (>@ Secretariats—Lessons Learned), and partnership programs do not usually assume their irrelevance. As a result, everyone tends to buckle up and keep it all going, even if that means shape-shifting missions and objectives over iterative partnership program phases. To be fair, it is also true that the international challenges partners set out to conquer tend to persist as much as the partnership programs perpetuate.

Consistent with the theme that trust funds dominate the scene, a common scenario is for international partnership programs to last as long as their trust funds. There is no bright line rule to that effect—a trust-funded partnership program could, for example, readily convert to a coordination partnership (>@ Typology—Coordination Partnerships)—but the reality of what powers a partnership program (adequate funding) makes the end of the funding stream a logical end to the partnership program.

Then again, international partnership programs could, and probably should, anticipate their wind-downs. Creating a "sustainable" partnership program does not mean the partnership program itself has to last and last. It more sensibly means that the benefit and impact are sustained, ideally for those who were to be helped and with respect to the matter to be addressed, with lasting effect. The topic of exit in this sense is more about how to handle the partnership program, rather than just terminating or limiting the endeavor. Winding down in that sense may even become a question of ramping up—putting into place what all can ensure sustained impact, even after the partnership program comes to a close.

Winding down may be a matter of ramping up.

Ramp up to roll out; step up to step out.

This takes some thought, and the sooner considered, the smoother the ramp up and roll out. Is it capacity building to the point of maturity? Is it a catalytic effect to spur other endeavors? Is it a spin-off into more suitable hands? There are various ways to step up and step out, and each one is as contextual as the partnership program itself. This takes us back to the concept of life cycle that started this chapter. Exit necessarily comes at the end, but its seed and structure can already be positioned at the beginning.

Conclusion

Do what you want, say what you will, prepare what you can—it may never come out exactly as planned. Business review is an ongoing process, and business risks are ever in flux. International partnership programs require an alertness of engagement and a finger on the pulse by all partners; namely, by the people involved—the individual representatives and their respective managers. Keep it like rock and like water, with a systematic, disciplined approach for starting out and checking in, plus a reservoir of resources for issues as they arise. And keep an eye on the folks involved, which is what we take up in the next chapter.

5

PARTNERS AND PEOPLE

When it comes to opportunities and risks, it starts with the partners themselves. When it comes to institutional partners, as is structurally customary for international partnership programs, it also starts with the people who represent them. This can get interesting. Institutional partners come together for their institutional qualities, and the individual faces of those institutions are expected to reflect those qualities. And yet, we are all personalities, organic to the core. Here are worthwhile considerations to keep in mind when matching partners and their people for partnership program purposes.

Choosing Partners

Getting all partners on the same page, with key details, is an important preparatory test for the long term. Partners in international partnership programs are usually invited or self-selected, with a good dose of politics in the mix. The choice of partner may be a foregone conclusion, but there is still no point in establishing an international partnership program with partners that are not going to partner well.

International partnership programs are by-and-large informal arrangements, featuring a degree of flexibility that is not customary for partnerships that take the form of legally incorporated entities, like dedicated entity partnerships. Without the direct and intended applicability of domestic statutes and courts, partners rely more on each other to follow through on their commitments, intentions, and expectations. (>@ Partnering Internationally) More than most partners may realize, international partnership programs are for like-minded organizations that come together to achieve something they collectively believe in. (>@ Decision Making) They are not usually treated as resolution mechanisms for ironing out differences or debating societies focused on argumentation. Particularly in the development arena, the point is implementation and impact, and that requires a commonality of spirit and perspective.

With more attention to country ownership and developing country voice, and the proliferation of issue-oriented organizations, not to mention a general trend toward inclusivity, the partnership tent has gotten larger. What used to be a gentlemen's club—basically states and their multilaterals—is now a much broader palette of entities and interests. Nowadays the question of like-mindedness is not theoretical. Should we bring in the NGO that has been so critical in its views because it is also critical to get its buy-in? Is there enough common ground that consensus can be sustained?

This applies both upstream and downstream. Among the differences between procurement contracts and grants is that, broadly speaking, procurement selection is based on fair competition and grant selection is based on good fit. Grant recipients do not compete; they are chosen. It is accordingly not by chance that grant recipients—downstream beneficiaries—can be viewed as partners. (>@ Fund Use Responsibility—Implementation Responsibility)

Often the test is compatibility—not only with each other, but also with the ambitions of the partnership program. How much diversity of involvement and how many views can be included without jeopardizing the goals of the partnership program? How much diversity is needed for the best mix of inputs, comparative advantage, and legitimacy to realize the goals of the partnership? The sum total of partners in a partnership program needs to add up to promising prospects for implementation and achievement. Otherwise the whole endeavor is a non-starter.

THE DIVERSITY SWEET SPOT

LESS DIVERSITY   MORE DIVERSITY

poor buy-in   **promising prospects**   poor consensus

Engaging the Private Sector

As a special category of partner, private sector entities pose particular challenges for international partnership programs. Private sector companies and their associated foundations may have deep pockets and wish to contribute to international efforts. Or they may simply wish to collaborate with international partners without being donors, especially when it comes to setting standards or other policy initiatives that can affect their businesses. It is not always obvious that private sector participants are compatible with international partners in international partnership programs. They well may be, but this is a case of heightened scrutiny, where partners are justified in putting the question to the test. Even when interests appear to overlap, it is prudent to double check the real motives and confirm real compatibility of prospective private sector participants.

Double check the real motives; confirm real compatibility.

Including private players in international partnership programs is not a bad thing, and public-private partnerships can be a good thing. However, the healthy assumption should be that public and private entities come from different places when they come together. By their very DNA, private sector entities are a different species. They have to contend with mandatory rules and requirements—some statutory, some tax-driven, some jurisprudential—that set them apart from international and domestic public sector actors. This is true even for philanthropic actors, who are typically also motivated by their specific funding source, personality, legacy, or agenda. Even with shared goals, this sets them apart from public entities using public funds with direct and usually greater responsibilities to the public.

Without this public nexus, private sector entities are bound to have a different set of incentives, especially the for-profit entities. Corporate business interests, like maximizing profit and promoting shareholder gain, do not inherently dovetail with development or other public sector objectives. Commercial ventures, in particular, are in it for themselves, rather than primarily for others, if only because they are duty-bound to maximize their own value—potentially at the expense of others and always in competition with their competitors.

Needless to say, international partnership program engagement with the private sector should be consistent with the partnership program's interests and objectives. Concretely:

- Partnership program participants, including the supporting entity, should take care that partnership program goals are not undermined or abused by private sector business interests.

- Partnership program participants should ensure that private sector partners will not use the partnership program to seek a competitive advantage over non-partnering competitors.

- Partnership program participants should watch that other private sector entities not perceive selective or unfair bias on the part of the partnership program.

- Partnership program participants should avoid partnering with private sector entities that do not share their overall objectives and values or have questionable track records.

Level Playing Fields, Open Access, and Codes of Conduct

Business interests of prospective private sector partners merit more of a prior soak and scrub:

Level Playing Field: Selective invitations to participate can be a point of sensitivity in ensuring a level playing field. Although partnering is based on compatibility, that may not be enough in competitive settings. In effect, the choice of private sector partner is an anti-competitive exercise that could use an extra effort to avoid playing favorites. Maybe our director knows and can vouch for their CEO, or maybe they came to us with a great proposal, but that may not justify exclusive partnering, especially if competitor companies want a seat at the table, too.

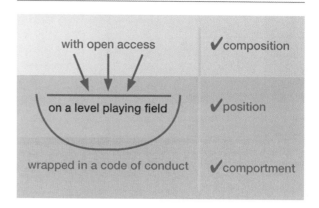

Open Access: Structurally speaking, a relatively safe approach is open access. Rather than be selective and exclusive, partners can design entry points that are open and inclusive. This eliminates the possibility of selective advantage because everyone can be advantaged by partnership program association. Then again, going this route can be hard, both because it can strain the numbers and work against compatibility. So the exercise is delicate and may mean a separate advisory body or working group as a private sector arm of the partnership program, or some other ringfenced, managed workaround. (>@ Trade-Offs—The Horizontal Buy-In Spectrum—Workarounds)

Code of Conduct: Another assist in managing private sector participation is a code of conduct. It need not be long or detailed, but is a way to set some ground rules or expectations or even just send signals for good behavior on the part of partners. Three simple statements can make this clear:

1 By participating in the partnership program, the partners are not endorsing any specific product, technology, service, project, activity, or event that is used, produced, or undertaken by any of the partners.

2 No partner may use, display, or otherwise manipulate the name, logo, or other material of the partnership program in public or private communications, advertisements, or in any other manner without prior consent of the [secretariat].

3 Cooperation among the partners in connection with the partnership program is not intended to confer special advantage or preference to any of the partners.

Along these lines, the association with private sector participants, especially for-profit entities, carries a special element of *reputational risk* for international partnership programs. Some supporting entities are known to undertake due diligence exercises on prospective private sector partners, including as cash donors or in-kind contributors, to make sure there are no skeletons in the closet, like ill-gotten gains or past practices, that would haunt their association later. It does not take a cynic to realize that a potential partner could be more interested in getting good press for marketing purposes or even whitewashing its past and rehabilitating its name than supporting a global public good. While dangled funds may be tempting, they may not be worth the reputational risk of NGOs calling out the association.

Whether private sector entities are more effectively crowded into partnership programs, or rather catalyzed or leveraged while still outside the partnership program, is something to be evaluated case-by-case. In defining what's in and what's out (>@ Typology—The Broader Landscape of Partnership Programs—Umbrella Arrangements), partnership programs can have close relationships or triggering effects with the private sector without bringing the entities themselves under the partnership program umbrella and attaching membership and brand. Private sector entities can contribute or collaborate without being "partners" per se. Or if they become partners, they can be donors without governing body membership; or they can be downstream implementers without being upstream decision makers; or they can provide expertise and sector-specific feedback in separate advisory processes or bodies without having core responsibilities. Figuring out the role of the private sector in international partnership programs can be a heightened exercise of the ten tips— like be clear, clean, modular, contextual, and aware—to align interests and incentives for impact. (>@ Ten Tried and True Tips)

Crowding In Expertise

Unless an international partnership program is purely political, it is about content. With content in the form of advocacy, knowledge, technical assistance, projects, or whatever else the partners have in mind, technical expertise has to reside somewhere in the partnership program. If the governing body has purview over technical aspects, whether strategic or operational, one might expect governing body participants to have the requisite expertise. However, since representatives are often assigned with other criteria in mind (>@ Governing Bodies—Participation), that might not be the case, and it might not be sufficient. Instead, there are other ways to make sure a partnership program has a functioning portfolio based on sound expertise.

Crowding in expertise can be a matter of both partners and people, in various combinations, with more or less structure. Three conduits for expert contributions are outlined here.

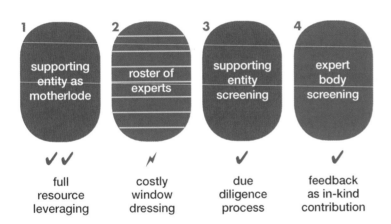

CROWDING IN TECHNICAL EXPERTISE

1. supporting entity as motherlode — ✔✔ full resource leveraging

2. roster of experts — ✗ costly window dressing

3. supporting entity screening — ✔ due diligence process

4. expert body screening — ✔ feedback as in-kind contribution

Secretariat

An immediate answer, the ultimate gap-filler, for all manner of expertise is the secretariat. If the supporting entity is willing—and especially if the partnership model is one-stop-shop—the secretariat (or trustee performing secretariat-type functions) can jump in. That may operate by default (>@ Custodial Effect), but, unless this is a limited secretariat, it is likely also by design. One of the great benefits of choosing international organizations like MDBs as supporting entities is the breadth and depth of expertise they offer. It is like tapping into a motherlode of resources.

In addition to robust operating frameworks that equip them as fiduciaries, major multilateral organizations also have country contacts, broad perspectives, international ownership and buy-in, implementation ability, and more. Especially rich is the extensive technical expertise in what can be an amazing aggregation of academic degrees and operational heft. If the subject matter is, say, sustainable fisheries, technical experts are available or can be hired as consultants to do the country-level studies or project implementation. If the partnership program needs better indicators for its results framework, those M&E experts are available, too. And if, heaven forbid, allegations of fraud or corruption surface, there is surely a department that deals with that—and will, if a trust fund is involved.

Technical expertise from supporting entities can be like an insurance policy, come what may. (>@ Custodial Effect) Implicitly or explicitly, the ability of a secretariat to play a substantive role can be a powerful factor in the choice of supporting entity. Once chosen, however, all partners should be clear on the degree of reliance partners intend to place on the secretariat's substantive contributions. For a solid foundation, supporting entities need to accept the ensuing degree of expectation and exposure, while all other partners need to accept the corollary degree of control and cost for this in-depth engagement.

Roster of Experts

Another way to draw in technical expertise is to set up a roster of experts that can be tapped as needed to provide informed feedback. This is not an additional entity or body, but rather a feature or activity that becomes part of the partnership program's process or work program. The list of experts can be controlled by the governing body or by the secretariat, depending on how much say the governing body wants. Specific assignments are usually implemented by the secretariat, which provides the administrative support, including the procurement logistics and legal entity status if contracting is involved.

While a roster of experts may sound helpful in theory, they are challenging in practice. For one, they can be costly, especially cumulatively, over time. For another, they are transaction intensive, as in pulling the list together, vetting and confirming participation, arranging engagements, chasing feedback, and, if applicable, making payments. This can be a relatively heavy lift for the secretariat. Third, they can produce significant decision-making delays for the time it takes to send materials out, get feedback in, distribute it, and absorb it, especially if some experts are less timely than others. And fourth, although touted for their objective or even independent advice, these expert lists are usually products of insider contacts and friendly views—not to mention that many experts tread lightly to get additional work and referrals—which undercuts the main purpose of seeking unvarnished views from the "outside." All in all, partnership programs might think twice about adding this to their structure. Those that have often end up wondering whether it was a good idea.

Secondary Body

A third way to bring in expertise is to create a secondary partnership body that convenes the expertise, as a support to the governing body and its decision flows. This secondary body can readily be tasked with providing preliminary comments that can serve as advice, or with making preliminary decisions—like picking out top candidates or top project proposals vis-à-vis governing body-approved criteria—that can serve as recommendations, to the governing body for a final decision. This kind of feedback or screening function can stay light, or it can be more structured. It can be performed by the secretariat/trustee supporting entity (part of the motherlode and fiduciary function) or a separate body with partners or other participants.

- **Supporting entity screening.** With minimal additional structure, the supporting entity may be willing to convene a group of expert staff internally, drawn from relevant units across the institution— either as a dedicated committee set up for the partnership program or as part of regular operational processes. If these staff do not charge their time to the trust fund, this becomes an in-kind contribution from the supporting entity, which also benefits in managing its risk profile. Normally, whenever the trustee or secretariat has implementation or supervision responsibility for partnership program activities, some internal pre-screening is already built into project procedures as part of the supporting entity's robust operating framework. Project appraisals can be diligent and detailed affairs, an impressive exercise in expertise. This kind of internally provided expert vetting is a major driver of one-stop-shop popularity and a major factor in choosing downstream fiduciaries for international platforms. The downside of this approach is that the supporting entity has complete say over the kinds of expertise brought to bear. Then again, that kind of complete delegation may be exactly what the partners want.

- **Expert body screening.** With somewhat more structure, if the point is outside expertise and the goal is broader credibility, the governing body can, with secretariat support, convene a group of external experts. A typical model is a technical advisory committee (TAC) that widens the circle of expertise directly associated with the partnership program. (>@ Trade-Offs—Horizontal Buy-In Spectrum) By tapping into relevant expertise, an expert body can go into the weeds and allow the main governing body to stay high level and strategic. It helps for the secretariat and governing body to have a presence on the expert body to keep inputs aligned within the broader partnership program. Overall, partnership programs can benefit from greater buy-in, the international community can benefit from greater collaboration, and participants may like being associated with a visible player in the arena. As a result, outside participation can also be in-kind if participants are willing and able to pay their way, often a non-issue for NGOs and private sector companies, but more of an issue when trying to ensure developing country voice. The downsides of a TAC include the logistics of supporting another body, plus no assurance of true expertise, especially if this is a self-selected group. The choice of expert may fall prey to some of the same challenges partners face with rosters of experts.

Less structure: lean on inhouse expertise.

More structure: convene external expertise.

Being a Good Partner

A big factor in successfully launching and running international partnership programs is strong partner motivation to combine resources, create multiplier effects, and succeed. In partnership programs that work, partners recognize that they rely on each other to make it work. Supporting entities, in particular, realize that partnership programs cannot work without their active outreach and ongoing engagement. Whatever the challenges, partners need to bring their good will and seek to be good partners.

Being a "good" partner means different things for different roles and can, as everything, vary according to the circumstances. However, generally speaking, it does not take contractual commitments and legal obligations for partners to understand the importance of stepping up to their respective roles. Just as engagement across the partnership program can bring synergies greater than the sum of the parts, weak links among partners can do the reverse. (What is the opposite of synergies? Dysergies? We need that word!)

For the lawyers in the room, this is not about legal line-drawing. When partners create expectations within the partnership program, even if they are not legally binding, they merit being viewed as commitments for practical purposes—certainly if the expectations generate reliance and letdowns portend reputational risk.

Even though international partners are institutional, and roles are functional, being a good partner also turns on the individual people involved, perhaps the most important factor of all. Putting the right people in the right positions can be the biggest determinant of a venture's success or failure, confirming the oldest truism in the world: that people count. Partnership programs that cannot get off the ground may be more challenged by lack of suited personnel or lack of necessary expertise—including structuring and design expertise—than any other inherent problem. Look to see if the working staff, including the policy and legal teams, understand what they are doing. For partnership programs that teeter from one crisis to another, spin their wheels or unravel, look around as well. Likely a key individual or two are not up to the task, or loyalties are conflicted (>@ Secretariats—Embedded, Inhouse Secretariats—Challenges), or understanding is limited (>@ Governing Bodies—Participation), or staffing is stretched (>@ Secretariats—Inhouse Secretariat Roles).

There is no substitute for a good mix of partners and people to get the job done. Neither structure and design, nor funds and events, can supplant the need for compatible partners and conscientious engagement, or for competent staff with relevant experience, requisite skill sets, and ready institutional support.

compatible partners

+

conscientious engagement

+

competent staff

"Good" in Practical Terms

What are the hallmarks of a good partner?

- **For the supporting entity,** it is better to be direct and straightforward about what is available and feasible, rather than be coy, complex, or confused. Just do it or say it; this is Relationship Building 101. It is not inherently bad to have restraints and requirements that affect the partnership program, but it is bad if they pop up to everyone's surprise long down the road or result in long, unanticipated delays for getting things done.

- **For the donors,** it is much appreciated if funds are as free and clear as possible, reflecting the pooled effort and enabling core support, rather than restricted, conditioned, tied, earmarked, or even preferenced. This may not always be possible, given domestic constraints, but donor-specific demands beyond the collective framework are usually cumulatively unwieldy and not scalable. That can put a drag on everything.

- **For the governing body,** it is encouraged to take the assignment seriously. This is in fact a real role with real responsibility, to whatever degree agreed by the partners. Free riders are not helpful when the point is collaborative input. Holdouts are also not helpful if objections are more for posturing than substance. Constructive governance engagement does not come by osmosis, but takes continuity, preparation, and follow through.

- **For the secretariat,** it can be a thankless job, as with administrative and clerical staff around the world. Secretariat functions are usually more multidimensional than any other role—stretched in all directions, looking both inward and outward; expected to be organized, fair, diplomatic, caring, consequential, and responsive; charged with compliance, consistency, and the ability to turn on a dime. Proactive, protective, pro-partnership secretariats do all this, all at once. As far as roles go, this one is often underappreciated, but hopefully not under-resourced.

- **For the trustee,** it helps to project and provide competence and confidence. Even if not part of the job description, trust is something partners look for in a trustee. When a trustee does not run a tight ship, in good times and in bad, the rest of the partnership program may slop around and drift into a sandbank or two, with ensuing ripple effects. As the contractual linchpin, for itself and other supporting entity roles, the trustee has to know and manage the agreed terms.

- **For the downstream fiduciary,** best be all over it. This is where the rubber hits the road, where funds get used and things happen. Well-cooked going in, well-monitored throughout, well-adjusted as needed, and well-reported up the chain. Whether the partnership program achieves anything, or instead corrects course to make it work or learns lessons to make it worthwhile, that rests first and foremost on the shoulders of those working downstream.

These are of course pretty subjective assessments, and there is much more to each role than noted here. Plus every case is different. However, even just letting the question of what makes for a good partner percolate may help lead to better partners for better partnerships. And if the upshot is raised expectations, good partners will also seek to be clear from the get-go about what they can and will, or won't, do.

Conclusion

If international partnership programs are understood to be organic, then it is no stretch to appreciate partner behavior, as institutions and individuals, as part of that fabric. It also becomes clear that this fabric, which holds everything together, is a combination of culture and commonality. And that points to an appreciation of partnership programs as an accretive exercise, where continuity counts and history matters, where experiences are shared and lessons learned, where time and effort put in over time determine what comes out.

If it is worth attending meetings, it is worth attending to who attends. If it is worth investing in the endeavor, it is worth investing in the partners and their people as the center and soul of the partnership program. At the end of the day, partners are personalities, and the sum of them, for better or worse, makes the partnership program.

Convening in a combination of culture and commonality, where continuity counts and history matters.

PART 3

KEY ELABORATIONS

In this Part, we take some deeper dives on select topics that can make a big difference.

1 Partnering Internationally

Benefits of partnering in the international arena are best preserved if they are better appreciated, including in terms of what law applies and how that affects governing bodies.

2 Decision Making

Here we explore the virtues of consensus decision making and the benefits of no objection decision making, breaking each mode down and showing exactly how it works.

3 Supporting Entities

In full recognition of the central supporting entity role, we unpack what that means for partners, including the supporting entities themselves.

4 Custodial Effect

In this chapter, we highlight the unacknowledged role of the partnership program "custodian," which usually attaches to the legal entity function and fills in as needed.

5 Synergistic Conflicts

By taking a closer look at "conflicts of interest" in partnership programs, we discover inherent and intentional features that are in fact valuable partnership synergies.

6 Trustee Types

From full trustees to limited trustees, and modular combinations and downstream variations, different options let partners position trustees to fit partnership program purposes.

7 Use of Funds

This chapter gives us a chance to consider fund use not just as a trust fund matter but more broadly from partnership program perspectives.

8 Fund Use Responsibility

As a corollary to fund use, here we look at different kinds of responsibility: implementation responsibility, two kinds of fiduciary responsibility, and collective oversight responsibility.

1 PARTNERING INTERNATIONALLY

A salient theme throughout this book has been the open, creative space the international arena affords partners, particularly when considered in relation to partnering initiatives that are embodied in legally incorporated structures beholden to domestic laws. This assertion deserves some backing and unpacking. First, we can consider what source of law actually applies to international partnership programs. And second, we can appreciate how that particularly impacts representation on the governing body, where most of the partners participate.

Applicable Law

Is Anybody Home? That might have been a more apt title for this section about what legally governs international partnership programs—if only to grab your attention. I can already see the non-lawyers scooting for the aisle. If you are tempted to skip to the next section, you may be forgiven, since in practice most partners seem to have skipped out on this subject as well. But stick with it for a moment; it may prove worth your while.

To put it bluntly, this topic is generally so orphaned that not only is the answer missing but the question is usually AWOL, too. Most international partnership programs do not specify the laws by which they are governed, not just because partners do not know, but because they do not even ask. The best we can usually do in this situation is extrapolate—and of course, alternatively, hope it never matters.

What is going on with this obliviousness? For starters, partners rarely need to consider the topic because it rarely comes up—which is, in a way, a good thing. International partnership programs may not be saints, but to date, they have been remarkably free of legal claims. They have had the luxury of coasting on mostly unchallenged track records, feeling assured that if issues arise, they will get managed, and if claims are brought, they will get resolved. With so few points of contention and so little potential consequence in practice (knock on wood), there is practically no need to talk about governing law, or so it seems.

Should we care? The only times governing law may really matter is when there is a dispute between partners or a claim by outsiders (so-called third parties) that needs resolution. Even though governing law also has implications for validity, effectiveness, execution, and interpretation of partnership documents, the rubber only hits the road when parties in disagreement or others with a claim want to pin responsibility or liability. The fortuitous infrequency of such scenarios in international partnership programs has thus far allowed partners to treat this as a non-issue. But good luck is not good practice. So let's review a few things about how this works in context, while considering both potential benefits of operating by default and potential risks of inattention.

Extrapolating

What we can determine in the absence of partners having determined it for themselves?

1. **By Nature.** A ready answer of what legally applies is that international law governs the agreements of subjects of international law, be they states or international (intergovernmental) organizations created by states or other international organizations, unless otherwise specified. That holds for a sizeable majority of partnership programs that engage only international players with international legal personalities, who are primarily operating in the international arena. It may not hold as well for non-international subjects that join in (like private foundations, NGOs, CSOs, and private companies) or for others that are just affected by international partnership programs (like beneficiaries). But even if international law does not apply to a partnership program per se, it is always a backdrop that may imply various rights and obligations for its international partners.

2. **By Default.** International law as governing law is also a good assumption to the extent it may afford real benefits to the partners. Or to put it in the reverse, at least in the case of international, intergovernmental organizations, because they are characteristically not bound by any domestic legal environment, they can avoid the more prescriptive and constraining laws of national jurisdictions. Without national moorings, international law can apply by default. Indeed, in being an "international" partnership, an important way to keep a level playing field among members is to steer clear of any specific national context.

3. **By Supporting Entity.** The central role of supporting entities (>@ Supporting Entities; >@ Custodial Effect) does a lot to characterize the governing law of international partnership programs. If the supporting entity is an international organization, itself governed by international law, this will color much of the operative legal environment. To the extent the partnership program consists of the supporting entity's work program— particularly as convener, secretariat, trustee, governing body chair, implementer, or other roles that go to the crux of partnership program operations—international law already applies in this way.

Good luck is not good practice.

International law:

1. by nature
2. by default
3. by supporting entity
4. by preservation
5. by half

4. **By Preservation.** When considering where international partnership programs are the most vulnerable, at least with respect to potential disputes with third parties, an alert lawyer will likely talk to you about privileges and immunities (P&I). To the extent that P&I applies, international partnership programs operate in a protected zone—as to staff, archives, property, and more. (>@ Supporting Entities—Basic Elements) International partners may assume they will always have P&I protection, but this is being increasingly challenged. Come crunch time, you can expect partners to try to enforce their special international P&I status if they can.

5. **By Half.** Admittedly, positioning international law as governing law is only half an answer, since any general reference to "international law" is itself a source of ambiguity. Without going into a treatise here, suffice it to say it is usually a bundling of various sources, including the institutional rules of the parties by virtue of their governing documents, relevant treaties, customary international law as reflected in broad international practice, and gap-filling, ground-truthing general principles of law. Taken as a whole, that is not all too precise.

Articulating

A natural place for partners to specify the choice of governing law would be in the agreements or documents that establish the international partnership program—the constitutive documents, like charters, and, in the case of trust-funded partnership programs, the contribution agreements. However, when international partnership programs, particularly their governing bodies, arise informally (>@ Governing Bodies—Informal vs. Formal), there is no driver to direct attention to the choice of applicable law. Being informal, partners tend to focus on the good (coming together), not the bad (falling apart), and usually don't go there (no prenups).

Ambiguous silence, rather than articulated clarity.

As a result, charters set out all sorts of basic understandings, but typically not the applicable law. In part, that is because adopted charters are not usually thought of as agreements, at least not formally signed ones. Without a signature, a charter might not even make it to the legal department. And that presumes a partnership program even has a charter or equivalent document, which, although considered good practice, is not a given. If partners are silent about their partnering generally, it's safe to assume they are silent about their applicable law.

Contribution agreements, as originating documents for many trust-funded partnership programs, have a better chance of explicitly referring to applicable law. In contrast to charters, which may have ambiguous legal status (binding or nonbinding? expectations or commitments?), contribution agreements are the real deal with formal signatures. Well, except when they are *not* intended to be agreements. As it turns out, the informality of international partnership programs can carry right over into the signed legal terms. No one wants to give contribution agreements treaty status (for a variety of reasons, including to avoid treaty formalities). For some, that includes overt measures to avoid contractualizing (like calling it an "arrangement," rather than an "agreement"). Referring to applicable law would be tantamount to admitting legal agreement status. As a result, when it comes to common denominators, getting everyone on the same page for the governing law in trust fund contexts often equals silence. Everyone shares in the ambiguity.

This kind of studied ambiguity can work as long as nothing goes awry. It can, however, be a liability if something does. For partners that want a lower risk profile, there is room to consider the question of applicable law, but it first needs to be asked. If that is not done early on by the partners themselves, those asking may someday come from outside with third party claims. It may also be that the spirit of inclusion, by bringing more and more non-international participants into the international partnership program fold, will provoke a closer look at the governing law that partners collectively choose for themselves in partnering.

Governing Body Ramifications

When governing bodies meet in international space, they still want their feet on the ground. We have talked about the kinds of reinforcement that can help representatives stand firmly with one foot in their home entity and one foot in the international partnership program, bridging the two. (>@ Governing Bodies—Reinforcement) They take their home identity with them into the informal governing body and have to square the two aspects in their day-to-day. Fortunately, this is relatively easy when international or national civil servants take up roles in informal, international partnership programs, where the fit is more natural. We can readily see this by comparison with dedicated entity partnerships. (>@ Typology—The Even Broader Landscape of Structured Partnerships)

Avoiding Dual Loyalties

Partnering through dedicated entity partnerships, with corporate governance, may be problematic for international partners. Asking for dual loyalty can be asking for trouble, and partnerships that convene in the form of incorporated legal entities, like dedicated entity partnerships, spell that kind of trouble for national governments and multilaterals trying to join corporate boards. National and international civil servants generally owe their loyalty to their respective institutions, even when corporate entities, with their statutorily imposed fiduciary duties, want that loyalty instead. (>@ Governing Bodies—Applicable Duties)

This gets particularly tough for international partners whose governing documents require sole loyalty to themselves, leaving little room for loyalty to anything else. For example, the International Bank for Reconstruction and Development (World Bank) Articles of Agreement, Section 5(c) states, "The President, officers and staff of the Bank, in the discharge of their offices, **owe their duty entirely to the Bank and to no other authority**. Each [country] member of the Bank shall respect the international character of this duty and shall refrain from all attempts to influence any of them in the discharge of their duties." (Emphasis added.)

By contrast, informal partnership programs allow partners to convene in a group without giving up their original and primary duties of loyalty and care to their own entities. Nor do they require fealty to the partnership. International partnership programs are normally gatherings or alliances around a common purpose, where each partnering entity keeps its own separate identity without being legally subsumed into or overridden by a partnership program identity. Individual representatives can make decisions, joining in the consensus or not, in the interests of their respective member entities without running afoul of any fiduciary duties to the partnership program. There are no such fiduciary duties, and there are no outside legal statutes or other imposed sources that creep in to tell international partners what kinds of duties they have to each other or toward their informal, international partnerships.

In practice, representatives sitting on governing bodies usually have their partnership program's interests at heart, even if they are not duty-bound. This works because partners convene on the basis of common interests and, if the partnership program is well-established, a solid common foundation. However, at the margin, in the event of conflict, a representative is free to follow directives or comply with requirements from home even knowing this might damage the business of the partnership program or the interests of other partners. If, for example, a representative decides not to approve a project for any reason, on the basis of instructions from the home ministry, that representative can legitimately block the approval, even if that goes against the interests of the partnership program as a whole.

A Note on Terminology

Because they are not incorporated entities, international partnership programs are encouraged to avoid corporate terms like *board*, *directors*, or *CEO*, which flag corporate duties and potential liabilities. Better words include *council*, *committee*, *members*, and *program heads*. Although high-profile, branded initiatives may wish to emphasize their importance and credentials (good enough to be corporate), or curry an air of independence (good enough to stand on their own), there is something to be said for low-key language that reflects the advantages of being an international partnership program.

In fact, international partnership programs do not have their own interests as such, at least not in a way that needs to be observed by the partners. A partnership program's interests are but a summation of each partner's interests and do not somehow morph into a separate set of interests that pose legal obligations. This reflects the informal nature of international partnership programs, without a legal personality or its own legal identity as a partnership program. The possibility, for example, that not doing a proposed project could hurt the partnership program is therefore not a factor in terms of legal duties. In international partnership programs, representatives have full discretion to act in the complete interest of their own member entities. Whether they end up choosing to act in a way that harms the partnership program is another matter. (>@ Partners and People—Choosing Partners)

Managing Corporate Settings

As we've seen, international partners engaged in international partnership programs present a natural match, especially when it comes to governing bodies. Like-minded and like-situated partners sit well together. But we have also seen that international partners can be relative misfits in corporate settings. (>@ Governing Bodies—Informal vs. Formal) And yet, blocking international partners from the corporate boards of dedicated entity partnerships is not a good answer when everyone wants to collaborate. We can keep underscoring that the structure of dedicated entity partnerships is not conducive to international characteristics, but there will still be cases where international partners want to sit on corporate boards as partners of—and part of—domestically incorporated legal entities.

So how do you fit a round peg into a square hole? Simply ignoring the matter is not very buttoned-down. Since most domestic, statutory regimes expect full fealty from board members to the interests of the incorporated entity, anyone who is not free and clear to consistently attend to the interests of the corporate

> Like-minded and like-situated partners sit well together.

entity takes a risk sitting on the board. And making this common practice does not make it less acute, especially if there has been no due diligence on corporate duties and liabilities in the relevant jurisdiction or confirmation that relevant insurance policies are in place. The assumption seems to be that interests will always align, and claims will never be made. That is, however, a big assumption, especially when personal liability is at stake.

What to do? One compromise is to have international participants, like international organizations, sit as observers, without decision-making rights or responsibilities. This is often the quickest, least controversial route to a resolution—but potentially at the cost of real influence. Another avenue used by some international organizations is to hire consultants for designated board positions, rather than assign regular staff. But here, too, this may be formality over function, since even those consultants are staff.

The other approach is by assertion. As with conflicts of interest, which this in effect is (interests of the corporate entity conflicting with interests of the representative's home base), a promising avenue is to disclose and manage. (>@ Synergistic Conflicts) The key disclosure statement is that the individual representative of an international member entity is sitting as an *institutional representative in an institutional capacity*, not in a personal capacity. This puts other board members on notice and may provide some breathing room for international representatives to stay true to their international status. It may not override statutory law, but makes clear that the international member entity expects to bring its interests to bear. Ideally, this is not just a verbal disclosure but something that surfaces in the dedicated entity partnership's formal articles, bylaws, *statuts*, or the like. This kind of disclosure can also connect back to any P&I protections by reinforcing that international representatives, by participating, are doing the work of their international member entities. (>@ Secretariats—Embedded, Inhouse Secretariats)

Conclusion

In the international arena, where partners collaborate on achieving global public goods and eliminating global public bads, along with many other efforts, creative partnering ranges from structures in international spaces where domestic laws do not reside to places where domestic law and international characteristics overlap. Whether an international partnership effort is framed by the absence or presence of applicable domestic laws has considerable bearing on how partners can engage with each other. International partnership programs usually find their comfort zone outside of legally incorporated structures that answer to national legal contexts. That is where international partners can truly be themselves, including with duties of loyalty to their own institutions and P&I protections to boot.

This, however, implies more certainty than may be warranted. It takes some guesswork to answer the question of applicable governing law for many international partnership programs, even after considering who the partners are and what the set-up is. As with much about international partnership programs, much may depend on the particular circumstances. Where partners see no clear answer, even the question is probably out of sight. That is all well and good if all stays good. Sooner or later, however, the question may come home to roost, at which point partners will be looking for answers.

International partners can be themselves in the international arena.

2 DECISION MAKING

Partnership programs are by definition undertaken in partnership, and that typically means some degree of shared decision making in ongoing operations. (>@ Structure—Collectivizing) Most partnership programs are a combination of shared and unilateral decisions. Sometimes only inputs are shared, where the governing body is advisory, but this chapter focuses on governing bodies that make partnership program decisions, whether high-level strategic, micromanaged, or otherwise. The usual partnership programs delegate fiduciary and implementation responsibility to specific functions—such as the secretariat, trustee, and other downstream fiduciaries—carried by specific entities. These functions and entities then make their own decisions in line with their responsibilities, sometimes with partnership input, but primarily without. Governing body decision making, by contrast, is multilateral. Although decisions are typically teed up by other partnership functions—for example, in the form of work plans or project proposals, via the trustee, secretariat, or downstream fiduciaries—the deciding yea or nay is collective.

What Matters?

When establishing international partnership programs, participants not only agree on who makes decisions about what but also in what manner. In other words, partners need to decide—as part of the initial design—what method of shared decision making they will use. To this end:

1 Partners want to be **clear**, so the rules can be followed, not made up or reinterpreted later when it comes time to decide.

2 Partners want to be **efficient**, so incentives and procedures accommodate relevant views and result in outcomes.

3 Partners want to **protect** themselves, so their exposure to and association with the partnership program can be managed.

With these goals in mind, should international partners choose voting rules with majority or supermajority control and dissenting views? Or is it better to require consensus, which allows individual vetoes? With consensus, any governing body member can affect every other member, since just one member can override all others by blocking a decision. However, without consensus, all other members can affect any member, since a fraction of members can force decisions that another member does not condone. On the basis of partnership program values and partner risk profiles, what level of decision making allows every decision maker to have what all partners consider to be an *adequate* voice?

It bears repeating:

A partnership works best if it works for all partners.

In the private sector, where productivity and profitability are paramount, decision making on corporate boards usually features a voting mechanism. Voting mechanisms are based on numbers and allow fractions of all voters (factions or not) to disagree. Voting mechanisms can be set up to always reach a result—no tie, no stalemate, no paralysis, just an outcome. In this way, voting ensures finality, even if that ends up creating winners and losers. In the public sector, however, international partnership programs emphasize collaboration and inclusion. This calls for a different kind of decision making, one that prioritizes harmony and collective buy-in.

In international partnership programs, the answer is usually that every decision maker gets a dispositive voice. Enter consensus decision making that is based on shared consent and leaves no one behind.

Consensus (Physical Decision Making)

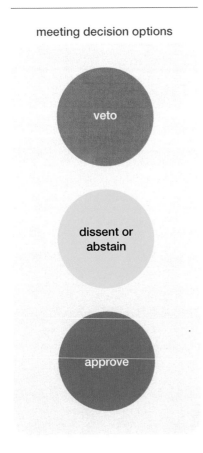

CONSENSUS DECISION MAKING

meeting decision options

veto

dissent or abstain

approve

Consensus decision making is by definition collaborative—the goal is to reach consensus. It puts a premium on recognizing each partner and valuing each voice. It presumes a certain amount of common ground, always helped by like-mindedness around the table (>@ Partners and People—Choosing Partners), but also puts in the effort to make up the difference. It is not willing to leave viewpoints behind if they are significant enough to hold up a decision. In the spirit of cooperation, which includes balancing the needs of individual partners, consensus also allows for shades of gray. If needed, each decision-making member has an effective veto. However, each decision-making member also has the right to dissent on the record without vetoing, as well as the right to abstain on the record without deciding. Effective consensus decision making allows for gradations.

A controversial decision point can be handled first through discussion, to try to reach common ground, and then through differing positions on the record in the minutes, before it results in a blocked decision. Even after a blocked decision, partners can continue the search for common ground to reach agreement. This gives the governing body chair and all the members a number of variations and iterations to reach an outcome that lets the partnership proceed as a whole. This assures solid buy-in, however assembled, before proceeding. The only scenario without solid buy-in is one that does not proceed, but even this outcome retains an invitation to try some more and the possibility that some commonly agreed solution can still be found. In this way, consensus decision making is a deliberative process as much as a decision point.

In maximizing buy-in and minimizing blockage, consensus is supremely suited to international partnership programs. Not surprisingly, most international partnership programs in the development arena use consensus decision making, although not always with the degree of clarity and modularity presented here. Even international partnership programs with voting tend to strive for consensus before taking any actual votes.

Yes Words

Back to terminology, what is the difference between *approve* and *endorse*? How about *adopt* and *ratify*? The bottom line is nothing; they all add up to the same thing: that the outcome is accepted. They each reflect a decision point. Granted, there are slight nuances as to when different terms are best. *Adoption* typically describes a legal procedure for a document or amendment to the document. *Endorse* and *ratify* are usually used in reaction, as a response to something already decided or developed. The critical point is whether the decision-making mode, whatever verb is used, gives the ability to veto or object and thereby block the decision. *Approve* in that sense is not the only label for signaling decision-making status. Even governing bodies that merely *endorse* or *ratify* have approval rights if they can choose not to.

Sample Consensus Clause for Charters

It does not take much text to capture gradations of consensus. The following can be added to the charter of an international partnership program:

> *Decisions by the Governing Body are made by consensus. Consensus need not reflect unanimity. A dissenting Member [decision maker] may choose to state an objection to be recorded in the meeting minutes, while also clarifying whether the statement is for the record only or intended to preclude agreement. Alternatively, a Member may choose to abstain. The Chair articulates the consensus view.*

In making consensus decisions, three features are key:

1. Consensus flexibly need not mean absolute unanimity, but can **allow for dissent and abstention**, as long as the dissenting view is not presented as an objection to block an agreement.
2. Consensus prophylactically **acts as a safeguard**, allowing every decision-making partner to have an effective veto to ensure that only collectively acceptable decisions go forward.
3. Consensus democratically gives every decision-making partner an **equal veto** to decide, as well as some non-decision-making partners an **equal voice** to contribute.

Just as there is no one solution for development, there is no one model for partnering. It depends on what the partners want, reflecting what their individual interests and requirements can sustain in a harmonized, shared setting. This usually requires sustained consensus, enough to create a sustainable partnership platform. Partnership programs can remain stable and effective over time with an equitable approach where all governing body decision makers have the same status, and where partnership activities proceed only if all key partners agree. Adhering to consensus decision making may not always achieve the lowest common denominators, (>@ Trade-Offs—The Central Harmonization Spectrum) but it preserves enough granularity to sustain partner interest and still meet shared objectives.

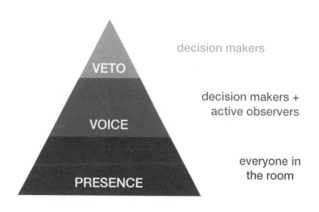

decision makers

decision makers + active observers

everyone in the room

An effective culture of consensus is based on informed, transparent decision making. Consensus approvals are meaningful if they reflect underlying agreement. The process of establishing consensus starts long before the governing body meets, and often continues well after. True consensus is typified by iterative decision making that is as much bottom up (for example, with broad downstream input and hands-on secretariat preparation) as top down (for example, with key partner/donor support and chair management). The pressure to keep secretariats lean belies their critical value in managing the wide coordination needed for effective and sustained consensus to undergird ongoing operations. (>@ Secretariats—Lessons Learned) Maintaining consensus both enables and promotes leeway and adaptability over time, with the flexibility to make changes along the way and the buy-in to keep those changes grounded. (>@ Like Rock, Like Water)

> **Consensus is common ground to sustain a cooperative approach toward collective action.**

The Virtues of Consensus Decision Making

It is worth elaborating why consensus works so well for international partnership programs, especially compared to voting arrangements. Four dynamics come to mind:

1. **Consensus encourages a constructive spirit.** Particularly with respect to international partnership programs, consensus is well-suited to partner objectives. These initiatives are usually designed for collective action precisely to enable partners to coordinate views and activities on a common platform, to leverage each other as a collective. This is best served by full consensus. When partners give themselves license to proceed on something less than consensus, the collaborative nature of the endeavor becomes diluted or even frayed. Dissenting partners can become corrosive over time, undermining the common foundation, collective buy-in, and collaborative results. International partners usually consider it worth the extra effort to attain and preserve consensus so as to promote the very collaboration they staked out as part of their original goal. When partners worry from inception that consensus will paralyze decision making or create inefficiencies and delays, it is worth asking whether the group that will be convening has enough common ground to sustain a cooperative approach toward collective action. (>@ Partners and People—Choosing Partners)

2. **Consensus creates a level playing field among partners.** In an environment where questions of voice, rank, hierarchy of fund flows, and prerogative have some bearing, consensus-based decision making gives baseline comfort that no single partner can be overruled. The tyranny of the majority (or two-thirds or whatever fraction) is never a factor with consensus. Every voice has a full say, in each case equal to all the others. Admittedly, international partners have to be comfortable with this paradigm—donors, for example, have to leave room for seated beneficiary countries to hold sway on decisions—and this puts a premium on diplomacy as a way to have influence and reconcile differences. Consensus ultimately puts real authority behind the rhetoric of inclusion, if that is what the partners truly intend.

3. **Consensus protects partners from unacceptable positions and outcomes.** By requiring approval (or at least no blocking disapproval) from every partner, and by validating disapproval (the blocking kind) by any partner, consensus effectively means that every partner has a veto. As potent as this may be, it also tends to inculcate a culture of engagement—positioning matters well in advance, massaging differences with greater attention, repositioning proposals with constructive deliberation—that rarely culminates in a final veto. And yet, a potential veto provides a valuable backstop for every partner seeking to manage its interests, even when kept in the back pocket. Consensus is the ultimate diplomatic lever to democratically ensure every partner's interests.

4. **Consensus is a primary risk management tool for supporting entities.** Supporting entities have a special need to manage their risk profiles. For entities providing trustee and secretariat functions, it is essential that the partnership program stay on track. The supporting entity's close identification with the partnership program—including associated exposure to other partner actions—heightens its need to help shape the partnership program and match its accountability with authority. (>@ Supporting Entities—Basic Elements—Risk Profile) If the supporting entity positions itself as a decision maker within the governing body, consensus can be its protector—not as a special right of consent, golden share, or unilateral veto, but more diplomatically, on a par with every other partner.

No Objection (Virtual Decision Making)

As a rule, international partnership programs also allow shared decision making to occur outside of physical meetings. The occasional partnership program relies entirely on shared decision making without meetings, but that is still more common than partnership programs that do not allow any decision making between meetings. It is simply too easy for partners to make decisions by email or other electronic platforms to preclude this virtual option. Sooner or later, partners will need to make decisions on matters for

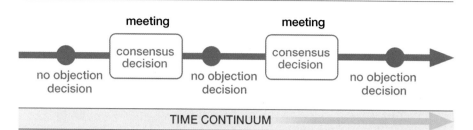

TIME CONTINUUM

which the time and expense of a whole meeting is not justified. And yet, the mission presses and work goes on. With virtual, electronic decision making, partners can provide their input from anywhere at any time within a prescribed timeframe in response to a prescribed request.

This is known as "no objection" decision making, so called because the absence of an objection creates a decision. It is completely straightforward in principle, but can be delicate in the execution. (>@ Ten To-Do's next page) Someone has to be in charge, with an active hand in the logistics. This active management lets the deciding partners stay passive. That active player is usually the secretariat, in which case the secretariat's roles and responsibilities listed in the charter would include "handling no objection processes."

No objection processes operate just like consensus at a physical meeting. If no one blocks the proposal, the matter is approved. All decision makers are responsible for deciding their position within the set time period in the same way that they cannot undo a meeting consensus after the meeting is over. All governing body participants—decision-making and non-decision-making—are invited to weigh in during meetings and over email. Only decision-making members can veto in physical meetings or object in no objection processes.

Note in particular that secretariats are not responsible for confirming that recipients actually received or read no objection request emails, as long as they went to the addresses provided by the participants. It is usually advisable to make governing body members and observers responsible for getting the proper email addresses for their designated representatives to the secretariat, after which the secretariat simply sends accordingly.

Virtually, you can respond from anywhere at any time—or not.

────────── ● ──────────

What Is the Difference Between Consensus and No Objection Decision Making?

It's simple—and good to distinguish to keep things clear. Consensus decisions happen during **physical meetings in real time**, whether together in a room or connected by audio, video, or other technology. No objection decisions happen as **digital exchanges over time**, usually through a string of emails with everyone involved on the same distribution list. Both are finite processes with set participants on a set decision point with set procedures in a set time period. So the only real difference is simultaneous, contemporaneous, physical space vs. iterative, extenuated, virtual space.

────────── ● ──────────

The Ten To-Do's of No Objection Decision Making

In basic outline, the no objection procedure goes like this:

1 The secretariat sends an email to all governing body decision makers and observers with a decision request, stating the decision point in clear terms, specifying a set review period, and including any accompanying documentation. For this purpose, the secretariat should keep a current list of regular governing body participants, as the designated representatives for both decision-making members and non-decision-making standing observers.

2 The set time period runs, during which time any decision maker can email back an objection (cc'ed to the whole group). An objection is entirely within the decision maker's discretion.

3 Within the set time period, decision makers and observers can also send questions and comments, which can elicit further reactions. Questions and comments by themselves do not amount to objections.

4 The secretariat keeps tabs on email traffic, making sure all exchanges are visible to the full distribution list.

5 By the end of the set time period, it remains up to each decision maker to decide whether to object (or not). Decision makers (but not observers) can object and block a decision for any reason, including while waiting for an acceptable answer to a question, needing more time or information for review, or with a request to postpone the decision to a physical meeting.

6 Decision makers have multiple options before the period runs out: (1) they can state objections intended to block decisions; (2) they can rescind their own previously stated objections; (3) they can state dissenting views without objecting; (4) they can abstain on the record; or (5) last but not least, they can effectively abstain/tacitly approve by simply staying silent.

NO OBJECTION DECISION MAKING

virtual decision options

1. state an objection
2. rescind an objection
3. dissent without objecting
4. abstain on the record
5. stay silent to proceed

7 The secretariat manages the process, including potentially extending the review period to deal with feedback (assuming the extension does not cause other problems) or restarting the review with a new time period for a reformulated request. For aspects that are controversial, the secretariat usually engages the chair and potentially all the members to find a way forward.

8 Decision makers who stay silent are presumed to have no objection. This is not necessarily the same as approving, but may of course be perceived as approval. As long as (1) the secretariat sent the email to the right representatives (this goes to the role of partners to provide proper email addresses); and (2) all recipients were privy to all subsequent exchanges (this goes to the role of the secretariat to keep tabs), then failure to object within the set time period is considered a final lack of objection.

9 The decision point is considered (deemed) approved at the end of the set time period if there has been no objection.

10 Once the set time period has passed, the secretariat, potentially in coordination with the chair, informs all participants of the outcome with an email confirming the decision (or not).

Voting (Not Recommended)

For all the reasons that consensus and no objection decisions fit the profile of collaborative, cooperative international partnership programs, voting does not. Voting opens the door to dissenting partners and minority blocs, which ushers in disruption and divisiveness. Holding a minority view in a partnership program can become unsustainable, if only because it associates the partner with something disagreeable (or even unacceptable) and may pose a reputational risk for that partner. If material enough, a partner can presumably pull out of the partnership program when that happens. Even if partnership program documents do not explicitly contain exit provisions, international partnership programs are informal and consensual, and no one is forced to stay. (>@ Risk and Review—At the Back End)

Voting is a potential way to weed out those who do not agree, but not a way to maintain inclusivity or achieve buy-in. It can also get especially complicated for dissatisfied donors, whose funds may continue to finance partnership program activities (as part of commingled trust fund pools) and, once committed downstream, cannot simply be reclaimed. Usually only pro rata funds that are uncommitted can be withdrawn, sometimes not until the trust fund closes. This can mean once a donor, always a donor, even after an exit.

Interestingly, many decision-making bodies that have voting mechanisms on paper use consensus decision making in practice, precisely because of the divisiveness caused by overriding objections. And yet, partners may say that consensus is not good or safe enough, that it risks paralyzing the partnership program. They may be willing to strive for consensus, but still view voting as a necessary last resort. But let's think about that. If business paralysis is really a concern, it may be that there are not sufficiently like-minded, like-purposed partners around the table. It may be that the premise of the partnership needs revisiting. International partnership programs are not for-profit concerns that have to answer to corporate shareholders, where governing body members have legal duties to the partnership entity, or public markets. They are instead informal arrangements that intentionally allow selectively chosen decision makers to reflect their own interests and, more importantly, can usually afford to prioritize consensus.

> Dissenting partners and minority blocs can lead to division and disruption.

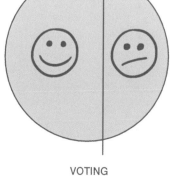

CONSENSUS   VOTING

Far from being an effective last resort, voting as a way to resolve divided partner views can instead become a winding downward spiral for the partnership program. However, if a voting option is nonetheless considered imperative, there may be some ways to cushion the impact—not that any of these steps make voting any more recommended:

1 Supporting entities managing their exposure risk may feel that they, in particular, need to keep a veto. An explicit clause can indicate that any vote to proceed must include the supporting entity, or at least that this rule applies in certain circumstances—like any time a decision point affects supporting entity-managed trust funds or potentially conflicts with supporting entity policies and procedures. This effectively gives the supporting entity a special right of consent (or special veto), an approach that can be used for other partners with other sensitivities as well.

2 If differing views are endemic to a particular category of partner—like private sector companies that have competing business interests—and those differences can be isolated from or withstood by the rest of the governing body, fractional voting could be made to apply only to that ringfenced group, while consensus applies to all the rest.

3 If the rule is consensus with last resort recourse to a vote, the threshold to take a last recourse vote might also be set at consensus. This separates the matter being decided from a decision about the decision making. In other words, decisions are by consensus unless the members decide by consensus to allow a fractional vote. The upshot is that a member can allow a vote to be taken, knowing the decision could garner enough votes, even if the member then votes against (akin to a non-blocking dissent).

4 A fourth option is to specify that recourse to voting would be exceptional and only after consultation by the chair with any parties dissenting from consensus. In addition to flagging voting as the rare case, this (1) puts the burden on the chair to handle proactively; and (2) couches a voting decision in prior consultations.

None of these workarounds changes the fundamental nature of voting and its potential fractionalizing of the governing body. If fractionalized too much, the center may not hold. Most international partnership programs are better off nurturing their center than allowing for splits and splinters.

No splits, no splinters.

No Shared Decision Making

For completeness, we can consider structured partnerships that have no shared decision making once established. This occurs with embedded partnerships, where key decisions are made upfront, and subsequent implementation is entirely delegated to a trustee or other supporting entity. (>@ Typology—The Even Broader Landscape of Structured Partnerships) Coordination partnerships, on the other hand, while on the light end of partnership program structure, may still have things to decide, like when and where to meet next, or whether to allow new participants, thus making the decision-making methodology relevant even here. Coordination partnerships are perhaps particularly prone to consensus, since the whole point is convening to share and coordinate. International partnership programs with advisory or consultative governing bodies operate in the same vein. Even though these bodies do not carry decision making roles and responsibilities, they may, at the margin, still have things to decide. Across the board, partnership programs that have any degree of shared decision making, even logistical or menial decision making, can benefit from establishing at the outset how to make those decisions as a group.

Conclusion

Players like to know the rules of the game before they begin to play. While there are a number of things for partners to agree on upfront when establishing international partnership programs, decision-making rules are on the short list. This includes questions of who decides what, which involves defining the composition of the governing body and the scope of its decision making. It also relates to the process, including who can provide input and who has a determinative say. Consensus and no objection decision making are well-suited to international partnership programs because they give every decision maker an equal voice and an equal veto, thereby striving for full buy-in and agreement.

In this sense, decision making is also about both rights and responsibilities—on the one hand, the right to make a decision and potentially block a decision, and on the other hand, the responsibility for outcomes and ramifications of decisions. Once a partner is designated a decision maker, then *not* deciding is a decision, and not being prepared for a decision is likewise a decision. (>@ Partners and People—Being a Good Partner) Having taken on a decision-making role, a partner becomes responsible for engagement (or lack thereof) both at the member level and the individual representative level. (>@ Governing Bodies—Participation) This may not quite amount to legal responsibility and liability (>@ Fund Use Responsibility—Collective Responsibility), but we still own what we do or don't do.

When it comes to governing bodies, partners may have choices about whether to engage as decision makers, observers, or not at all. Clear rules of the road can help them choose and follow through.

Decision rights come with decision responsibilities.

3 SUPPORTING ENTITIES

It's odd. When creating international partnership programs, you would think partners would focus on themselves and put their partnerships front and center. But no, money is the magnet, and partners tend to focus on funding vehicles, like trust funds. In trust-funded partnership programs, partners commonly view the world in terms of fund flows first, with the trustee in the middle, defined by agreements that channel money in and out. If partners instead put the focus on partners and their partnering, shared governance emerges front and center. That puts a spotlight on the governing body, which in turn shines a light on its supporting secretariat. And this can bring the supporting entity that houses the secretariat out of the shadows.

Giving the supporting entity its due is not instinctive but crucial. Failure to do so can lead to major misunderstandings and challenges, becoming a major strain on the partnership program over time.

Baselines

For each international partnership program that relies on an embedded or inhouse secretariat (>@ Secretariats) or a full or limited trustee (>@ Trust Funds; Trustee Types), it is essential to understand and articulate from the start what that entails: *reliance on an existing supporting entity*. Conversations on the topic are best welcomed and not glossed over. A supporting entity can explain its institutional set-up diplomatically, since it is what it is. Messages from the supporting entity about its management, rules, control, and risk approach need not be off-putting to participants, and certainly should not be read to signal that the supporting entity is retreating from its partnership engagement. In the same way that active collaboration and shared decision making are visible and real to the partners, the supporting entity's day-to-day operations for the partnership program deserve amplification, so as to be appreciated and accommodated.

To establish a solid foundation, supporting entities need a chance to lay out their baselines, both the benefits and limits of what they can provide in their various roles. Partners need a reciprocal chance to confirm that the set-up works for them. This confirmation can be facilitated through the development of a charter or similar constitutive document. Otherwise a partnership program may end up playing *tug-of-war with itself* down the road. And once that happens, there is less energy left to do what partners first set out to do.

For ease of description, the focus in this chapter is on the secretariat. This is by way of example, since elements that apply to the secretariat may also be extrapolated to other roles undertaken by the supporting entity, particularly that of the trustee. These support functions rest on the supporting entity in different ways—for example, one can say the secretariat acts as an agent on behalf of the partners, while the trustee acts as a contracting principal on behalf of itself (>@ Trustee Types—Trustee Entity)—but the nub is the same. To understand the role of the support function within the partnership program, it is important to understand that function in relation to its home base, the supporting entity.

Basic Elements

An inhouse secretariat typically presents three things worth articulating in the charter or equivalent document:

1 An inhouse secretariat consists of *supporting entity staff.*

2 It operates under *supporting entity management.*

3 It is governed by *supporting entity policies and procedures.*

This makes sense, since the embedded secretariat is part of the larger whole, not something that exists separately from the supporting entity. It also means that activities undertaken by secretariat staff are part of the supporting entity's work program. Even though these activities may be for and on behalf of the partnership program, the relationship of secretariat staff to the supporting entity is fully integrated. Indeed, partnership program participants rely on the supporting entity to hire and manage these individuals, since the governing body has neither the bandwidth nor legal entity status to perform this day-to-day role. Naturally, the supporting entity does so on the basis of its own policies and procedures.

Can this be done differently? Can the partnership program substitute its own set of rules or judgments for those of the supporting entity? That depends on how much ground the supporting entity is willing to cede to the governing body. Perhaps the supporting entity has special policies and procedures to accommodate partnership programs, or perhaps it is just a matter of negotiations. Perhaps, for example, the supporting entity is willing to allow an external

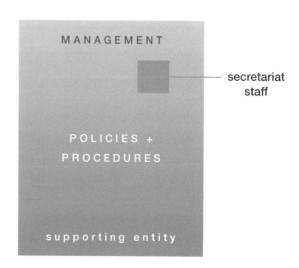

MANAGEMENT

secretariat staff

POLICIES + PROCEDURES

supporting entity

member of the governing body to participate in the shortlisting process for the head of the secretariat, as long as the final decision rests with supporting entity management—a request that may be considered out of line or possibly within manageable bounds.

In the end, international partnership programs are not legal entities and cannot replace supporting entity legal functions, like hiring and procuring. The more the supporting entity deviates from its standard approaches, the more difficult it becomes to scale the support and ensure full compliance with nonstandard aspects. The partnership program may not be able to have it both ways—benefiting from the supporting entity's robust operating framework and day-to-day management while at the same time supplanting this operating framework and management with special rules and exceptions. Partners should in any case not be surprised if the supporting entity pushes back and persists with its own rules and judgments.

Privileges and Immunities

One of the backdrops to all this is P&I. Without going into a legal dissertation here, P&I is one of the special benefits that can come with international organization support, accruing to UN agencies, MDBs, and other international organizations to varying degrees and under different international instruments and agreements. International partnership programs can derive significant benefit from engaging supporting entities with P&I.

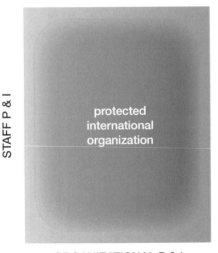

PRIVILEGES & IMMUNITIES

STAFF P & I

protected international organization

ARCHIVAL P & I

ORGANIZATIONAL P & I

In general, these supporting entities can operate with multiple forms of P&I: (1) for the international organization overall, including making its property and assets immune from search and seizure (organizational immunity); (2) for its staff doing official acts, making them immune to judicial process (staff immunity); and (3) for its documents and records, making them "inviolable" (archival immunity). This kind of immunity is usually justified by "functional necessity," meaning international organizations, their officials, and their agents enjoy such immunities as are necessary for their effective functioning as organizations without undue interference from governments or others.

While this kind of P&I does not cover everything the partnership program (or its individual partners) does, it may shield the parts undertaken by the protected supporting entity. In the case of one-stop-shops, that can be most of the partnership program. In the case of international platforms, that can cover the limited trustee and secretariat plus any downstream implementation or supervision by the protected entity. Meanwhile sovereign states have their own immunities so that most if not all of the other governing body participants have protections as well.

Even when immunities are available, however, it works only if two things are true:

- relevant staff are considered staff of the protected entity; and

- relevant activities are considered part of the protected entity's work program.

As a result, any moves to distance staff and activities from the protected entity can enter a danger zone. If partners treat supporting entity staff and activities as belonging exclusively to the partnership program— even though the partnership program is not a legal personality or entity per se—or if supporting entity staff seek or appear to operate outside of supporting entity management and rules, they can put these P&I at risk.

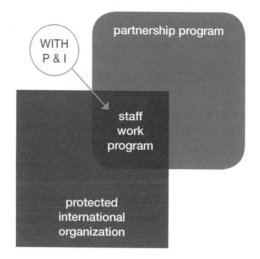

Secretariat staff may think twice if they realize that business cards containing only the partnership program name, without any reference to their supporting entity employer, could leave them individually exposed. This also brings risk to the supporting entity, which hired these staff under their expectations of protection. And it is ultimately risky for other partners. Presumably, they too have an interest in preserving P&I for the supporting entity, the seat of their venture, to keep an overall low-risk profile.

On this front as well, partnership programs cannot have it both ways. They cannot seek to co-opt inhouse secretariats as their own and expect to keep benefits like P&I that attach to the supporting entities. Prudence suggests that inhouse secretariats be recognizable as part of their supporting entities, even as they are cobranded as part of their partnership programs, to keep staff and activities properly aligned. Both participants and the broader public should be able to recognize that inhouse secretariats are part of the supporting entities, and secretariat staff should understand and communicate that they perform their duties and obligations as supporting entity staff. This deliberate clarity and transparency can help avoid tensions among partners and may help keep supporting entity P&I from being challenged.

Risk Profile

Another backdrop is the supporting entity's own risk profile, primarily, but not only, in terms of reputational risk. With one or more supporting roles— commonly secretariat, trustee, implementer, supervisor, decision maker, and more—the supporting entity becomes inextricably entwined with the partnership program, at the root of it, as it were. The supporting entity has to be comfortable in this position, where it is exposed by association to every activity and aspect of the partnership program. Delineating and delimiting roles and responsibilities may help keep problematic partner behavior from tainting the rest, but only to a degree. There is usually still some residual reputational exposure for the supporting entity simply by the central nature of its involvement.

Among the ways to protect the supporting entity's risk profile is to let the supporting entity be the governing body chair, especially when the chair participates in the decision making, manages the deliberations, and articulates the outcome of consensus decision making. This is particularly common in one-stop-shops, as a clear way to match a high degree of responsibility with significant control and influence. By contrast, this supporting entity chair role is not as common in international platforms, where supporting entity roles are typically kept limited and reserved, administrative rather than substantive (>@ Typology—International Platforms). However, even in these cases,

Managing the Supporting Entity's Risk Profile

On the home front, the work of the partnership program needs to align with the supporting entity's institutional mandate and direction for it to be legitimately involved.

Both factors give the supporting entity an interest in shaping how the partnership program operates and evolves.

On the partner front, the engagement of every partner has a bearing on the supporting entity and how the supporting entity is perceived, sometimes with partners as shareholders.

Matching accountability with authority.

supporting entities could legitimately decide they have so much exposure that there is more risk in deferring to others than in getting substantively involved. With that calculus, a supporting entity could buck convention and negotiate a seat at the table of an international platform, with a full say in the decision making. (>@ Risk and Review—Risk Innovation)

Another effective way to match accountability and authority is to give the supporting entity secretariat a central clearing house role that lets it act as gatekeeper. (>@ Secretariats—Inhouse Secretariat Roles) This could affect, for example, how charter amendments are handled. If, as is normally the case, the governing body is positioned to adopt the charter, it can also amend the charter. However, by requiring any charter changes to route through the secretariat before reaching the governing body—everything has to be teed up in advance, not simply tabled at a meeting—the supporting entity can discreetly and efficiently make sure nothing reaches the governing body that has not been vetted against its own policies and procedures.

This secretariat compliance role would not be by way of subterfuge. It would be open and transparent, acknowledged and accepted, as a way of letting the supporting entity keep things smooth, while also managing its own risk profile. This might not be as critical for a one-stop-shop where the supporting entity is already substantively involved as a decision maker. It might also be less critical in international platform cases where the supporting entity is not a decision maker but nonetheless holds a right of consent over changes that affect its functions and claims prevalence in cases of conflict between its internal policies and any charter changes. Regardless, however, this gatekeeper role can help assure orderly proceedings.

Nuclear Option

What if the partnership program drifts too far from its supporting entity base? What if it does things that are untenable for the supporting entity, outside its mandate or beyond its risk appetite? Whether incrementally over time or in one fell swoop, that can happen if a supporting entity has too little say.

In structures where the supporting entity (read: both trustee and secretariat) defers to other partners for governing body decision making, the partnership terms are likely to include an explicit clause granting the supporting entity the right to terminate or exit. This can be at will or for cause (legal-speak for without or with justification), but the latitude is normally wide enough that the supporting entity is never in a position where it is bound to do something against its own internal rules or beyond its mandate.

Where this shows up frequently is in a standard legal clause in contribution agreements with limited trustees. Through this clause, international platforms typically pre-position the ultimate, final option of a supporting entity exit—the so-called nuclear option. The secretariat role might also need this option, but if the secretariat and trustee are part of the same supporting entity, one nuclear option is presumably enough. Pulling this trigger is rare and extreme (I have seen it threatened once and leveraged once), if only because that can truly explode the partnership program into smithereens. Before it is pulled, the looming prospect focuses the minds.

Even in cases where the right to terminate is not explicit, it seems to be de facto understood. The supporting entity would say it cannot be forced to do something that violates its own requirements, especially if some of the partners are also beholden to those requirements as shareholders of the supporting entity. Partners might claim reliance on supporting entity functions to keep it from exiting, but that would normally not be enough to make the supporting entity go against its own rules. Informal partnership programs generally have enough room in their informality for any partner, including supporting entities, to walk at any time—even if that means weighing the reputational risk of continuing under untenable circumstances vs. decamping into ignominy.

When it comes to escape valves, it is of course better to be explicit than implicit. But it is even better to have understandings and accommodation mechanisms that manage challenges long before they come to nuclear stand-offs. This means first understanding the supporting entity's baselines and then directly anchoring the partnership program's foundations in them. Short of triggering the nuclear option, measures that can help frame supporting entity participation include some that were already mentioned, and then some:

- Securing a clearing house, gatekeeper, and compliance role for the secretariat
- Granting rights of fund transfer suspension to the trustee, while things are sorted out
- Keeping the final decision for hiring and firing of the secretariat head in the hands of the supporting entity
- Including the supporting entity as a decision-making member of the governing body, potentially through one or more of its roles, including as chair
- Granting specific rights of approval or consent on aspects that affect supporting entity interests

All of these measures have one thing in common: They let the supporting entity stay true to its own institutional requirements and manage its own risk profile. Without that, the supporting entity will not last long, nor will the partnership program in its current guise. If a partnership program needs a supporting entity to function, then the supporting entity functions, like trustee and secretariat, need to function fully within the supporting entity.

Tongue twister:

A fully functioning supporting entity has functions functioning fully within the supporting entity.

Duality and Balance

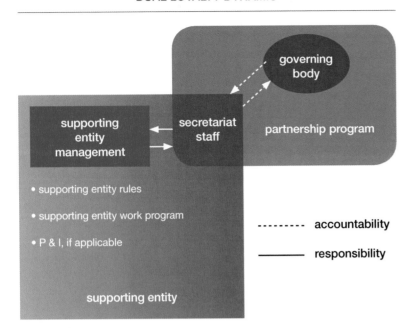

- supporting entity rules
- supporting entity work program
- P & I, if applicable

supporting entity

governing body

secretariat staff

supporting entity management

partnership program

- - - - - - - - **accountability**

———— **responsibility**

The predominance of the supporting entity does not mean inhouse secretariats are free to ignore partnership program participants and the governing bodies they support. This would not make sense, since the secretariat exists to provide that support. Instead, although the first allegiance is to the supporting entity, the second allegiance to the partnership program is close behind. Inhouse secretariats that belong to the supporting entity are still accountable to the partners. Secretariat staff work for the supporting entity and *report to their managers*, but also work in support of the partnership program and *provide reports to participants*.

Pro-partner. In practice, supporting entities can make their expectations of internal compliance and operational control known upfront and then acknowledge partners' expectations of collaboration along the way. For example, even if, technically, inhouse secretariats can be restructured at the initiative of supporting entity management, just like other supporting entity units, to do so unilaterally without at least some consultation with partners would seem inappropriate (then again, it may be the same partners as supporting entity shareholders that are mandating overall budget cuts). Similarly, although performance reviews are between the supporting entity managers and secretariat staff, it may be in the spirit of partnership to seek key partnership program participants' views on key staff positions, like the secretariat head. Hiring and firing decisions are up to the supporting entity, since they invoke serious human resources obligations and potential contract and benefits liabilities, but some limited partnership input could perhaps be accommodated up to a point.

Whoa partner! Deference to the partnership program does not, however, imply that supporting entities do everything partners instruct or request. Excess unilateralism can cut both ways. Partners may ask for blank check arrangements, but supporting entities should take care to resist them. That includes catch-all charter clauses for secretariat responsibilities, like "the secretariat also performs other functions assigned to it by the governing body." With this kind of charter clause, the sky is the limit, even though budget and resources are finite, and the secretariat loses all control. Cooperation is mutual, and that means acknowledging each other's boundaries and collaborating within them, while also seeking to meet each other's expectations and ambitions.

In the Middle

As every middle child knows, growing up in between has its family dynamics. Middle children are (stereo)typically known for their conflict-managing, compromise-finding, peace-loving ways. Embedded secretariats have a similar lot sitting between supporting entities and partners. It isn't always easy, and here are three ways that it can play out.

1. **Sensitivity.** International partnership programs call for sensitivity on all sides and in all directions. Supporting entity managers need to have their finger on the pulse of the partnership program. Partnership program participants—especially the chair, as the conduit for the governing body—need a good sense of the supporting entity. But the brunt is on secretariat heads, who are most successful when they navigate both sides of the coin, channeling information and interests up to their direct management, back to the partners, and around again, anticipating issues, closing gaps, and maneuvering frictions. It takes sensitivity and skill to protect the supporting entity's interests while also furthering the partnership program's interests. Secretariat heads need to be expert at *bridging the synergies and the frictions*.

2. **Neutrality.** Under these circumstances, it can be difficult for an inhouse secretariat to be a neutral convener. While an inhouse secretariat can offer to bring participants together in a balanced manner, without imposing its own agenda, it cannot completely disavow the institution within which it sits. Some secretariats fancy themselves "honest brokers," but for that, the supporting entity has to support the intention to stay neutral, without tilting or intervening—basically undergirding partners more than overseeing staff. Partners, too, have to believe the secretariat can play a neutral broker role despite its context, which can be a challenge in politically charged contexts where perceptions are easily swayed.

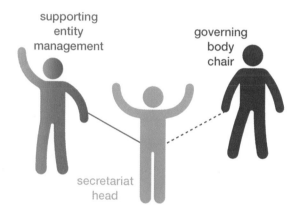

it's about people
and relationships

3. **Independence.** The role of the inhouse secretariat can also present a quandary when the governing body wants independent assessments or advice. This arises, for example, when individual consultants or firms are engaged to undertake "external" midterm reviews or "independent" evaluations, presumably at arm's-length, free from bias, and untainted by close associations or conflicts of interest. As the legal entity for the partnership program, it is usually the secretariat qua supporting entity that contracts the engagement, using its usual procurement procedures, a process that, technically, is not very independent. To help the case, however, these arrangements are typically referred to by the partners as "commissioning" (with the secretariat acting on governing body instructions), as opposed to regular contracting or procuring. To further help the case, the terms of reference for the engagement, prepared by the secretariat for approval by the governing body, can explicitly limit the secretariat's role, and thereby also the supporting entity, with no substantive responsibility for the outcome or substantive engagement in the process.

Calling It

Labels can be misleading. Some international partnership programs like to call themselves "independent," even when they benefit from an embedded secretariat. That is not quite right. Dedicated entity partnerships can be independent—they are stand-alone—but partnership programs that plug into one of the partners' already existing legal entities cannot. (>@ Typology—The Even Broader Landscape of Structured Partnerships) Partners might say that the inhouse secretariat is simply "located at" or "hosted by" the supporting entity, but that does not alter the fact that secretariat staff are part of the supporting entity, under its management, governed by its rules. A description of a secretariat and partnership program as being at "arm's length" under these circumstances would be inaccurate, as would claims that the whole partnership program is "owned" by the partners. Calling it something does not simply make it so. For international partnership programs, hybrid as they are, the reality is usually more complex.

In a similar vein, seconded staff who join the secretariat do not join an arm's-length relationship in which they stay part of their original employer entity. A secondment from one organization to another usually means the seconded staff person fully moves over to the second entity, effectively becoming staff of the second entity, under second entity management and subject to second entity rules for the period of the secondment. This means secondments do not result in "joint" secretariats, but rather merge staff into one and the same embedded secretariat. Using a limited trustee or giving more decision-making control to a governing body, as with international platforms, does not change the formula. A secretariat for an international platform is just as embedded in the supporting entity as for a one-stop-shop.

Bottom line, the tripartite essence of an inhouse secretariat—embedded staff, management, and rules—is unaffected by names, models, or partnership elements, except to the extent the housing supporting entity might explicitly allow otherwise, if it is willing and able.

Middle Ground?

Perhaps there is some middle ground for international partnership programs. Perhaps there is a model that lies between embedded, inhouse secretariats (all in) and outsourced, third-party service providers (all out). Some international organizations have offered "hosting" arrangements, whereby the supporting entity still participates as a partner (>@ International Partnership Programs—Collectives), but strips back some of its engagement, reframing the inhouse support terms as outsourced service terms instead. Whereas embedded secretariats tend to operate more informally and broadly vis-à-vis roles and responsibilities in a charter or similar document (>@ Custodial Effect), the hosting idea seeks to create a more arm's-length, circumscribed arrangement.

One of the goals in this third-way approach is to give both the partnership program and the secretariat/partner entity more certainty over the kind of resources being procured and provided. This can occur by limiting deliverables to an as-needed or as-requested basis off a menu of functions, more service provider than support partner. The secretariat/partner entity accordingly enters into a formal, contractual agreement with the partnership program. This agreement can feature a set of negotiated services, as well as a process for reconciling partnership program decisions that are at odds with supporting entity rules, potentially under a special policy regime of the secretariat/partner entity devised for just this kind of partnership program support.

But there is a problem. It takes two legal entities to enter into an enforceable contract. Because the legal entity for the partnership program is the secretariat/partner entity acting on behalf of the partnership program, that entity cannot enter into a contract with itself. And it cannot enter into a contract with the governing body of the partnership program either, since neither the governing body nor the partnership program is a legal entity. It is also especially awkward to have a partner enter into contracted, litigious-type footing with its own partnership or fellow partners, getting indemnifications and other recourse provisions, especially if that same partner also participates in the governing body. (Does it really expect to be held harmless for decisions it helped make?) And it is not clear to whom such recourse clauses would be directed; which is to say, from whom such indemnifications would come. The partnership program is not a legal personality that can receive enforceable claims, and governing body members are not stepping up as deep pockets.

This leaves the unwieldy possibility of having the secretariat/partner entity sign with every other partner individually, thereby treating partnership terms much like bilateral fund flow agreements and making the whole set-up a contractual joint venture more than an informal partnership. By this point, we are far afield from the flexibility, informality, efficiencies, and overall synergies of international partnership programs.

This middle ground is actually in the shoals. Setting up a contractual relationship between the supporting entity and the partnership program for which the contracting entity is both the supporting entity and a partner is a convoluted conundrum. This is the twilight of the twilight zone.

Here we have yet another one of the many reasons that secretariats embedded in their supporting entities are so common. Embedded secretariats do not rely on contractual underpinnings, when the relationship is really too incestuous to be arm's-length anyhow. Their engagement is more usefully defined in terms adopted by partners, like a charter. When the supporting entity is a partner, and other partners are shareholders of that same supporting entity, it is no surprise that a more integrated, wholesome approach—the informal, synergistic world of international partnership programs—is more feasible and favored.

Guiding Principles

Embedded, inhouse secretariats can be big business for international organizations like some of the MDBs and UN agencies. Even if they do not fully acknowledge this secretariat role (being more focused on trustees and trust funds than partnership aspects) and have little to no policies, procedures, or even guidance to support the role, they invariably back into this supporting entity position over and over again as a corollary to other collectives, like shared governance and branded platforms.

PARTNERSHIP PROGRAM SECRETARIAT OPTIONS

1	2	3
support partner	"host" partner	service provider
part of the partnership	? (neither/nor)	outside of the partnership

A Guiding Framework for Inhouse Secretariats

Drawing from a previous attempt to articulate parameters, here are some thoughts that spell out a holistic approach, presented as an initial template for an internal policy or guidance note. These Ten Tenets can also be extended to pick up other supporting entity roles, like trustee:

1 The partnership program secretariat based in the supporting entity is part of the supporting entity.

2 The supporting entity has ultimate authority over and responsibility for the secretariat.

3 The supporting entity's P&I [if applicable] applies to secretariat activities, as well as partnership program activities that are part of the supporting entity's work program.

4 Supporting entity staff rules apply to staff hired by, or seconded to, the supporting entity for, or otherwise assigned to, the secretariat.

5 Secretariat staff are covered by [relevant, if available] supporting entity insurance and security policies, including for travel and other risks.

6 Secretariat staff are expected to reflect their supporting entity status externally to partners and others , potentially in addition to their partnership program association.

7 Supporting entity administrative and operational policies apply to the secretariat, including with respect to partnership aspects handled by the secretariat.

8 Supporting entity managers are encouraged to develop terms of reference with secretariat heads, including about internal reporting requirements, external representation of the partnership program, balancing dual loyalties, and managing potential conflicts of interest.

9 In case of conflict, supporting entity rules and requirements, as interpreted by supporting entity management, prevail over partnership program rules and requirements, unless otherwise explicitly agreed.

10 Questions, concerns, or requests for exceptions may be raised with [fill in the blank].

For organizations that provide secretariat support across multiple partnership programs, a guidance note or policy paper for their staff—both secretariat and management—can lay out the issues and clarify expectations. This same document can also put partnership program participants on notice, particularly at inception, as well as the public at large (including third parties vis-à-vis P&I and potential third-party claims). The note can stay at the level of principles, to be applied in specific circumstances, rather than prescribe minutiae that vary case by case. It can also spell out where secretariat staff can go for internal interpretations and exceptions, since it is difficult to anticipate every scenario in advance.

Rules should not become strait jackets. They can support without restricting, harmonize without confining, and standardize the framework while still leaving room to contextualize the specifics.

Conclusion

In the classic international partnership program scenario, partners lean on one of their own to provide secretariat-type, administrative support functions without contractualizing the terms—and sometimes barely acknowledging the role. Meanwhile, at home base, the partner providing those support functions may have minimal if any institutional policies or procedures for this role, sometimes barely naming it. Is it any wonder that this can erupt into dissonance over time, either by partners who are chomping at the bit to be independent, prescriptive, or controlling, or by support organizations that are chafing to preserve standard practices, maintain control, and manage risks?

This need not be so. Partners can bring secretariat functions and supporting entity support out of the shadows and into the light, so that all partners, the supporting entity included, can coalesce around the same expectations and understandings. When it comes to supporting entities—those unsung heroes of partnership programs—it is worth speaking the unspoken and addressing the unaddressed.

This is all the more true in light of the custodial effect, which merits a whole additional chapter—coming up next.

THE PERENNIAL TUG-OF-WAR

other partners

supporting entity partner

partnership program

independence
control
wishes + needs

standard practices
control
risk management

4 CUSTODIAL EFFECT

All but the lightest international partnership programs need a custodian, an entity the participants can rely on to care for the partnership program. This role is rarely articulated and even less understood. It is more assumed than explicit, more de facto than deliberate. Greater visibility of this custodial effect can help both partners and the supporting entity clarify their needs and expectations before issues arise.

The Effect

Unarticulated but Assumed

Beyond specifically articulated functions—for example, receiving, managing, and disbursing funds through the trustee or supporting a governing body through the secretariat—there are any number of *residual functions* that are left unenumerated by the partners, but still carried out by the supporting entity. It is not feasible to exhaustively itemize every specific support task in a constitutive document. Instead, there may be a catch-all trustee or secretariat provision for "any required administrative support." More commonly, however, there is silence, and partners simply assume that someone, presumably the designated seat of certain administrative functions, will pick up all the rest. This assumed function is so essential that it deserves a name, so I have given it one.

I call this the "custodian role," a role that goes well beyond the mere provision of services and includes more than specifically assigned support functions. The custodian affects the very essence and reputation of the partners and the program, as caretaker, guardian, steward, butler, protector, and more of the partnership program.

The supporting entity as:

1. custodian
2. caretaker
3. guardian
4. steward
5. butler
6. protector
7. and more

Defaulting to the Secretariat

In practice, this default responsibility usually ends up with the secretariat or its administrative equivalent (which could also be the trustee performing secretariat-type functions). For example, when it comes to setting up the partnership program's website, most likely the secretariat obtains the server (from its own institution or outsourced) and becomes the contact for any issues. When it comes to printing brochures, getting office supplies, or mailing communications, the secretariat readily avails itself of its supporting entity resources. If the governing body commissions an evaluation, the secretariat is normally expected to hire the firm or consultant. If the partnership program needs legal advice, the first recourse is usually to the supporting entity legal staff already assigned to the secretariat. If the partnership program wants to enter into a memorandum of understanding, the signature on behalf of the partnership program is normally provided by the supporting entity on behalf of the partners, as coordinated through the secretariat.

In all these scenarios, it is almost always the secretariat role that steps up to provide the needed support, whether or not it has been explicitly asked or assigned to provide it. These extra functions seem to come with the territory of being a secretariat and end up with the entity that houses it.

Providing the Legal Entity

For practical reasons, an effective custodian role necessarily connects to a legal entity. On the one hand, some partnership program aspects that need to be carried out by a legal entity are expressly assigned to specific functions. For example, the receipt of funds invariably requires a contractual arrangement, which is only valid and enforceable between legal entities. As a matter of fund flows, this legal function is normally assigned to and performed by the trustee—or rather, by the trustee's legal entity. On the other hand, there are any number of non-trust-fund-related matters that also need a legal home. For example, the partnership program needs staff, space, supplies, and digital assets. Whether these are owned, leased, hired, or contracted, they are legally arranged.

As a result, partners that expect dedicated support and operations, like a designated program head and supporting team, or a branded website, need some legal entity to provide related legal functions. Options are basically to (1) outsource the role under service terms to a third-party provider; (2) have the partnership program be its own legal personality; or (3) find an existing legal entity among its partners.

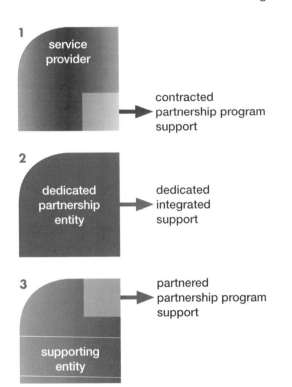

1 Option one, outsourcing, is a limited way to get well-integrated support. As a commercial transaction, it provides defined and costed support without the synergies of staying within the family. International partnership programs usually like to rely on legal entities that are closer to home, especially if that includes P&I and shareholder relationships.

2 Option two, establishing a new, dedicated legal entity, is not just closer to home: It *is* home. There is no question that the new entity, the dedicated entity partnership, will be the primary legal entity across the board—that is why it was being set up. Partners know where to go to get their dedicated legal entity support. But it is a heavy lift and may be more than partners want or can afford. (>@ Typology—The Even Broader Landscape of Structured Partnerships)

3 Option three, relying on an existing legal entity that is not uniquely dedicated to the partnership program but is a partner, is a tried and true international partnership program choice. The support from the undergirding legal entity—the partner *qua* secretariat *qua* supporting entity—is not exclusively "dedicated" to the partnership program in the sense of option two, but is no less essential and just as presumed.

Option three, the embedded secretariat in a partnering supporting entity, lends itself to custodial help. Whereas option one is usually less than custodial, and option two is ultimately more than custodial, option three is most likely to fill in just the interstices when and where needed.

Mutual Respect

Respecting the Legal Entity

The coupling of administrative responsibility with legal responsibility is so functionally necessary that any deviation can hinder a partnership program's ability to function. A partnership program can, for example, ill afford a secretariat supporting entity that refuses to provide a "signing" function on behalf of the partnership program. If not this entity, then who? A signature delegated to another individual partner loses its neutral, representative quality. A signature delegated to a limited trustee or other specific function may mix unrelated activities and transgress defined responsibilities. Without a secretariat signing function, the partnership program is unable to enter into procurement, hiring, or consulting contracts, or memorialize its understandings with others, short of some complex workaround like having all partners sign individually.

Even so, partners should appreciate that this legal personality backstop is not a blank check. The supporting entity is usually willing to be the legal conduit for the partnership program, but within bounds. Not only is the legal entity always subject to its own policies and procedures but also its own risk profile. Under a mantle of overall cooperation, the supporting entity should at all times, at the margin, retain the discretion not to enter into specific arrangements on behalf of the partnership program.

As custodian, the secretariat function is thus well-advised to preserve enough space to **operate within its own comfort zone**. Partner expectations need to be set and managed accordingly. As a matter of good practice, the secretariat's roles and responsibilities are best overtly couched within the supporting entity's institutional rules and management discretion, especially in recognition of custodial creep. (>@ Supporting Entities)

Respecting the Partners

Sometimes the custodial instincts of the secretariat cause it to fill in on its own. As a matter of authority and accountability, however, the secretariat should **reflect partnership program buy-in** through legitimate, agreed decision-making processes and allocations of responsibility before making legal statements or commitments on behalf of the partnership program. For example, in signing a memorandum of understanding (MoU) for the partnership program:

1. **As to authority**, the secretariat can act in a representative role only if it has secured legitimate authority to sign or act for the partnership program. This could be on a blanket basis through delegated authority in a document (for example, an enumerated role in the charter) or on a case-by-case basis through a proper governing body decision (for example, consensus approval of a specific proposed MoU).

2. **As to accountability**, the secretariat as legal entity (supporting entity) should be clearly characterized in the document and signatory line as representing, or acting on behalf of, the partnership program. The document can additionally clarify that the signing entity is *not* acting as a principal in its own right. This is especially helpful for supporting entities seen as deep pockets, including as a signal to potential third-party claimants. As we have seen elsewhere (>@ Trust Funds—Trustees), when rebutting presumptions, it can be useful to say something in both the positive and the negative.

The secretariat legal entity should, on the one hand, remain responsive to partnership program needs and maintain efficient partnership program operations and, on the other hand, refrain from acting unilaterally outside of partnership terms and partner consensus.

The Need for Balance

Being a custodian for a partnership program can be a complex balancing act, with limits on both ends:

- On the one hand, when the secretariat picks up assumed roles and responsibilities, it should be careful about assuming the partnership program's buy-in.

- On the other hand, when a partnership program benefits from a legal entity's assumption of activities, partners should be careful about assuming that this default engagement is unbounded at the behest of the partners.

The penumbra of activities that are conducted by the partnership program's administrative base—including through its legal entity status—puts a premium on the supporting entity both in terms of expectations and exposure. For the supporting entity, however, the custodian role has both sides of the coin: it affords control, and it increases exposure. More control usually means better risk management, but it also means greater responsibility with more risk exposure. Where the balance of risk falls, and whether it is better to insert oneself or not, is always the $64,000 question. (>@ Risk and Review—Risk Innovation)

This is a business trade-off that the supporting entity needs to consider carefully when stepping up to the administrative/legal entity functions of an international partnership program. It can embrace this comprehensive role—thereby maximizing efficient operations and minimizing partnership risks—but must also manage that role in terms of legitimacy vis-à-vis its partners and acceptability vis-à-vis its own institution.

The custodian role has both sides of the risk coin:

- It affords control (risk management).

- It increases responsibility (risk exposure).

Where is the point of minimum risk?

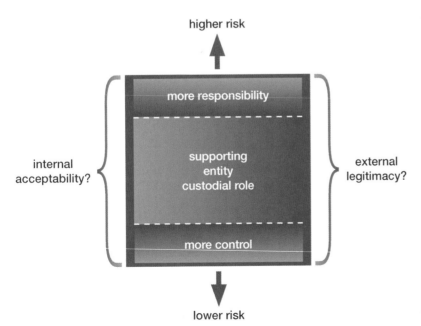

higher risk

more responsibility

supporting entity custodial role

internal acceptability?

external legitimacy?

more control

lower risk

Policy Limits

Let's consider again that a supporting entity is not dedicated entirely to an international partnership program, in contrast to a new legal entity established exclusively for and dedicated fully to a specific partnership program. The supporting entity has a lot of other things going on. Its support of the partnership program has to fit within a larger operating framework, rather than operate within a framework designed just by and for the partners. Any efforts by the partnership program to develop its own operating environment (for example, seeking to enact partnership program–specific operating policies) can quickly run afoul of the existing policies and procedures of the supporting entity. For this all to function, partnership program activities should be subordinated to these existing policies and procedures, at least where they would otherwise conflict.

Within those limitations, however, the reverse is also true. Efforts by secretariat staff to fill the gap must be consistent with the partnership program's agreed baseline terms, like the charter and contribution agreements, and decisions by the governing body. The secretariat as custodian of the partnership program should stay true to its own operating and legitimizing environment, as well as that of the partnership program.

Needless to say, it is crucial for these two operating contexts to remain compatible, both a lawyer's job in drafting and a working staff chore in operating. Keeping this all aligned is key for the supporting entity sitting in the middle so as not to end up in two dissonant universes, beholden to two sets of divergent terms. As we have seen, there are ways to manage these dynamics over time. (>@ Supporting Entities—Basic Elements—Nuclear Option)

With Vigilance

Good Housekeeping

Typically, partners expect a low risk, high integrity partnership program. It behooves the secretariat to seek the same, especially with its central role and degree of reputational exposure. In this regard, good business practice suggests that this default role be not only reactive but also proactive. As between the secretariat and the governing body, both of whom have an interest in keeping things on an even keel, good housekeeping generally falls to the secretariat more than to the governing body. The secretariat has an administrative seat with ongoing operational functions and is active day-to-day, whereas the governing body meets only periodically with limited functions. Even the governing body chair, with engagement at a higher level, is usually ill-suited for proactive, micro-stewardship.

Whether specifically assigned or not, preparing and confirming accurate meeting minutes, managing transparent and unambiguous no objection decision processes, maintaining comprehensive and properly disclosed/undisclosed files and archives, monitoring press and public commentary, and handling inquiries and claims, these and other tasks receive more or less diligent attention in a partnership program depending on the secretariat's performance. A proactive secretariat takes vigilant, sensitive responsibility for such activities as a matter of course—in effect, acting as a custodian for the sake of its own institution, not just for the sake of the partnership program and other partners. A proactive custodian supports the good reputation of everyone involved in all the many details as—or before—they arise.

Not a Magnet

In articulating the usually unspoken dimensions of the partnership program "custodian," the idea is not to introduce new elements into the international partnership program landscape, but rather to put a label on an aspect that already exists. Both the custodial entity and other partners have an interest in clarifying expectations and responsibilities assumed in a custodial capacity. Recognizing a custodian role is not, however, tantamount to saddling the custodial entity with all the partnership program woes that no one else wants.

Good housekeeping: low risk, high integrity.

Nor does it give the custodian license to undertake all sorts of gap-filling. For example, it does not mean the custodial entity suddenly becomes the legitimate target for all legal claims against the partnership program. Nor does it mean that the custodial entity could or should jump into rescue mode when other roles are underperformed. (>@ Secretariats—Inhouse Secretariat Roles) While keeping the custodian unnamed and unnoticed neglects a key structural element, there is admittedly also some delicacy—some risk—in noting and naming this function.

In Practice

One-Stop-Shops

In one-stop-shops, the custodial effect is full-on, like a penumbra-plus package of support. Since the sum of support functions is housed in the one-stop-shop supporting entity, the partnership program is already poised to fully benefit from the supporting entity's custodial function. It is generally understood that this all-in support includes keeping minutes and records, handling no objection processes, maintaining the website, and doing other overall housekeeping. It is also generally understood that the one-stop-shop supporting entity is the legal entity for partnership program business, in terms of hiring staff and consultants, providing space and security, signing partnership agreements, and much more. However, while this default role can and does encompass many things, it is always governed by the supporting entity's policies and procedures and framed by its institutional assessments of risk—thus occurring within the limits of what the supporting entity is able and willing to do. From the start, it is important for both the one-stop-shop entity and the other partners to understand these dynamics and set their expectations accordingly.

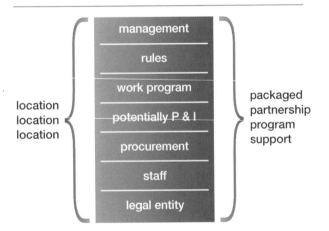

SUPPORTING ENTITY

location
location
location

management
rules
work program
potentially P & I
procurement
staff
legal entity

packaged partnership program support

International Platforms

The same can be said of international platforms that feature a limited trustee role and support from a secretariat—the applicable operating environment of the supporting entity needs to be reflected in partner expectations. Here the trustee role is clearly defined because of its limited nature, and the additional secretariat role is usually described as a distinct part of the partnership program, whether provided by a different entity or simply a different part of the trustee entity. The governing body usually has a heightened role, so that its support function also tends to get a heightened status. This would seem to bode well since it gives the secretariat more focused attention.

Indeed, because roles and responsibilities are usually more explicitly negotiated and described in international platforms, partners may get the impression that that is all there is to it. But that's not how it works in the drafting. Ironically, precisely because international platforms tend to be more "as negotiated" than standard, not every detail, like ones easily taken for granted, may get attention upfront. With more line-drawing between roles, there is also greater room for gaps; and yet the need for a comprehensive legal entity and proactive caretaking function is no less crucial.

With a limited trustee and a limited secretariat, not all the support functions readily provided in a comprehensive one-stop-shop are as quick to find their home in an international platform. In the end, after setting limits around the trustee and the secretariat, the remainder may fall to the governing body, particularly if the governing body has overarching strategic and oversight responsibility. That may come as a surprise to the governing body, whose members are unlikely to realize they are in the default position holding the bag. In international platforms then, it is all the more important for the custodian role—this unenumerated, filler function—to be better understood, negotiated, allocated, and accepted.

More line-drawing leaves more room for gaps and more need for filler.

Conclusion

As with any other partner, the custodial entity retains discretion in whether to explicitly accept various responsibilities within the partnership program. It still needs to follow its own policies and procedures and manage its own risk profile. And meanwhile, the partnership program—the collective participants—at least theoretically (if not legally) retain responsibility as a whole for aspects that have not been delegated to and accepted by one or the other partner.

The partnership program's custodial, legal entity—whether by design or default—does well to recognize the added *expectations and exposure* the custodial role can bring and then articulate any *requirements or limitations* to the other partners. In turn, the other partners will want to come to terms with any such requirements or limitations and address any gaps or conflicts, as mutually agreed within the partnership program.

5 SYNERGISTIC CONFLICTS

"Conflicts of interest" is a legal concept, a business judgment, and a term of art. There are conflicts of interest and there are synergies, and sometimes there are both together. In international partnership programs, they regularly unite, with relationships that may be simultaneously conflicted and collaborative. Putting too much emphasis on "conflicts" can undermine the whole point of the partnership program. This chapter is an invitation for partners to let collaboration trump conflict.

People love to zero in on conflicts of interest, like detectives on the prowl. More often than not, however, when people refer to "conflicts of interest," they are not actually talking about specific conflicts, but rather some other suspect or subpar behavior. Like throwing everything into the kitchen sink, "conflicts of interest" (also referred to as COI) tends to be a buzzword repository for all sorts of strange and sundry dirty dishes. It is easy to say "this raises conflicts of interest" and cast a pall, but the analysis is often lacking. Before jumping to conclusions, it is worth applying a little discipline to the topic.

Points of Order

First, to avoid confusion, conflicts of interest (potentially problematic) are not the same thing as conflicting interests (perfectly normal). Partner A is a beneficiary with a prevailing interest in getting the project done quickly, while Partner B is a donor with a prevailing interest in getting the project done carefully. These interests are in conflict and lead to different views—that is normal and perfectly okay. This is what negotiations and compromise are all about: resolving conflicting positions, bridging the gap, and coming to agreement. This is a "conflict of interests" (plural interests), which is not the same as a "conflict of interest" (singular interest).

The pernicious matter of conflict of interest, singular, is more nuanced and complex. A summary high-level description of the term "conflict of interest" is *a tendency toward untoward bias in favor of one factor at the expense of another*, as when judgment is impaired by outside obligations or interests. This bias in decision making is considered morally problematic because it unfairly skews the result—unfair because it is not transparent to others, nor within the expected rules of the game. It takes an inappropriate toll on something or someone. Exactly how this plays out in practice depends on where the tensions lie. Ultimately it is not the conflict itself that is the main problem, but the perception of bias that arises, the subsurface bias it causes, and the skewed outcome that can result.

> **Conflict of interest: a tendency toward untoward bias**

conflict of interest	→	perceived / actual decision-making bias	→	potentially skewed outcome

Second, a "conflict of interest" can happen on two different planes: *institutional and individual*. On the institutional plane, competing interests within the same institution can skew results. On the individual plane, divided loyalties within the same individual can also skew results. There is value in knowing exactly where the conflict lies when aiming for the kitchen sink. (>@ next page)

Third, conflicts of interest may present in three different ways: *actual, potential, or perceived*. Even if they may not all result in skewed decision making, they can all affect the partnership program's reputation and operations.

Fourth, the upshot of conflicts of interest is *selective bias*, which causes a decision to be made for the wrong reasons. In international partnership programs, participants are usually expected to act above board and fairly. This is not a dog-eat-dog corporate environment where competition rules. Instead, the point is cooperation and collaboration. Fairness standards come into play when the participants, particularly supporting entities, get to choose from among various possibilities. These could include with whom to collaborate, to whom to provide grants, from whom to procure services, and generally how to engage with others—in other words, who gets the benefits. If decision making is driven by allegiances extraneous to the subject matter, off-piste competing interests, divided loyalties, or distracting incentives, then inappropriate bias can cause subjective results that are neither sound nor fair.

Two Levels of COI

■ **Competing interests (institutional).** It is quite common for a supporting entity of a partnership program to perform multiple roles—this is, for example, the hallmark of one-stop-shops. As part of these multiple roles, the supporting entity may take on various roles, like the fiduciary role of a trustee, and various responsibilities, like program implementation through an inhouse secretariat. These roles and responsibilities are usually accompanied by outside expectations of proper and uncompromised execution. The supporting entity may, however, have difficulty meeting those expectations when interests or even requirements of these multiple roles conflict. Even if duties and commitments are not overtly compromised, the supporting entity may remain vulnerable to perceptions that proper execution is less than assured.

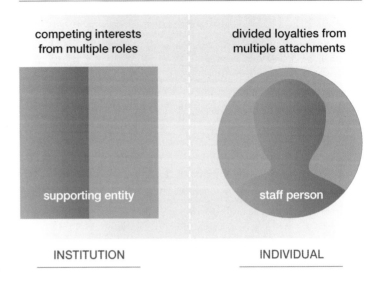

CONFLICTS OF INTEREST

competing interests from multiple roles

supporting entity

INSTITUTION

divided loyalties from multiple attachments

staff person

INDIVIDUAL

For example, if a secretariat head is underperforming to the point where results are suffering, a "proper" response might be to exit the individual—except that the supporting entity may be conflicted by its role as hiring manager and the inclination to protect that individual for internal political or potential liability reasons. This is a case where the interests of the secretariat acting on behalf of the partnership program are competing with the interests of the institution that is the secretariat. Partners might say the supporting entity has a conflict of interest, pitching its own interests vs. those of the partnership program.

■ **Divided loyalties (individual).** Not only do partner entities take on multiple roles in partnership programs, but individuals engaged in partnership programs may also be subject to multiple sets of expectations. This is a conflict of interest at the staff level, not the entity level. When a staff person carries responsibilities vis-à-vis an outside element (like sitting on a dedicated entity partnership's corporate board), those responsibilities may diverge and conflict with the staff person's responsibilities to her or his employer. Such conflicts can interfere with institutional obligations and undercut proper execution, in either or both directions. This includes undermining staff loyalty to the employer entity, an especially serious issue if the governing documents of that entity call for undivided loyalty. These divided loyalty situations are not limited to staff assigned (in whole or in part) directly to a particular partnership program, but can also affect other support staff, such as supporting entity lawyers assigned to help with inhouse secretariat implementation or corporate board representation, as part of the supporting entity's own business.

For example, a staff person assigned to represent her or his institution on the corporate board of another legal entity, like a dedicated entity partnership, normally needs to sit on that body in an institutional capacity, with full duty and loyalty to the home institution. (>@ Governing Bodies—Informal vs. Formal Partnerships) This duty to home typically includes a duty of staff to inform direct management of things that pose reputational risks or could otherwise harm or affect the employer institution's operations. If confidential information about alleged fraud is presented to the corporate board, that staff person should be able to share the information institutionally with her or his own management at her or his own discretion. If the corporate entity were to disallow this kind of sharing of confidential information up the staff person's management chain, it would put the staff person in an untenable position of divided loyalties. (This does not, however, go both ways. Corruption allegations surfacing within the supporting entity cannot be shared willy-nilly with partners, but only in accordance with the supporting entity's policies and procedures, since staff are bound by those. That may well mean withholding information from partners for a while until substantiated. Home entity rules rule.)

Three Kinds of COI

1 Actual conflicts of interest are those that actually arise in practice, that exist, and that may in fact result in inappropriate decisions and results.

2 Potential conflicts of interest are possible or foreseeable under the circumstances. The difference between potential and actual conflicts is slight—they both harbor the prospect of inappropriate decision making.

3 Perceived conflicts of interest are those that seem to exist, that are perceived by others as potentially or actually affecting practice, even if they do not. Perceived conflicts may or may not reflect actual or potential conflicts. If they do not, the issue is more a matter of communication than conflict.

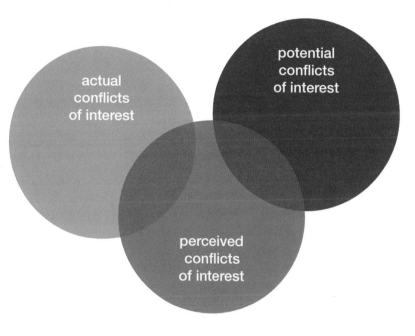

Once again, I'm confused.

Five Examples of COI

What does biased decision making look like concretely? For example:

1 Decisions are based on connections more than merit or content.

2 Decisions are made for kickback benefits or other personal gain.

3 Decision-making criteria are not objective or transparent, and hide bias.

4 Decision makers apply self-interested or other inappropriate factors.

5 Decisions promote an uneven playing field or confer unfair advantage.

Seeing and Seeking Synergies

Strict constructionists say conflicts of interest must be either avoided or eliminated, *punto*. However, there are virtually no strict constructionists that design international partnership programs, especially trust-funded, development partnership programs—those structures would likely be ruled out from the start. That is because "conflicts of interest" are endemic to these structured partnerships, embedded in their very fabric. There is practically no avoiding them if the point is greater upstream/downstream collaboration.

This is not to take conflicts of interest lightly. Partners should always stay attuned to the potential for improperly biased decision making and operations. However, certain types of "conflicts" are innate to collective mechanisms and collaborative platforms. Anyone who starts piping up about structural conflicts of interest in international partnership programs, especially in development, does so at the risk of undoing the very benefits the partnership programs are seeking to achieve.

One person's conflicts are another person's synergies.

Upstream/Downstream Synergies

To take the classic example, the very notion of upstream and downstream collaboration—where funders, implementers, and beneficiaries sit at the decision-making table together—can be considered a conflict of interest. Implementers and beneficiaries may try to influence funders to make decisions in their favor, to skew the outcomes to their benefit, potentially at the cost of other implementers and beneficiaries, so the reasoning goes. But isn't that exactly the point? Implementers and beneficiaries are not chosen from a competitive marketplace, but as partners. Having decisions skew in their favor is what funders actually seek to do, country ownership and all.

The point of development aid is to help implementers implement and beneficiaries benefit. To that end, it is not only valid to have downstream implementers and beneficiaries comment on what they want and how it is going for them—thereby affecting the upstream decision making—it is intended and imperative.

To put it another way, what looks like a conflict in a competitive marketplace is actually a synergy in an international development context. It is synergizing, rather than skewing, to coordinate, bring in country voice, recognize country priorities, generate lessons learned, and validate results. This all relies on having the upstream and downstream participants share views, influence each other's decisions, and even make shared decisions—in true collaboration, not as conflicts of interest. Here, funding allocations are not about the market's power of the purse, but rather the international partners' power of the purse, appropriately tempered by the recipients of that power.

On occasion, the suggestion that a beneficiary country sit as a member of the governing body, as a full partner, has been met with a stern diagnosis of "conflict of interest"—

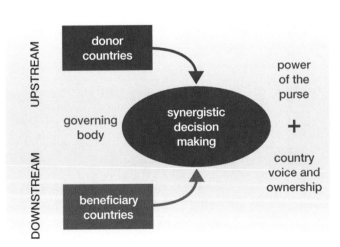

effectively saying this is not allowed. But that is like wearing blinders. If the seminal 2005 Paris Declaration on Aid Effectiveness and its progeny stood for anything, it was the principle that upstream and downstream actors would do development together, that donors and fiduciaries would work harder to give status and credence to the countries and beneficiaries they purport to want to help. Citing "conflicts of interest" as a reason to disinvite the parties that were supposed to be empowered seems misplaced.

Multiple Role Synergies

The same applies to one-stop-shops. One might say they are a hornet's nest of conflicts of interest, except that all the ways internal decision making can be skewed are actually the flip side of synergies that donors and other partners so enjoy. Partners love the one-stop-shop approach for its comprehensive suite of support, the full package that leverages the full heft of the supporting entity for the full benefit of the partnership program. This soup-to-nuts approach has been validated time and again. The results speak for themselves, and partners continue the uptake. The whole point is that the trustee and secretariat (support) functions are internally coordinated, along with the governing body member/chair (upstream) and implementing (downstream) functions, so the partnership program has a seamless, coherent, active home, and other partners can rest easy. Rather than view each role in isolation and say the supporting entity is conflicted with itself, this model of collaborative synergy has trumped conflict of interest concerns in partnership program after partnership program.

Just by breaking out the different roles into trustee, secretariat, chair, and more does not mean they need to be mapped into conflicts of interest. The secretariat will indeed be influenced by what the trustee thinks, and the chair may well favor his or her internal colleagues' interests, but that presumably reflects the charter, which has already established that institutional management and internal rules of the supporting entity prevail. In the spirit of partnership, all of the partnership program's support functions have to work together for the overall collaboration to work. This works especially well within one and the same institution, particularly if other partners are also shareholders, keeping an internal eye on support operations. Taken as a whole, this is a story of synergies, not an account of conflicts of interest.

SYNERGISTIC OPERATIONS

business context	potential roles
	chair
	donor
management	decision maker
operating framework	secretariat
	trustee
staff	implementer
	supervisor

supporting entity

Disclosing and Managing Conflicts

When it comes to conflicts of interest, international partnership programs can often disclose and manage rather than avoid and eliminate. Purported conflicts of interest—actual, potential, and perceived—that may be seen to arise from the very essence of the partnership program can be recast as synergies. If they are appreciated for their inclusive rather than distorting qualities, their positive effects can prevail. It is usually enough for participants to understand the structure, accept the rules of the road, appreciate the intentions, and proceed with eyes wide open. A charter adopted by the governing body is, in that sense, a blueprint for letting participants be clear about relationships and responsibilities, thereby moving beyond concerns of conflicts of interest to endorsements of synergies.

Disclose and manage.

Beware of strict constructionists that undercut the very essence of international partnership programs.

This is not to say that international partnership programs are immune from harmful conflicts of interest, some of which are described later in this chapter. For individual decision points, managing conflicted decision making may well justify recusal, which is when the conflicted party or person takes her- or himself out of the decision, typically as a one-off response to a specific case. Structurally, however, because conflicts of interest are both inherent in the multiple roles that some partners perform and integral to the inclusive partnering that all partners share, completely avoiding or eliminating them can produce extreme and unsustainable results. Taking a strict constructionist view would effectively undercut key principles for engaging in international partnership programs in the first place.

On multiple roles, the supporting entity is crucially placed to hold things together by coordinating its various roles internally—like secretariat, trustee, chair, implementer—rather than keeping aspects artificially separate. Partners are apt to feel the pain if this internal cohesion breaks down. Similarly, an internal lawyer should be able to support multiple partnering roles comprehensively and coherently, rather than insisting on different lawyers for different functions within the same entity because of alleged conflicts of interest. All internal lawyers work for and ultimately protect the same institution and perform under the same senior management. Separating them into role-specific silos usually wipes out important benefits to both the supporting entity and all partners. If some of the partnership program participants are at odds with the supporting entity's governing environment, this kind of siloed legal support can even exacerbate tensions.

you should be feeling like this

In this vein, the supporting entity has an interest in managing its overall risk profile regardless of any individual functions it performs—something that is true of every partner. It has to be able to influence decision making and its own participation enough to comfortably engage. Claiming that a supporting entity cannot be a decision maker or have rights of consent because it is conflicted ignores the nature of the engagement and the extent of exposure. Similarly, beneficiary countries should be able to influence decisions with country voice in favor of country priorities and consistent with country contours. Implementing entities, too, cannot be made to implement things except in ways they are prepared to implement. These are chosen partners, not competitive bidders, whose downstream participation has upstream relevance. "Conflicting" out these views in some purist fashion would cut at the quintessence of international partnership programs.

In the end, conflict of interest risks should be weighed against partnership and performance benefits, rather than viewed in the abstract. On balance, international partnership programs and their intertwined partnership structures usually carry a welcome bias, based on interests that are acknowledged and appreciated, even encouraged. In international partnership programs, especially in the development arena, there is plenty of room to disclose and manage what might at first appear to be conflicts of interest in ways that promote sensitive, inclusive, above-board, development-promoting decision making and operations.

In search of:
sensitive,
inclusive,
above-board,
development-promoting,
partnership structures

Conflicts to Avoid

After explaining why cooperative/collaborative partnership elements are more about partnership synergies than conflicts of interest, it is still appropriate to look at real conflicts of interest that partnership programs might face. These certainly come up and can arise in connection with any participant. A look at potential pitfalls for supporting entities across a few functions can be instructive across the board:

- trust fund management

- governing body representation

- inhouse secretariat support

In most cases, these pitfalls can be managed through transparent decision making, objective standards, and adequate reporting. What at first glance might look like a conflict of interest could, on further contemplation, have a justification or different interpretation. Whether something is ultimately deemed a conflict of interest or whether behavior is truly out of line is not always easy to pin down, and this often leads partners to disclose, manage, and trust. Yes, the availability of trust, based on strong relationships and proven track records, is a valuable addition to the mix. To a noteworthy degree, partners trust the supporting entity and other partners to do the right thing—to act in the interests of the partnership program's goals—on the basis of common understandings and a solid history of interaction and support.

Heffalump Traps

Without wishing to cast aspersions or imply that potential issues raised here are likely to arise, we can still—for the sake of a fuller landscape—take a closer look at the supporting entity and where it could go astray in a few of its roles. As Winnie-the-Pooh knows, some of these heffalump traps may be easy enough to fall into, even as you're just walking along.

Potential pitfalls as:

1. trustee
2. governing body participant
3. inhouse secretariat

■ *As trustee.* The trustee has a fiduciary duty to manage donor funds on terms agreed with the donors, usually with significant residual discretion. Partners can watch for COI dynamics when the supporting entity's role as trustee may be

- affected by internal pressures to use funds to finance its own staff or the inhouse secretariat—more than may be in the interests of the donors or partnership program overall;

- unduly influenced by relationships with outside parties to develop proposals from which those parties may benefit—for reasons outside the partnership program's objectives; or

- unduly influenced in allocating funds by its own programming elsewhere—in ways that favor those internal programs at the expense of other intended recipients.

■ *As governing body participant.* A supporting entity representative on a governing body is there for the partnership program while also carrying duties to her or his own institution. This is ultimately about clarity of interests more than COI, so note that

- international organization staff serving as institutional representatives on governing bodies—whether informal bodies of international partnership programs or corporate boards of formal legal entities—need room to meet obligations and interests of their own organizations, even if they conflict with partnership program interests; and

- international organization staff serving on outside boards related to their staff work might be tempted to favor individual over institutional interests, but are best fully integrated into their own home base and management structures for good coordination, integrity, P&I protection, and continuity management. (>@ Governing Bodies—Informal vs. Formal)

- **As inhouse secretariat.** For supporting entity staff with a duty of loyalty to the supporting entity, setting some clear rules may preclude COI. Supporting entities can consider clarifying that

  - supporting entity staff must first observe any loyalties or duties to their own entity, since running a secretariat from within a supporting entity means not running roughshod over supporting entity management, rules, and interests;

  - supporting entity staff can seek to meet partner expectations and further partnership program interests as long as everyone understands this is ultimately within supporting entity management, rules, and interests; and

  - partnership program participants interested in hiring and firing decisions about key support staff must take a back seat to the supporting entity's relationship with its staff under their terms of employment.

Conclusion

Labeling something a conflict of interest can be a first step to recognizing tensions that arise within international partnership program structures. This can then open the door to managing any risk, bias, or wrongdoing, rather than shutting the door to engagement. By acknowledging that relationships appearing to give rise to conflicts of interest may also be creating valued synergies, partners can reframe issues into opportunities to test and pursue what matters most.

When it comes to international partnership programs, partners can take care not to let an abstract focus on conflicts drive out an appreciation of synergies. The same structure that appears to pose a conflict of interest may be leveraging exactly those synergies that let the partnership program become sustainable, effective, and impactful. Claims of conflict of interest are always worth a second look, first to see what is actually in conflict, and second to see if a synergistic lens justifies collaborative, coordinated, leveraged, and inclusive structures.

Try opening the door to managing, not shutting the door to engaging.

6 TRUSTEE TYPES

This is the first of three chapters that consider trust fund aspects in greater detail. In succession, we take up the who (focus on the trustee; this chapter), the what (focus on fund use; >@ Use of Funds), and the how (focus on responsibility for that fund use; >@ Fund Use Responsibility). The trustee typically has a prominent place at the center of international partnership programs. Whether the trust fund accounts are chock full or scraping the barrel, the trustee has a crucial role in trust-funded partnership program operations. A trustee that handles large sums needs to be no less dexterous than a trustee that handles small sums. Always, the nature of the trustee should be chosen to match the context.

Variety

International trustees come in different flavors, from plain vanilla to soursop-sopadilla, and that enables international partners to position trustees according to their tastes. For partners that are not long at the table, plain vanilla trustees simply take funds and implement on behalf of donors with little to no fanfare, no bells and whistles, using standard operating procedures and getting on with it. At the far end of the spectrum, these are embedded partnerships, where the partnering basically occurs upfront, only long enough to position the trustee to follow through as agreed. (>@ Typology—The Even Broader Landscape of Structured Partnerships)

For partners with more complex tastes, there are more exotic varieties, where international partners push the envelope of innovation to stretch trustee roles in conjunction with market mechanisms, special purpose vehicles, treasury operations, and other arrangements and add-ons. We won't go into those innovations here; that would be the subject of another book. However, if there is a fiduciary role to be played somewhere in the structure, and the purposes of the endeavor fit within the trustee entity's institutional mandate—and all parties are willing to take the time, effort, and cost to explore intricate structural avenues—there may be room to define and agree on a distinctive flavor of international trustee for a specific case with sui generis features. Remember, an international trustee is not defined by statute or jurisprudence, but by the parties. (>@ Trust Funds—Trustees)

In general, the trustee is where fund flow terms and governance terms converge most acutely. Donors want their requirements and conditions legally memorialized at the point of contribution, usually on a bilateral basis. In an international partnership program, these bilateral contributions occur within a multilateral context, commonly through multi-donor trust funds with shared governance. This multilateral convening features a series of collectives, of which pooled funding is only part of the mix. (>@ International Partnership Programs—Collectivizing) To see this played out more concretely, we can again compare one-stop-shops with international platforms and get the lay of the land. This lets us compare two fiduciary flavors: **full trustees** and **limited trustees**.

One-Stop-Shops—Full Trustees

One-stop-shops feature the full trustee, who has fiduciary responsibility from top to bottom. As a result, in most one-stop-shops, the focus tends to be on the trust fund first and partnership second. All elements converge around the commingled account—the contributions and contribution agreements that flow into it, the activities and grant agreements that flow out of it, with shared governance but a complementary feature. The trustee is the center of attention, like the hub of a wheel around which all spokes turn. Shared governance is defined primarily in relation to funding—what is needed to direct or decide funding allocations—with the overall focus on proposal generation, funding coordination, and funded results. In many cases, the trustee prefers to keep its management of the trust fund in the foreground, while minimizing any shared governance that comes along.

The trustee is where fund flows and governance terms converge most acutely.

This is the international partnership program world inverted, when the design exercise zeros in on the trust fund, rather than the partnership program. Instead of focusing first on the partnership being convened and then incorporating the supporting elements, like funding vehicles, the trust fund becomes the starting point, from which the structure looks upward and downward. It is tempting to say that replacing partners with accounts as the focal point is akin to defining corporations as persons. Real people become secondary to legal constructs.

In one-stop-shops, however, this trustee-centric view of the world is by design. The legal entity acting as trustee (as financial manager and fiduciary) can also act as convener, broker, secretariat, governing body member, chair, possibly donor, and implementing and supervising entity—participating as an outsized partner, not a mere contractor—and accordingly with a lot of heft. As quid pro quo for all the benefits to donors and others of the full package of support and the full capacity of the supporting entity, the one-stop-shop world revolves around the policies, procedures, and management of this trustee-partner institution.

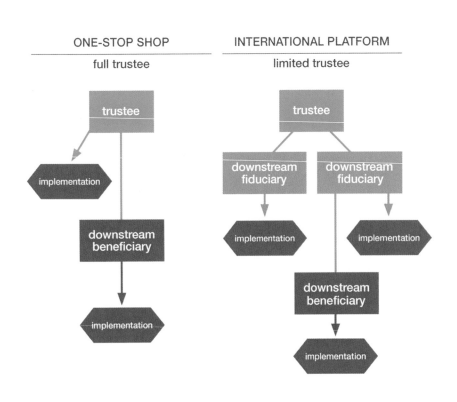

ONE-STOP SHOP — full trustee

INTERNATIONAL PLATFORM — limited trustee

With such broad exposure to the partners and such deep association with the international partnership program, this trustee-plus entity is necessarily under pressure to keep control of the partnership program, both to manage the entity's risk profile and stay within its mandate, rules, and regulations. What better way to circumscribe the partnership dynamics and handle external relations (from the trustee entity's point of view) than to define the partnership program as secondary to the trust fund. With the trustee in charge, this proves a better fit for the institution than establishing the partnership centrally with the trust fund as an add-on. If the trust fund is the core, the trustee is king, and the trustee entity reigns. Donors and other partners get their piece, in the gallery, in exchange for putting the onus on the trustee—a worthy exchange for many.

International Platforms—Limited Trustees

International platforms feature the limited trustee, which has responsibility only for the central trust fund within an extended partnership arrangement. This trust fund is often the impetus for the partnership program, but the focus is on the platform as a whole, including the governing body upstream and the implementing partners downstream. International platforms, especially the large ones, can be like mini-businesses, often convened by the trustee entity, but usually in the context of a broader international push and largely contoured by the contributors and their sizeable contributions. Donors typically end up in the driver's seat more than the trustee—such is the value of money—and often drive greater customization.

Despite what are at times expansive accommodations, the limited trustee is by design limited in one crucial way: its fiduciary responsibility. International platforms are best viewed as a series of building blocks, a structure that connects and aligns an interlocking set of players and functions. It has a common core—common mission, common strategy, common governance, common funding—supported by distinct, modular functions, of which the trustee is but one, and only one, of a number of key players. In the fund flows profile, the international platform trustee is just a starting point down the fund flows chain, to be followed by other entities, usually other fiduciary entities (which can include the same legal entity as the trustee entity, albeit in a distinct function).

The Not-So-Limited Limited Trustee

To be sure, "limited" trustees are hardly limited when it comes to what they can do, especially given financial management demands that come with hundreds of millions, if not billions, in contributions. This greater flow of funds can justify and pay for greater complexity, be it multi-currency operations, multi-window financial tracking, multi-year cash and promissory note installments, long-term loan-accompanying operations, and other financial management bells and whistles. Limited trustees backed by sophisticated inhouse treasury departments can also provide a range of other financial management services, including bonds, hedges, insurance mechanisms, and monetized carbon credits. Having room to customize or come up with innovative financing can be one of their main selling points, particularly in comparison to one-stop-shop trustees that normally conform to standard approaches under set policy frameworks. Being limited as a fiduciary does not have to mean being limited in every other way.

As negotiated and agreed within this modular context, the international platform trustee limits its responsibilities to *only the funds that it holds*—starting upon receipt and ending upon transfer. This is the linchpin to engaging multiple downstream entities, each with its own fiduciary framework, each with the trust of the donors to implement and supervise responsibly. When the international platform trustee transfers the funds, it also transfers the fiduciary responsibility—two in one. If drafted clearly, a clean handover lets the original trustee be "limited" from legal, accounting, operating, and risk perspectives. This is quite the contrast to a one-stop-shop trustee who takes it all on.

Compared with one-stop-shops, limited trusteeship goes against the grain. Donors would rather have more fiduciaries on the hook, not less, and they know the one they started with. Any trustee that wants to limit its fiduciary responsibility has to bend over backwards to make those limitations clear. Usually rights and obligations in contribution agreements are spelled out in the positive—"the trustee shall." For limited trustees, however, obligations are best spelled out in the positive *and* negative. (>@ Fund Use Responsibility—Transferred (No) Responsibility) But the vigilance does not stop there. It is not enough to limit the trustee with contractual positives and negatives if the same legal entity is also providing other support roles, like the secretariat. For that, let me explain about ensuring clean handovers and avoiding backdoor trustees, all for the sake of no messy middle.

The limited trustee is a two-fer: passing funds and fiduciary responsibility.

Clean Handovers Downstream

International platforms can be thought of as a pass-the-baton relay between the limited trustee and downstream fiduciaries. Either the original trustee has fund use responsibility or each of the others does; no gap, no overlap. The transfer should be a **clean handover, with a clear and complete shift in the chain of responsibility**. In this context, an unbounded secretariat can expand, or be perceived as expanding, the limitations set on the trustee and the responsibilities the trustee transfers downstream. Both the secretariat and trustee together must take care to operate within their respective limits and not overstep their respective bounds.

Once funds are transferred downstream by the limited trustee, the downstream fiduciary kicks in, acting effectively as a full trustee one tier down. In this way, an international platform structure combines a limited trustee role with full trustee-like roles. Explained this way, it becomes clear that, from a structural perspective, international platforms combine multiple, disaggregated, second-tier trustee-like functions under a single, centralized, first-tier trustee function. This is like putting several smaller sub-trust funds under a larger super-trust fund, with one big—and crucial—difference: each of the underlying trust funds operates on the basis of its own rules.

Major pause to contemplate. This is a big deal and worth repeating: Because international platforms are outward-looking paradigms of mutual respect, they let **downstream fiduciaries implement on the basis of their own rules**, the mantra being their own "applicable policies and procedures." The limited trustee is not imposing its own rules, nor is it supervising. In an ideal scenario, downstream fiduciaries are treated in full as replacement trustees, with complete reliance by donors on each of their respective operating frameworks, which they follow independently and without interference from above. Their obligations for fund use are only and directly to the donors whose funds they are using and the governing body that approved the funding terms for that use, legally bypassing the originating trustee.

Of course, since donors are legal entities, and informal partnership program governing bodies are not, the contractualization and enforceability of fund use obligations in most cases rest with the donors alone. (>@ Fund Use Responsibility—Collective Responsibility) That said, in more innovative cases, downstream obligations to donors, specifically around recourse and remedies, can be negotiated as collective procedures that involve governing bodies—yet another form of partnership program collectivizing. (>@ Fund Use Responsibility—Transferred (No) Responsibility)

Considering how difficult it is to slot one fiduciary under another, where rules may be similar, but not quite the same, and where efficient and effective functioning depends on consistency with internal procedures and systems, this modularity around applicable rules is arguably the single most valuable feature of limited-trustee international platforms. But it has to be clean, clear, and complete to work.

original trustee
= limited trustee

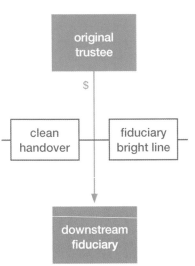

downstream fiduciary
≅ full trustee

What's the key to the limited trustee? Clean and clear modularity around downstream "applicable rules."

The Trustee-Secretariat Axis

The trustee-secretariat support axis within one and the same entity is a very common, almost customary feature in international partnership programs. (>@ Secretariats—Embedded, Inhouse Secretariats) It applies by definition to one-stop-shops, so much so that the two roles often meld into one (the trustee), and it is also a frequent feature of international platforms. When it comes to limiting the trustee in international platforms, that task is usually coupled with limiting the other partnership program functions provided by the same supporting entity. The concern is that the supporting entity not become a backdoor trustee through the secretariat or other roles.

For example, a secretariat that not only compiles progress reports but also does desk reviews with substantive comments on results, is crossing the line into trustee-type responsibility. By doing so, the secretariat is providing a form of fiduciary support, undercutting the intention of keeping the original trustee role limited and out of the downstream fiduciary kitchen. Similarly, if the secretariat agrees to establish and apply accreditation criteria to determine eligible downstream fiduciaries, it is now weighing in on substantive fiduciary standards that belong to the governing body. This goes beyond administrative (limited) support functions and supplants the responsibility that donors through the governing body are meant to bear.

This concern about keeping the supporting entity in a box typically also dictates that the supporting entity not have a decision-making role on the governing body. While this is a valid position, it is not immutable. The supporting entity can instead position its role with more nuance if it is also a partner. Should its balance of engagement be more supporting or shaping, or both? As a trustee and secretariat, it is supporting; as a partner, it could legitimately also shape. Even in international platforms, where the baselines are modular limits, partners can consider engaging the supporting entity as an institution that additionally has a full and equal say in determining the direction of the partnership program. (>@ Governing Bodies—Supporting Entities)

Modular Combinations

We have seen how trustees fit into the two ends of the spectrum—one-stop-shops and international platforms—and how these two types variously maximize, minimize, or modulate different elements of shared and stand-alone responsibility. To round out the picture, a few words should be added to underscore the modularity of trustee functions as a matter of partnership program structure. As noted, it always depends on what the supporting entity is willing to do and what other partners, especially donors, are willing to accept, but the "mix + match" approach potentially offers more possibilities than partners may realize.

In a fit-for-purpose design, it is important to consider where the comparative advantages lie, who is best positioned to play what roles, and where layers are needed or can be avoided. These tests are directly relevant to fiduciary functions—as a measure of the partners' risk appetites, as a reflection of the implementing entities' operating frameworks, and as a function of cost, efficiency, and ownership. It may well be that what looks like a more

With a limited trustee, don't let the secretariat become a backdoor trustee.

Trust Fund Structures

Let's briefly scan the spectrum again, to see how this all lines up. You can have:

1. **One simple bucket**—a single, commingled trustee-level account, as one entry point for donors, each with a contribution agreement, feeding into one set scope of trustee-implemented activities (one-stop-shops)

2. **One bucket with multiple, separate spouts**—a single commingled trustee-level account, again as one entry point for donors, but feeding into separate, independent implementation channels by multiple, usually fiduciary, entities (international platforms)

3. **One bucket with partitions**—also a single trust fund, one entry point for donors with one contribution agreement, but that lets donors direct their funds to multiple, distinct, trustee-level accounts/windows, usually tagged to specific sectors, themes, or countries (earmarking)

4. **Multiple buckets**—multiple trust funds, each a different entry point and different contribution agreements for donors, potentially under an overarching governance arrangement (umbrella arrangements)

For completeness, it is possible to mix and match. A single partnership program can draw from all of the above, including with a single trust fund that is part one-stop-shop (category 1) and has added pass-through implementation channels (category 2) and/or windows (category 3). Each trust fund in multiple-bucket arrangements (category 4) can be its own combination of categories, all depending on what partners want, what trustees are willing to do, and how bespoke the design is allowed to be. This layering—whether within the same trust fund or across multiple trust funds—is not as bad as fractals, but partners should weigh the options, knowing that each iteration creates another compounding layer of cost and complexity.

To put them in context, international platforms are characterized by multiple spouts (category 2) that often flow into trust funds run by the fiduciary recipients (categories 5 and 6). They start from the premise that implementation is disaggregated by entity, but keep a convenient single point of entry for donors. In this way, international platforms are hybrids. Much like partnership programs are hybrids (new shared governance, existing support) between fully embedded and fully dedicated partnerships (>@ Typology—Light to Heavy), international platforms are also hybrids (shared entry; separate implementation) between one-stop-shops and umbrella arrangements. They combine collectivized advantages at the top (upstream) with disaggregated advantages at the bottom (downstream). To paraphrase Goldilocks again, assuming she is an internationalist, the answer may be not too hot, not too cold, but in between, just right.

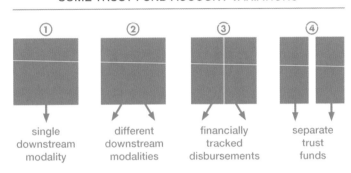

SOME TRUST FUND ACCOUNT VARIATIONS

① single downstream modality ② different downstream modalities ③ financially tracked disbursements ④ separate trust funds

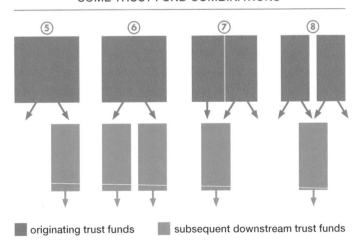

SOME TRUST FUND COMBINATIONS

⑤ ⑥ ⑦ ⑧

■ originating trust funds   ■ subsequent downstream trust funds

complex structure is actually the simplest. For example, it is far more complex to layer one fiduciary entity over another fiduciary entity in order to apply only one set of rules (even if one set of rules sounds simpler) than to allow each robust fiduciary to apply its own rules when it has the funds. An international partnership program that wants a single point of entry through one trustee/supporting entity, but also wants more than one downstream fiduciary entity, each operating on the basis of its own rules, can consider a modified one-stop-shop. It may be that using a full trustee up top, but building in limited trustee roles with fiduciary carve-outs down below, could work the best.

These are business choices. Whether it is better to make the whole trust fund operate with a full trustee (one-stop-shop), or just part of it (mix + match), or move everything into a limited trustee model (international platform), or break it all out into separate full trustees (umbrella arrangement), or something different (innovate!), is part of the design conversation partners can have. The point is to converge around fit-for-purpose structures that leverage comparative advantages, while keeping it clear, clean, and simple to maximize sustainability, efficiency, and impact.

Trustee Entity

Now a few words about the trustee entity, to peer into what may seem like a black box. The international trustee, whether full or limited, is not a stand-alone function. It is embedded in an existing entity, deriving its legal status—which ideally includes privileges and immunities—from its home base. This is more than a trivial association; it is integral to the trustee's being and ability to perform. The trustee is directly identified and closely integrated with the trustee entity, even more so than the secretariat with the secretariat supporting entity (often the same entity). Legally speaking, both functions are fully embedded in their entities, but operationally the relationships are quite different. While the secretariat exists for and because of the partnership program, particularly in relation to the governing body, the trustee operates in its own right. The trustee steps up as a principal, not an agent, and commits to contractual terms that are expected to be enforceable. Contracted under fund flow agreements, the trustee is effectively the trustee *entity*, the legal entity that provides the legal status needed to sign enforceable agreements.

From an entity perspective, the trustee function has an inward-outward dimension (trustee entity—donors), as with secretariats (supporting entity—governing body; >@ Secretariats—Lessons Learned). In both cases, the legal entity creates the inward dynamic, while the partnership element creates the outward dynamic. However, vis-à-vis the outer element, the dynamic is exactly opposite. The trustee's fiduciary role under fund flow agreements is designed to create a separation from donors. Donors explicitly shift responsibility for fund use away from themselves over to the trustee. By contrast, the secretariat's support role under the constitutive documents brings the secretariat closer to the donors and other governing body members. Donors and other governing body members typically pull the secretariat in toward them, as agent on their behalf, in support of the overall partnership program. (>@ Secretariats) At the same time, donors want an arm's-length relationship with the trustee and legally distance themselves from the entity and fund use responsibility.

The donor-trustee at arm's length

vs.

the donor-secretariat embrace.

It helps to understand this difference. When the supporting entity and the trustee entity are the same legal entity, the same organization, as is often the case, these divergent dynamics—the simultaneous push and pull of partner engagement—can be the root cause of crossed wires and fraying frictions if they are not well understood.

Trustee Costs

As long as we are on the subject of the trustee entity, it is also useful to add a few words on trustee costs, and with that a word on supporting entity costs generally. As with the secretariat, trustee support provided by international organizations is usually provided on a full cost recovery basis with varied funding models.

In one-stop-shops, trustee full cost recovery is typically standardized as part of the overall fee or cost structure of the trust fund, in addition to or wrapped in with other support costs, like secretariat-type functions and institutional overhead. The biggest line item is usually staff costs. Amounts are usually part of the business model and memorialized bilaterally with donors—for fairness, usually one-size-fits-all as one of the common terms for a multi-donor fund—and are not under the purview of the broader governing body. If linked directly to cash flows, fees may be charged as fixed percentages on either inflows (contributions) or outflows (transfers/grants).

In international platforms, trustee costs are usually also based on full cost recovery, but often presented as an estimated budget, along with a separate secretariat budget, for governing body approval. This is commensurate with the more central role of the governing body, the distinct role of the secretariat, and the modular, open participation design that treats costs across more players (supporting and fiduciary entities) more transparently. It also reflects greater, potentially non-standard financial management complexity that is more typical of larger international platforms. Expenses may depend, for example, on the number of donors, agreements, and deposits; the size, currency, and frequency of contributions; the amounts held in balance subject to investment management costs and fees; the number of windows and related maintenance; the number of operating currencies; and more. To be sure, the more features, the more cost. To achieve full cost recovery, if the principle is actual costs, the approved budget is usually automatically topped up (or docked) at the fiscal year-end to make up any difference.

More features, more cost.

Fixed fees are, of course, approximations, whereas actual expenditures are real. Under a fixed fee regime, trustee (and secretariat) entities may pitch higher fees that err on the side of caution, or place more limits on the support they provide. Under an expenditure regime, trustees and secretariats may get approval for estimated budgets that are then reconciled to cover actual costs either above or below the estimates. Either way, these support functions need sustainable budget models that keep them out of the red, unless other business lines or revenues are available to subsidize partnership program support. But this kind of subsidizing, which amounts to an in-kind contribution from supporting entities, is normally not available—and even less scalable. As a result, supporting entity pressure for total cost recovery can clash with donor preferences for low-cost structures. Donors shop around and compare rates, at times scrutinizing trust fund numbers without fully appreciating partnership program aspects. In the end, efficiency gains go only so far, and you get what you pay for. The degree of trustee/secretariat support and *ability* to engage ultimately reflects the degree of donor support and *willingness* to engage.

Conclusion

With the centrality of funds, and the corresponding centrality of trust funds, in international partnership programs, it may seem almost futile or even counterproductive to keep preaching "it's the partnership that matters!" But from a structural point of view, it really does. Even in giving trust funds their due and trustees their deference, it is the larger context that determines their fit and validates their usefulness.

Figuring out how the trustee fits into the upstream and into the downstream, and how it relates to the secretariat and potentially other fiduciaries, is an exercise that focuses on roles and entities—the trustee vis-à-vis bodies, functions, and organizations that bring their respective parameters. Four things are important here for placement of the trustee vis-à-vis other elements:

1. a seamless, no-gap fit

2. a clean, non-overlapping fit

3. a clear, well-delineated fit

4. a synergistic, complementary fit

In the next two chapters, we'll see how the trustee fits in with use—what constitutes proper fund use and how responsibility for proper use can be apportioned. As we look more closely, keep an eye on the trustee and watch where design decisions can take that role when international partnership programs operationalize their trust funds to maximum advantage.

If you are reading this any later than 12:01

Make yourself some tea and go to bed.

7

USE OF FUNDS

International partnership programs often come in the trust-funded variety. This signals a partnership program with branded activities that are centrally funded, and potentially also centrally implemented, enough to justify establishment of one or more dedicated trust funds. This then also makes the use of the funds a central focus for the partnership program, not just for the donors, but all partners.

When it comes to trust funds, it is important to keep track of two things: proper fund use and effective impact. Both are results of the partnership program, one in financial terms, confirmed by financial reports and audits, and one in activity terms, measured by progress reports and evaluations. While proper fund use is expected, and even contractually obligated, effective impact is hoped for. Visibility about fund use usually means bad press, while visibility of impact is leveraged for good press. With these and other differences, proper fund use usually gets less attention than positive program results. Partners much prefer to talk about performance indicators and M&E (monitoring and evaluation) than about eligible expenditures and audits. And yet, bad news on fund use—especially fraud and corruption—can be more toxic to a partnership program than bad news on results. While assessments of progress can be managed and massaged, it is harder to scrub and soften a diagnosis of missing funds.

Proper vs. Improper Use

Logically, use of funds can be divided into proper and improper use. These might seem to be direct opposites—proper fund use is defined within a certain scope of what is allowed, and improper fund use is anything outside that scope—but there is more to it. Improper fund use—or, more malevolently, fund *misuse*—can include other carve-outs from the broad rubric of what is allowed. Off-limits or at least questionable scenarios might include the following:

- tied funds—funds from a donor that are used to benefit the donor, as in using funds contributed to a trust fund to hire staff or consultants that are nationals of the donor country;

- conflicted funds—funds that are used for or by someone under biased circumstances in connection with a conflict of interest (>@ Synergistic Conflicts);

- nontransparent funds—funds that are intentionally below the radar, rather than acknowledged and above board, as when a recipient country resists public disclosure of a grant agreement;

- diverted funds—under the AML/CFT rubric (anti-money laundering and combating financing of terrorism), funds that end up in the wrong hands for the wrong purposes; and

- harmful funds—funds for activities that cause or trigger harm or damage to individuals, communities, or environments.

1. tied funds
2. conflicted funds
3. nontransparent funds
4. diverted funds
5. harmful funds

And then there are the four horsemen of ill repute, from which fund misuse can arise (in legalese):

- fraud—an act or omission, including misrepresentation, that knowingly or recklessly misleads, or attempts to mislead, a party to obtain financial or other benefit or to avoid an obligation;

- corruption—offering, giving, receiving, or soliciting, directly or indirectly, anything of value to improperly influence the actions of another party;

- coercion—impairing or harming, or threatening to impair or harm, directly or indirectly, any party or property of the party to improperly influence the actions of a party; and

- collusion—an arrangement between two or more parties designed to achieve an improper purpose, including to improperly influence another party.

1. fraud
2. corruption
3. coercion
4. collusion

When thinking about fund use in partnership programs, it is both a matter of sticking within the bounds of what is contractually allowed and keeping to the overall objectives, without diverting benefits, enabling ulterior motives, or causing harm. Fund use in this sense dovetails with partnership program results. In terms of good stewardship and reputational risk, it is a topic not only for accountants but all partners—and by extension also the donors' taxpayers. In most international partnership programs, the use of public sector funds, like ODA for development purposes, puts heightened scrutiny on the way in which funds are used, from the public for the public, as a public good.

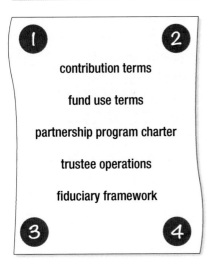

contribution terms

fund use terms

partnership program charter

trustee operations

fiduciary framework

Four Corners of
the Agreement:

What you see is
what you get;

what you agree is
what you've got.

Four Corners of the Agreement

International partnership programs conveniently allow donors and other partners to pick and choose where they want to engage and what they want to be responsible for. In this largely design-your-own environment, the primary way partners deal with the tedious topic of fund use is to hand it over to a fiduciary, like a trustee. The trust fund approach to humanitarian and development finance effectively outsources the drudgery of ensuring funds are properly used. This delegation of responsibility even outsources the meanings behind "proper" and "improper," with expectations that the trustee or other fiduciary entity supply the whole package of terms.

Crucially, the international trustee steps up to negotiated terms—usually within the four corners of contribution agreements—as opposed to some broader trust jurisprudence arising from civil codes, common law, statutes, or courts. As a result, the contribution agreement often acts as the point of entry for a donor both into the trust fund and the broader partnership program. In an ideal scenario:

- To align with the international partnership program, the contribution agreement incorporates by reference the partnership program's charter and potentially other key documents.

- To align with the trustee's fiduciary framework, it also incorporates by reference the relevant "applicable policies and procedures" of the trustee for implementing and supervising.

Following this approach, governing trust fund/trustee terms are as negotiated and agreed, not as regulated or adjudicated.

Eligible Expenditures

The specific scope of eligible expenditures is one part of the negotiated contribution agreement. These specified terms around objectives, activities, and eligible categories vary from trust fund to trust fund and are developed to fit the context, case-by-case. The actual description in each case depends on what the donors (collectively, for multi-donor trust funds) and trustee agree, which can be more or less detailed, more or less prescriptive, more or less inclusive or exclusive. For convenient drafting and easy reference, this description often shows up in an annex to the contribution agreement and is usually separated from standard terms, like those relating to trustee operations and obligations.

Applicable Policies and Procedures

This kind of contribution agreement usually relies on the tried and true shorthand of enlisting the fiduciary entity's operating framework—its "applicable policies and procedures"—as the governing framework for fund use. It takes but a sentence in the contribution agreement for the whole heft of the trustee/fiduciary entity to be brought to bear, including everything from substantive standards and process provisions to management discretion and responsibility. For multilateral organizations, like MDBs, this policy regime also happens to be under the watchful eye of donors doubling as shareholders, who may approve these policies at their board meetings. And so it comes full circle. Traditional sovereign donors provide funding under *applicable policies and procedures* knowing they have an overarching say in what standards are *applicable.*

Role of the Fiduciary

What does it mean to be a fiduciary? The fiduciary entity takes responsibility on behalf of donors for proper fund use. It accepts this responsibility at the same time it agrees to accept the funds. International partnership programs that rely on trust funds rely on the trustee as the main fiduciary and may also rely on downstream recipients as secondary fiduciaries.

- In the "full" trustee variant (think one-stop-shops), this fiduciary responsibility carries through to end use, even as the funds may pass from one hand to another. The trustee (or more broadly, the trustee entity) may use the funds itself or pass them on for another entity (a grant recipient) to use. In the first case, the trustee/trustee entity directly implements (what MDBs may call "bank execution"). In the second case, it supervises the grant recipient's implementation (what they may call "recipient execution"). The applicable operating framework of the full trustee, as full fiduciary, usually sets the terms and standards for this downstream supervision, unless otherwise negotiated in the contribution agreement. Downstream supervision usually includes rights by the trustee to conduct periodic supervisory missions and obligations of the grant recipients to keep accounts, provide reports, and commission audits.

- In the "limited" or "pass-through" trustee variant (think international platforms), this fiduciary responsibility attaches to the physical possession of the funds. Here the initial trustee is responsible for the funds it holds, no more and no less. As the funds flow through the chain of possession, so does the responsibility for their proper use. This is a kind of coupling, where both funds and responsibility pass downstream together. Usually this responsibility passes from fiduciary (trustee) to fiduciary (downstream fiduciary), although in a few, potentially challenging, cases, donors have allowed non-fiduciary, direct beneficiary recipients to become responsible for fund use without someone else supervising (sometimes called "direct access"). As a rule, fiduciaries do not supervise fiduciaries, and so this limited trustee approach defines "applicable policies and procedures" according to the fiduciary that gets the funds, not the one above, and then makes them applicable all the way down.

Clause 1: The terms of the charter, as modified from time to time, shall apply.

Clause 2: The applicable policies and procedures of the trustee shall apply.

Clause 3: . . . . . .

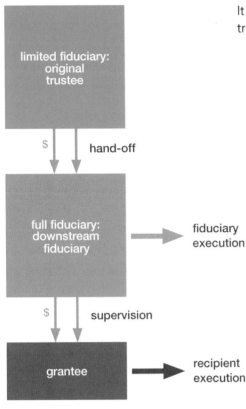

limited fiduciary: original trustee

$ hand-off

full fiduciary: downstream fiduciary → fiduciary execution

$ supervision

grantee → recipient execution

It is possible—and not uncommon—to mix and match these full and limited trustee flavors (>@ Trustee Types):

- On the one hand, a trustee can be both full and limited in the same trust fund with respect to different funds. While it may retain full fiduciary responsibility for most of the funds, a chunk could be transferred out on a limited trustee basis (sometimes called a "transfer out" or "pass-through"), as long as the terms are clear and transparent to the donors. These hybrid trust funds combine two trustee modalities not only to apportion responsibility, but also to apply different rules (applicable policies and procedures) to different implementation channels.

- On the other hand, because a limited trustee is almost always followed by a downstream fiduciary, this effectively puts a full trustee function under the limited trustee. This is how international platforms usually work and why they work so well. When downstream recipients take on fiduciary responsibility, they essentially act as full trustees one level down, often through their own second-level trust funds. This allows their individual operating frameworks to be leveraged all the remaining way to the end use of the funds, whether directly by the downstream fiduciary or subsequently by grant recipients. Structurally, this can position the equivalent of multiple full trustee trust funds under the central limited trustee trust fund, like roots off a trunk.

Providing "Concessionality"

There is yet another variation that can be mentioned as an example of the innovative scope around international trustees and the use of funds. Trust funds usually finance projects or activities, but they can also finance concessionality. "Concessionality" is understood to be lower than market rates of borrowing, which is typically what MDBs offer lower-income countries. Where donors wish to support and encourage global public goods that are provided at significant cost by middle-income countries (like hosting refugees), donors can use trust funds to turn regular loans into concessional loans that are normally not available to middle-income countries. In this approach, funds go directly to MDBs for their "use" in embedding those funds into their loan packages, resulting in an effective reduction of the borrowing rate—one way to achieve concessionality. The amount of funds provided can be calculated to meet certain pre-defined levels of concessionality on agreed terms.

This way of providing concessionality is not simply a matter of blended finance with a sidecar grant. Instead, it represents a full leveraging of MDB operations by letting funds become fully absorbed. "Providing concessionality" accordingly means MDB use of the funds to create an overall, integrated financing package that flows down as a composite loan to a borrower country, of which only the loan portion, not the concessionality portion, is then pro rata repaid. Because funds can be used only once, they are not used a second time to finance the downstream operation. In other words, although the funds increase the overall project budget, "use" is by the MDB, not the borrower. This has implications for fund use responsibilities (only in the hands of the MDB) and fund use risks (lower in the hands of the MDB). It also avoids additional appraisal or supervision costs charged to the trust fund, since they are already part of the MDB's operations. And ultimately, the benefit of the funds is not one-to-one as with a normal grant operation, but one-to-a-higher-number in leveraging the loan operation.

An Unbroken Chain

From a fund use perspective, this is key: in a normal fiduciary context, there is never a gap in the progression. Someone is always the fiduciary with responsibility to the donor, from the moment the funds are contributed to the time they are used, no matter how many transfers occur, no matter what funds or frameworks are involved. The donor hands the money off, and the ensuing progression is unbroken, link to link. From a legal perspective, the original terms agreed at the point of contribution set the baseline for any terms to follow. As funds move down the chain, the original terms flow down in one of three modes—(1) in their entirety, as is; (2) as a subset of the original scope of activities; or (3) based on standards that are higher than originally applicable.

1. **Straight flow-down:** The grant agreement says the same operating framework and scope apply as in the contribution agreement, and this operating framework and scope define how the grant agreement is handled.

2. **Subset flow-down:** The grant agreement applies the same operating framework, but adjusts the scope by limiting fund use to specific activities, like a particular project.

3. **Strengthened flow-down:** The grant agreement expands on the operating framework by spelling out additional protective, fiduciary terms, like third-party monitoring, more frequent procurement reviews, or project-specific environmental measures. This can be combined with (1) or (2).

Expenditures and Results

The link between what can be done and what actually gets done is a function of the international partnership program's governance, where "governance" is broadly understood to include both governing body and operational decisions. Since partnership programs are programmatic, this usually means a two-step process by which (1) the trust fund is given a broad scope of potential activities; and (2) subsequent decisions allocate specific funding to specific activities. Those subsequent decisions may be made by the trustee, the governing body, or some combination. (>@ International Partnership Programs—Shared Decision Making) For example, the governing body may consider specific funding requests to decide funding allocations on specified terms, or it may approve a high-level work plan after which the trustee follows through to decide specific grants and other expenditures. Or, in the alternative, the governing body may defer to trustee and secretariat functions for specific fund allocation decisions, either fully or with some degree of consultation.

In this programmatic context, it may be obvious that the defined scope for fund use should align with expected results. If, for example, a contribution agreement lists out activities that the trust fund may finance, the results framework should reflect intended progress resulting from those activities. In other words, partners should be deliberate in linking fund use and results. This linkage cues partners on how to prepare and position the results framework. It also positions what contributors can expect to take credit for. For results frameworks to be a realistic measure of what trust-funded activities can achieve, scoping proper fund use is the first step.

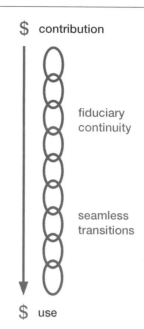

UNBROKEN CHAIN OF
FIDUCIARY RESPONSIBILITY

$ contribution

fiduciary
continuity

seamless
transitions

$ use

Fund use terms follow funds;

results follow fund use.

Repercussions

What happens if funds are misused? The usual remedy includes refunds, which means returning money to the trust fund, or possibly all the way back to individual donors on a pro rata basis. For development grants (recipient execution), this can be challenging. A low-income, developing country recipient that received grant funding to address poverty may not be in a good position to refund. Trustees and other fiduciaries may well look at the recipient's financial capacity to manage funds, as well as the project impact on the recipient and country as a whole, when considering a refund request. To soften the blow, refund demands can be tempered with specified undertakings to improve conditions or recouped through installment payments over time.

The role of the trustee/fiduciary in these cases is intricate. What did the fiduciary entity step up to, how far did its responsibility go? Is there donor recourse against the fiduciary, especially if the beneficiary recipient does not pay up? Contribution agreements can be relatively silent on remedies provisions, relying instead on applicable policies and procedures, and some trust in the trustee.

Importantly, the first principle is that the trustee (or other fiduciary entity) is not considered personally liable for recipient transgressions. Fund misuse by the recipient does not equate directly to trustee responsibility (the trustee does not control the recipient) and accordingly does not automatically extend to trustee liability. In managing the trust fund, the trustee is not guaranteeing proper fund use, just promising to supervise. That is a big difference. And yet, some level of supervision is expected—exactly in the manner and to the degree called for in the trustee's applicable policies and procedures (unless otherwise agreed).

The question then becomes: was the trustee negligent in following its applicable policies and procedures? Did the trustee properly apply its operating framework to supervise the recipient's fund use? The contribution agreement may not say one word about negligence or refunds, or trustee duty of care or liability, but if the trustee committed to following its applicable policies and procedures, then failure to do so properly—diligently and reasonably—could be a breach. And in that case, a refund may be proffered by the trustee if it acknowledges negligence.

In the end, when it comes to international trust funds, fiduciary liability tends to be a business equation more than a contractual result. The integrity of the trustee's business and the trustee's reputation are strong motivators for the trustee to pay the piper when the trustee falls asleep on the job. A track record of stepping up to fiduciary responsibilities, and taking the consequences if not, may give donors the comfort they need to continue their funding streams.

Conclusion

In ongoing international partnership program operations, donors and other partners are likely to focus on funded results more than fund use, at least until the proverbial mess hits the fan—although here's hoping it never does. In trust-funded partnership programs, this is by design, since trust funds allow donors and others to put the burden of fund use on other partners; namely, their fiduciary and implementing partners.

It is accordingly not happenstance that fund flows are premised on extensive deliberations and formal legalities. Donors rely on their fiduciaries to do as they have agreed, and these fiduciaries in turn rely on recipients to do as they have agreed. Use of funds rests on a serious hierarchy of responsibilities that involves a lot of down-in-the-weeds details that take a lot of articulating, aligning, and maintaining. But it does not take an accountant, lawyer, or trustee to recognize that fund misuse can severely impede a partnership program and lead to grave reputational and operational risk.

In this chapter, we have mostly addressed how proper and improper fund use gets defined. To fully appreciate fund use in international partnership programs overall, it also helps to understand who has what responsibility for following through. We'll look at that in the next chapter.

Donors rely on their fiduciaries;

fiduciaries rely on their recipients.

8 FUND USE RESPONSIBILITY

In designing international partnership programs, participants collectivize some things and allocate others. When it comes to trust funds, contributions are collectivized, but fund use responsibility gets allocated. More broadly:

- All partners are affected by fund use in the name of the partnership program.

- All partners have an interest in knowing that partnership program funds are properly and effectively used.

- Only designated partners have designated, individual responsibilities for proper fund use.

For all the emphasis in this book on collectivizing, that last point may seem out of step—collective, collective, not collective—but it makes sense, as we'll see.

Delineating Responsibility

Incoming funds and decision making about those funds can be "collectivized" as pooled funding and shared decision making (>@ International Partnership Programs—Collectivizing), but the responsibilities for fund use travel with the funds. Much as funds come into the partnership program from individual donors, funds also spread out to individual recipients. If you think about it, a partnership program that makes everyone responsible for every activity, even ones they do not control, probably would not last long. Partners have exposure to all activities reputationally and associationally, but giving them all actual responsibility for all activities would go too far.

International partnership programs are not normally joint ventures with joint and several liability, where everyone is equally liable for everything everyone else does in the partnership. It is also not a matter of saying whoever pays is responsible, but rather the opposite. With international trust funds, donors deliberately remove themselves from fund use responsibility. And it is also not a simple matter of saying whoever has or uses the funds is responsible. Most international partnership programs create layers and dispersions of responsibility. That makes the topic of fund use responsibility an interesting and important corollary to the topic of proper and effective fund use. (>@ Use of Funds)

From a structuring perspective, allocating fund use responsibility is a key element of international partnership program design. Trust-funded partnership programs, in particular, ascribe different responsibilities by layering trustees and downstream recipients. Operating through trust funds means that fund use responsibility rests on fiduciary responsibility. This fiduciary function may be a stand-alone role for a partner (for example, as trustee or downstream fiduciary only) or one of several roles (as trustee, plus secretariat and decision maker, as in one-stop-shops). The fiduciary entity may use the funds itself or devolve fund use to grantees for their use. This web of relationships needs structuring and defining to be sustainable, efficient, and effective.

In international trust-funded partnership programs, we can identify four common modes of fund use responsibility:

1 implementation responsibility

2 supervision responsibility

3 transferred (no) responsibility

4 collective responsibility

Some partnership programs operate with only one mode, most operate with a combination, and some even use all modes.

─────────────────────────── ● ───────────────────────────

What About Joint Responsibility?

Joint responsibility is not advised. Downstream implementers can cooperate, coordinate, and collaborate, but actually sharing responsibility creates a messy middle that is best avoided. This is particularly true from fiduciary and legal perspectives. (>@ Ten Tried and True Tips—Be Clean) When it comes to fund flows and fund use, partners should always know who is using and who is responsible—and overlapping two or more entities into joint relationships obscures that clarity. In this way, for example, partnership programs that operate on the basis of funding requests from downstream implementers are better off requiring separate proposals from individual entities, even if they come together as a package. The relevant proposals can articulate the same (shared) objectives, refer to an overall (total) project budget, and refer to each other. However, it should always be clear which funds flow to whom for what, separate and apart from other funding streams. This is attributable, auditable, and enforceable, all of which matters under fund flow agreements.

─────────────────────────── ● ───────────────────────────

Implementation Responsibility

Implementation responsibility is tied directly to fund use. It usually belongs to the entity making the actual payments to conduct activities, like payrolling staff and procuring consultants, goods, and services. In trust fund arrangements, implementation responsibility can lie with the same entity as the fiduciary entity (whether trustee or other downstream fiduciary), or it can drop a level and lie with a grantee entity. Whoever does the implementing does so as a matter of procurement. While procurement simply means procuring and paying for goods and services, procurement also represents direct implementation responsibility.

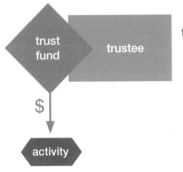

financial management and implementation responsibility

Procurement vs. Grantmaking

Have you ever wondered why trustees do not procure grants or enter into grant contracts? We usually say they *make* grants and enter into grant *agreements*. Why the difference? To follow where implementation responsibility lies, it helps to understand the difference between procurement and grantmaking.

In procurement situations, funds move from one entity to another, but implementation responsibility does not. A hired consultant, for example, does not become responsible to donors for fund use. Instead, that responsibility stays with the hiring entity, usually in a quid pro quo, delivery-for-payment relationship. The hiring (procuring) entity defines, controls, and owns the product that the consultant delivers.

Make, not procure, grants through grant *agreements*, not contracts.

In grantmaking, by contrast, the funds move and so does responsibility, as both shift from the funder/grantor to the recipient/grantee. Funds are provided for something under express terms of engagement, and once transferred, it is up to the recipient to use those funds and follow those terms. It becomes the recipient's implementation responsibility. Whereas a procurement situation generally sets up a service contract relationship, where control, responsibility, and ownership stay with the funder, a grant situation generally sets up an agreement relationship, where control, responsibility, and ownership shift to the recipient—in each case under agreed terms.

There are various other ways to describe the differences between procurement contracts and grant agreements. Procurements are for deliverables; grants usually are not. Procurement contracts usually call for specific delivery of a product or service to which payment is tied, whereas grant agreements are more aspirational, with expectations of reasonably diligent efforts. In some cases, grants are based on milestones, results, or other performance indicators to receive subsequent, tranched disbursements. Failure to meet those goals may mean no more money, but is not a contractual breach. In other words, grants are based on efforts and agreed activities more than delivery commitments. Arguably, a "best efforts" procurement contract, without a fixed delivery obligation, starts to look like a grant, but even grants with milestones are still not quid pro quo contracts.

Procurement rules for public funds are typically designed for standards like fairness, competition, economy, and transparency without favoritism, nepotism, discrimination, conflicts of interest, selective bias, and the like.

Interestingly, these enlightened procurement standards do not apply overtly to the selection of grantees. Grant recipients are viewed as partners instead of providers or vendors, and they are usually selected for their subjective fit rather than their ability to meet objective, competitive criteria. Choosing grant recipients may be relatively obvious when dealing with country projects that channel funds to relevant ministries and agencies, but for other grant recipients, they can just as easily be a matter of contacts, presence, or even happenstance. Grantors usually check potential grantees for adequate financial management systems and other capacity assessments to handle the funds, but it is not clear how much extra due diligence goes into vetting grant contenders. Even when grant recipients are chosen through a call for proposals, the final selection may still be based on subjective fit with the partnership program more than objective, competitive criteria. Grant recipients may even be known underperformers when the point of the grant funding is to assist capacity and institution building.

Since low-capacity grant recipients come with the territory, at least in the international development arena, donors and partners have had to consider ways to supplement recipient implementation to bolster proper and effective fund use. Part of this has to do with risk appetites. Donors and other partners are not monolithic when it comes to risk, and some circumstances may warrant higher-risk grantmaking. (>@ Risk and Review—Risk Innovation) However, mindful of their exposure, partnership program participants usually want fund use to be accompanied by good processes, standards, management, and system controls. If any of this is lacking in the grantee, partners tend to lean on fiduciary operations and other interventions to manage implementation risk from both fund use and impact perspectives. And that brings us to supervision responsibility.

> Grantmaking is also a two-fer:
>
> passing funds and implementation responsibility.

Supervision Responsibility

Supervision is another kind of fund use responsibility. In trust fund settings, supervision is an add-on to improve proper and effective fund use. It is a uniquely fiduciary function. It is also a discretionary function, and not all implementation is supervised, especially not if the recipient is also a fiduciary in its own right or has similarly robust operations. However, when engaging development recipients with lower capacity, system limitations, and institutional challenges, sometimes in conflict-affected and fragile countries, fiduciary supervision is usually a must-have for ODA donors.

Just as implementation responsibility is both about proper fund use (eligible expenditures) and effective fund use (progress and results), so too does supervision responsibility encompass both aspects. A fiduciary entity inserted between the upstream donors and the downstream recipients is there both to make sure money is not misused or made to disappear *and* to keep tabs on progress. An implementing entity provides both financial and progress reports, the supervising entity reviews both, and information on both fronts is usually passed on to donors and other partners.

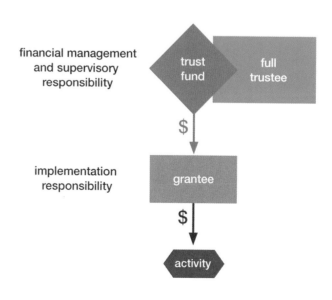

financial management and supervisory responsibility

trust fund — full trustee

$

implementation responsibility

grantee

$

activity

"Implementation support"
is supervision-plus,
both cop and coach.

Increasingly, international trustees are also leveraged through the supporting entity to do more than just supervise. This is sometimes called "implementation support," where it is clear that project implementation belongs to the recipient, but supervision can be hands-on supportive. MDBs are particularly attuned to this supervision-plus approach, since this broadened role reflects an overall shift in downstream operations, and not only with respect to trust funds. As both regulator and supporter, cop and coach, a trustee that is backed by comprehensive supporting entity engagement can promote proper fund use by also amply buttressing project implementation. This reflects a continuing emphasis on results and steady focus on impact.

As with implementation standards, the trustee contractually agrees in its contribution agreements with donors to follow the supervision standards and requirements set out in its applicable policies and procedures (or in the case of limited trustees, passed off to the applicable policies and procedures of any subsequent downstream fiduciaries—more on that in a bit). Although the donors and trustee could of course agree to modified operating terms, the reliance on existing policies and procedures is best preserved to the extent possible. Not only do the "applicable policies and procedures" present the baseline case, but they usually also enable more efficient, cost-effective, mainstreamed, and systems-supported fiduciary operations.

Why Add Supervision?

Donors do not need to use trust funds and trustees. They can—and do—provide funds bilaterally and directly to implementing end users, like country governments or NGOs, without adding a fiduciary layer, effectively doing the supervision themselves. However, there is often great relief in relegating this role to partner entities that are specifically set up to do so, especially when they feature

1. robust operating frameworks that embed internationally endorsed policies and procedures;

2. local staff spread out in all the key places or ready to travel if not already there;

3. systems and management structures geared to supporting this role; and

4. mature and well-developed recipient relationships from prior engagements.

In addition, the incentives to engage fiduciary entities is compounded by the collective leveraging opportunities provided by trust-funded partnership programs, in terms of scale, shared decision making, reinforced international consensus, increased visibility, and many other factors enabled with collectivizing. (>@ International Partnership Programs) It does not hurt that these types of fiduciary entities are often also multilaterals, where donors are shareholders and effectively supervise the supervisor, making this a double comfort zone. Few donors have the kind of staff, presence, and operating framework that these multilaterals have, preferring instead to maintain these multilaterals to do their bidding as fiduciaries.

For the full-fledged variant, fiduciary supervision is an amalgam of policies, procedures, systems, and activities, all bootstrapped into projects to make sure taxpayer money and other resources are well spent. This does not amount to guaranteed results, but is designed to manage inherently challenging and risky environments. Supervision of fund use and activities entails monitoring, reporting, and evaluating, sometimes more or less frequently, sometimes with desk reviews or on-site. Assessments are made regarding whether funds are spent within the agreed scope and with the hoped-for results.

Whether at the trust fund level (as part of trust fund design) or at the project level (as part of project design), these assessments typically measure use and performance against pre-defined categories, components, targets, objectives, or performance indicators. Standard reporting formats and periodicities tend to apply, but are sometimes augmented or altered in specific cases, either on the program level as part of partnership program or trust fund design (hopefully without creating added or conflicting policy layers, >@ Custodial Effect—Eyes Wide Open), or on the project level as part of project appraisal and negotiation. Disbursement levels are usually checked against activity progress, matching use to performance, sometimes to the point where, as mentioned, performance milestones are specifically used to trigger fund disbursements.

When implementation drops a tier from fiduciary to recipient in the context of supervised grantmaking, donors can effectively couple two divergent interests, thereby letting donors and other partners have their cake and eat it, too:

On the one hand, donors retain a tight rein and high standards on fund use and implementation with fiduciary supervision.

On the other hand, donors enable country ownership and local capacity building with recipient implementation.

Depending on the case, having everything implemented by fiduciaries might miss too many of the development objectives, but having everything implemented by beneficiary recipients might also put too much of those development objectives at risk. Although there are plenty of examples that do all of one or all of the other, there is a significant sweet spot in pairing the two. Let beneficiaries implement, and let fiduciaries supervise, each to their comparative advantage and development needs. For sure, this two-layer cake that donors not just get, but also eat, is pricier than the one-layer cake, but it still counts as "value for money" and "money for value." Is it any wonder that trust funds feature so prominently in international development contexts when the package serves multiple purposes, all so nicely wrapped up with a bow?

International partners seem to agree: Tiering responsibility gives value for money and money for value—worth the cost and worth the effort.

Conception to Completion

Supervision suggests an ex post role once the activity gets going, but supervision at the back end only works if measured against standards set at the front end. As a result, supervision usually covers the life cycle from conception to completion, with active input throughout preparation and implementation.

Over the years, pressure points and lessons learned have led to ever burgeoning standards for implementation under international partnership programs. This reflects both a maturing of the international development arena and a proliferation of issue advocates, and perhaps also some prompting from mistakes along the way. From financial management standards to procurement regimes, environmental safeguards, social safeguards, anti-corruption approaches, anti-terrorism lists, disclosure rules, gender inclusion, civil society voice, and climate change aspects, to name some—and no doubt with more focus areas to come—project checklists are long and demanding. These elements are brought to bear in often arduous upfront concept reviews and appraisal processes, with many sector-specialist cooks in the kitchen and many team member fingers in the pie, and then continue to permeate the supervisory role through to completion.

COMPLEMENTARY ENGAGEMENTS

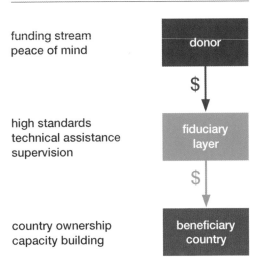

funding stream
peace of mind

high standards
technical assistance
supervision

country ownership
capacity building

Active supervision also entails active management, particularly if disbursements and performance are out of whack. Normally the supervising entity has a number of tools available, which can include rights to alter disbursement schedules, require more information, adjust work plans and budgets, or make various other modifications as needed. These may be in the hands of the fiduciary entity, as regulated by its applicable policies and procedures, without needing to revert to a fund-allocating governing body or individual donors for permission. They can also be encompassed within the terms of the grant agreement, without needing to get separate grantee consent or amendments. Depending on the nature of the adjustments, they may surface in the regular financial and progress reporting if material, or simply be part of the ordinary course.

The transaction burden of all this fiduciary infrastructure can be heavy, and support costs can be high. It is telling that in the development world and elsewhere, partners consider fully freighted supervision to be an acceptable and necessary means to promote safe fund use and effective project implementation. This risk-averse approach to trust fund implementation can dovetail neatly with supporting entity tendencies to run their trust funds like their other business lines, including the MDBs' more substantial loan and guarantee operations (also called "mainstreaming"). This ends up legitimizing the application of fiduciary standards built for large-scale projects even for partnership programs that seek to operate on a more nimble, fit-for-purpose scale.

Transferred (No) Responsibility

Implementation responsibility plus supervision responsibility equals full fiduciary support. A limited trustee is typically a layer on top of that. Limited trustees can come in different combinations (>@ Trustee Types), but in classic international platforms, adding a limited trustee on top of one or more downstream fiduciaries overseeing beneficiaries makes for a triple-decker layer cake. This apportionment of fiduciary responsibilities tracks different implementation roles—implementation as a central fund manager (financial management), followed by implementation as a supervisory guardian (project supervision), followed by implementation of on-the-ground activities (project management).

In this rubric, the first layer of responsibility is of a limited kind because it has a mouth but no tail. Funds are received, commingled, managed, and then disbursed—but in disbursing, any responsibility for them goes with them. While supervisory responsibility means responsibility does not end until the funds are fully spent, a limited trustee's transferred responsibility puts a cap on it long before. The limited trustee has the luxury of disavowing any responsibility for funds it does not hold. No responsibility on the part of the limited trustee is then replaced with delegated responsibility to the transferee (a downstream fiduciary entity) under a transfer agreement. In this way, one fiduciary is replaced by another as funds and responsibility are transferred downstream together, no gaps, no overlaps. (>@ Use of Funds—Role of the Fiduciary)

Why Add a Limited Trustee?

What is the value of inserting yet a third layer? The answer turns on maximizing modularity—collectivizing a diversified mechanism. The limited trustee is a pivot point. It first allows for the centralization of funds, commingled into one or more trust fund accounts, and then pivots to allow for diversified implementation, channeled to multiple full fiduciaries across a level playing field. Clearly there is no need for two fiduciaries at the same time for the same funds—one cook in the kitchen is enough, and way less expensive. So even as the original trustee pools and manages the funds, it remains in a fiduciary capacity only until the next fiduciary steps in and receives the funds. And meanwhile, the limited trustee continues to manage the remaining and replenishing trust fund balance.

The limited trustee model distinguishes between centralized, upstream fund management (as money comes in, is held, and disbursed) and decentralized, downstream fund management (after money is disbursed). In this way, it makes room for broader participation for implementation purposes, including by multiple peer institutions that have similarly robust operating frameworks. Each of these frameworks constitutes a separate and unique set of rules, even if they may be somewhat patterned after each other and approach a common international

The limited trustee pivot:

from a single trust fund to diversified implementation, with multiple fiduciaries, across a level playing field.

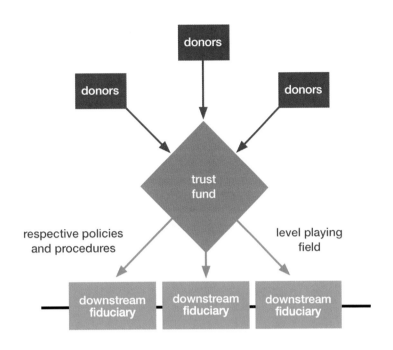

standard. Crucially, none of these institutions is inclined to be subordinate or to act as supervising layers to each other, since they are all generally good enough fiduciaries to be trustees themselves.

With a limited trustee, *donors get a single entry point*, only one contribution agreement to be signed, after which the trustee releases its role to accommodate multiple downstream fiduciaries. This efficiency is widely appreciated and serves as a simple and direct match for one governing body and one secretariat. In most cases, the *downstream fiduciaries participate on a par*, each eligible for funding in its own right and each with expectations of a level playing field in vying for funds.

The importance of maintaining this level playing field is heightened when the limited trustee entity also has a role as one of the downstream fiduciaries, potentially with an (actual or perceived) inside track. Mindful of these sensitivities, an effective limited trustee carefully reserves its role, so as to eliminate any prospect or perception of overreach and favoritism. Whatever role it plays, it seeks to do so neutrally and equally across all downstream transferees.

Managing the Accountability Gap

One missing piece in these limited trustee arrangements is the link between the upstream donor and the downstream recipient. Normally with a full trustee, the chain is unbroken, and all the donor needs is privity of contract with the trustee through the contribution agreement to get coverage vis-à-vis any recipients. However, when the limited trustee pivots, and it pivots both the funds *and* the fiduciary responsibility, the donor loses that privity to the follow-on fiduciary. It is now the trustee that has privity with the fiduciary through the transfer agreement—but in a way that disavows responsibility for any remedies. That leaves the donor with no direct link for recourse, whether through refunds or other remedies. This is known as the "accountability gap." A conscientious lawyer may fill the gap with third-party beneficiary rights in the original contribution agreement, which flow into the transfer agreement and let each donor, individually, step into the shoes of the trustee for remedies purposes. But that is not routine, and even that is not really enough.

In the spirit of collectives, the accountability gap is more suitably filled with a collective approach. Third-party beneficiary rights are still bilateral, donor by donor, which can become quite a tangle if every donor exerts its own approach to remedies in a multi-donor trust fund context. Have pity on the downstream fiduciary and beneficiary having to field a dozen avenues of attack! Better practice would be to negotiate collective arrangements for remedies that are more in the spirit of the pooled funding and the overall partnership program. These collective remedies arrangements can use the governing body as a conduit for handling trust fund issues that affect all donors and other partners. And that brings us more broadly to the role of the governing body.

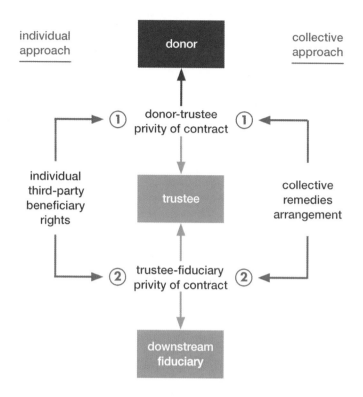

clauses included in the (1) contribution agreement and (2) transfer agreement

Collective Responsibility

The first three categories discussed so far are all downstream responsibilities—responsibility (1) through use; (2) from supervision; and (3) by delegation. These are operational responsibilities that figure directly into activities and project operations. There is also an upstream variant, a top-level layer of collective quasi-responsibility—that of the governing body.

Some international partnership programs position the governing body with fund-related roles and responsibilities; others do not. Pinning the exact scope of these responsibilities down can be hard, in part because governing bodies tend to articulate their roles more as rights, like approval rights, than obligations. Governing bodies may insert themselves in trustee operations, but still expect the trustee to be responsible. And yet, if the governing body makes fund allocation decisions, or decides who is eligible to be downstream fiduciaries, or has a strategic role in shaping the entire partnership program and its operations and activities, do any of these rights carry any responsibilities? What if something goes wrong—does the governing body simply point to others?

Do any of the governing body's rights carry any responsibilities?

We have already seen how international partnership programs combine structural and contractual aspects. (>@ Structure—Connecting Fund Flows and Decision Flows) Downstream responsibilities attach directly to fund flows and become contractualized. This gets attention because it behooves all parties to be clear on contract terms for fund use, especially those that spell out fiduciary obligations and carry liability. Fund flow agreements put things in black and white. By contrast, upstream decision responsibilities are more elusive. They arise from structure more than contract. They are not articulated or discussed nearly as much.

Broadly speaking, trust-funded partnership programs give donors and governing bodies rights to decide and influence, while giving support functions and fiduciaries obligations to perform. Although donors have payment obligations, and trustees and secretariats may have prior consent rights, these are more like exceptions that prove the rule. Fiduciary roles are primarily about responsibilities, while programmatic roles are more about authority. This does not mean governing bodies act with impunity, but in all likelihood, neither constitutive documents nor fund flow agreements make governing bodies expressly and consequentially responsible for their decisions. Governing body approvals tend to simply give license for others in the partnership program to pick up their responsibilities.

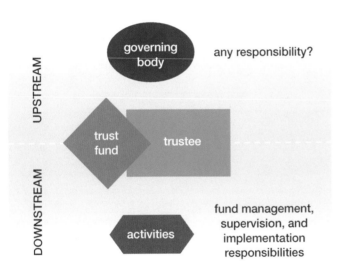

any responsibility?

fund management, supervision, and implementation responsibilities

Structure has a lot to do with this discrepancy. The individual nature of fiduciaries contrasts with the collective nature of governing bodies in a way that pins responsibility on individual entities (legal entities) more readily than collective amalgams (not legal entities). This is also a big reason why being a collective, without legal personality, makes the liability consequences of responsibility—recourse and remedies—harder to attach.

Legal recourse usually seeks a legal entity, which the governing body in informal partnership programs is not. And refunds usually seek a deep pocket, which the governing body as such does not have (not even the trust fund "belongs" to the governing body). Individual entities are the likely targets of any claims, and that largely spares the governing body per se, even when it heftily inserts itself into funding decisions and operations. Then, too, some potential claimants, like donors seeking refunds, are members of the governing body itself. In the intertwined world of international partnership programs—where donors are decision makers and in many cases also shareholders of the trustee and other fiduciaries—one would not expect the governing body as a collective to be a target for claims by its own members. The lack of legal personality and directly owned assets is also likely to shield it from claims by outsiders.

Governing bodies may find themselves acting imperviously, knowing they have relegated responsibility to specific partners and fronted their status as informal collectives. Their greatest fear may be reputational damage, which may carry consequence enough. In the end, one might conclude that their decisions are driven more by reputational risk than collective responsibility—more about themselves, than their intended beneficiaries. And yet, in the international arena, and especially in the development arena, it is the constant focus on doing good and making a difference that motivates the governing body. When it comes to responsibility, this means that the motivations of international partners are driven by ambitions to have positive impacts way more than any avoidance of negative consequences.

We talk about international partnership programs being more than the sum of their parts. But when it comes to the responsibilities of informal governing bodies, we have a case of less responsibility than the sum of their parts. For governing bodies, it would seem that doing right and good is more about laudable goals than loaded responsibilities.

A tendency of international partnership programs:

Responsibility gets designated downstream, but diffused upstream.

Conclusion

A large part of structuring international partnership programs is about defining roles and allocating responsibilities. Structuring often starts with a diagram showing the components—governing body, trust fund, trustee, secretariat, implementers—and then tracing the flows. (>@ Structure—Whiteboarding) Following the power, who is making decisions about what? Following the money, where is the money going from top to bottom? But it does not stop there. In addition to making decisions and flowing funds, partners need to think about operations and implementation. Partly this means looking at who has what rights, but mostly this means looking at who has what responsibilities.

Collectivized decision making can result in a diffusion of responsibilities. This is particularly true where the governing body is informal and without legal personality, as opposed to being part of a legal entity, like a corporate board. International partnership programs therefore have to be especially intentional in defining who carries implementation responsibility, including with respect to decisions made by their informal governing bodies. Fiduciary and implementing entities in turn have a greater interest in shaping what they supervise and implement. To this end, these entities usually take charge either on the basis of proposals they have submitted (having the "first say") or with final decision making about projects (having the "last say"). This lets them match their responsibility with authority.

Even if reputation counts for more than responsibility, governing bodies should aim to decide responsibly.

This may also suit governing bodies. And yet, even if governing bodies are more attuned to reputation than responsibility, they can recognize that their decisions have consequences and always aim to decide responsibly.

CONCLUDING REMARKS

We've been around the block a few times to get this far. Starting from vocabulary and definitions, we surveyed the landscape and zeroed in on international partnership programs. Then we looked at each component— governing body, secretariat, and trust fund—studying how it works, how it varies, and how it relates to the rest. From there, we took a business lens to think about how to set up the exercise, how to frame decisions, and how to take a comprehensive approach. And finally, we took a deeper dive on key topics that go to the essence.

That essence may start with a decision by international partners to convene in some form of informal, collective body, and already the structuring begins. This triggers the need for some form of administrative support, often provided by one of the partners as a supporting entity, and now the structuring is well under way. It may also lead to a trust fund or two when partners are willing to combine their dedicated funds, although it can instead or also rely on financing by any number or types of funding sources and vehicles.

With each added element, there is more to design. With every added layer, there are more dimensions to manage. But for every aspect that is shared, there is more potential for synergies. And all the while, context matters, with a view to creating a fit-for-purpose partnership program that is at once solid as rock and flexible as water.

It may not be as easy as 1, 2, 3, but along the way, we learned that a number of basic equations apply. We learned that international partnership program permutations equal countless business decisions. We also learned that a fit-for-purpose partnership program amounts to choices factored by context. We understood that collective action needs effective structure and design to equal expected results and impact. And in terms of collectives, we recognized that combinations can range from a denominator of one (full harmonization) to the total number of partners (full individualization). But most of all, we saw that, if successfully synergized, all partners together can equal more than the sum of each of their parts—otherwise what would be the point?

For all the variables and possible complexity, the mantra **KEEP IT SIMPLE** remains. Every choice along the way can be tested against this leitmotiv, even as the layers and elements add up. It helps to start with a couplet—*know your goals, know your roles*—to lead the way.

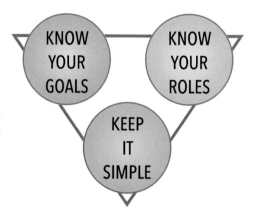

- **Goals:** What do you want to accomplish?
  What results do you want to share?

- **Roles:** What do you want to contribute?
  What resources are you willing to share?

Partners who know their individual goals and share their collective goals have an active compass to mark the path. Partners who know their individual roles and recognize each other's roles are wearing the boots to make the journey. Partnering may sometimes feel like a detour, but it is often the most effective way to move forward and reach the desired destination. As the saying goes: go alone, go fast; go together, go far.

The bottom line is to let the wide range of considerations and variety of options empower, rather than overwhelm. In practice, the available considerations and options may be more limited, depending on the specific context, but structure and design can always be informed by an appreciation of why things are the way they are and how they might be better. Is it true that international partnership programs are wonderfully complex and refreshingly simple, as claimed at the outset? This book may succeed in promoting sustainable, efficient, and impactful structured partnerships if partners can turn their complexity into simplicity—clear, clean, understood, and straightforward.

Once partners peer through the partnership lens, it colors every step they take. As individual partners, we take on an added dimension, a factor beyond ourselves. As collective partners, we become part of, shaped by, and enriched through the whole. When we are confronted with all the pervasive, growing, and unrelenting challenges in the world, it is easy to be pessimists. When we collect ourselves and combine our resources and forces, when we are energized and fortified by our collaboration, we can become optimists.

Ten Topnotch Traits

Under the rubric of structured partnerships in the international arena, this book has focused on international partnership programs. Although options for international collaboration go far beyond partnership programs, this focus seems justified by their potential. Before we conclude, here is a summarized shortlist of reasons why the kind of international partnership programs we have been unpacking together are such promising platforms:

1. **SPACE:** International partners convening and operating in the international arena benefit from a creative, informal, and modular space for collaboration.

2. **OPPORTUNITY:** Collectivized structures—like governing bodies, secretariats, and trust funds—increase opportunities for coordination, harmonization, and synergies.

3. **RESPONSIBILITY:** Collective input for shaping and decision making does not result in collective responsibility for implementation, but channels responsibility where it best belongs.

4. **COMPARATIVE ADVANTAGE:** Clean and clear allocation of roles and responsibilities enables partners to contribute in accordance with their comparative advantages.

5. **EXISTING ENTITY:** Partners that rely on existing supporting entities can lean on well-tuned operations, robust fiduciary frameworks, and proven track records.

6. **DEDICATION:** Supporting entities chosen from among partners are especially dedicated to making things happen, with all-encompassing support.

7. **SYNERGY:** Partners can comfortably and transparently perform multiple roles, both upstream and downstream, thereby leveraging structure and reinforcing synergies.

8. **LEVERAGE:** Shared governance through governing bodies allows partners to leverage each other's views and experience for greater buy-in and richer lessons learned.

9. **INCENTIVES:** Governing body engagement can create incentives for partners to keep participating and supporting, along with the collective ability to make changes over time.

10. **IMPACT:** Feedback loops that channel upstream, downstream, and back again enable partnership programs to grow, mature, and become more effective with greater impact.

We have learned a lot over the last decades. We have seen the hazards of going it alone, the pitfalls of letting the money lead, and the value of inclusive and constructive engagement. All partners come with their interests and ambitions, all of which deserve to be recognized and reconciled. International partnership programs are all different, depending on the circumstances and what is agreed, and all will differ over time, depending on what changes.

As with any ambition, international partners start with a destination on the horizon and strive for smooth steering along the way. As with anything organic, international partnership programs are never the same, neither in relation to each other nor in relation to themselves. They are, as they should be, infinitely varied and iteratively evolving. With the right lens, informed design, and sound structure, plus a good dose of common understanding and mutual respect—**enough rock and enough water**—they can be built to be fit, sail true, and deliver. That bodes well for the world.

INDEX

ABOUT THE AUTHOR

Andrea Emily Stumpf supports international partnership initiatives through her business, Structured Partnerships, based in the Washington, DC, area. Her experience draws from over ten years of partnership and operational practice at the World Bank, where she was Lead Counsel in the Legal Department. During this time, she worked with hundreds of partners on hundreds of partnership programs, large and small, mostly with trust funds, as an acknowledged expert in partnership program design and trust fund operations. She also supported World Bank loan operations in Africa and the Middle East. Andrea continues to advise clients at the World Bank, in addition to supporting a variety of other clients.

Prior to joining the World Bank, Andrea worked in the private sector for over ten years as inhouse counsel and in law firms. She handled legal matters for three global telecommunications companies, including support of multiple subsidiaries in emerging markets, complex commercial negotiations, and compliance aspects. Prior to her inhouse work, Andrea worked at two major international law firms, in Shearman & Sterling's Paris and New York offices and Morgan, Lewis & Bockius's New York office. In her law firm practice, she participated in cutting-edge global securities offerings and complex, multi-party mergers and acquisitions for major multinational corporations.

Andrea holds a JD from Yale Law School and a double major BA with honors in international studies and German from the University of North Carolina at Chapel Hill. Immediately following law school, she clerked for the late Judge Frank M. Johnson, Jr., a renowned judge on the Eleventh Circuit Court of Appeals.

ABOUT THE ILLUSTRATOR

The Illustrator supports her mother's work on international partnerships in many ways, including with her cats. She loves cats as much as her mother loves partnerships. When she is not drawing cats, sketching, or reading any book she can get her hands on, she is doing her homework, practicing trumpet, or playing soccer (preferably in the reverse order). That does not leave much time for cats, but fortunately just enough for this book. Meow.

Made in the USA
Middletown, DE
17 March 2021